WHAT WORKS

Assessment, Development, and Measurement

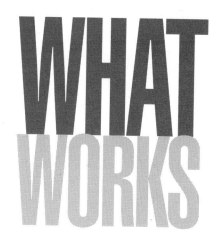

Dennis L. Johnson

AMERICAN SOCIETY FOR TRAINING & DEVELOPMENT

WHAT WORKS

Assessment,

Development, and

Measurement

- Competency Assessment Methods

- Learning Style

- Organizational Learning

- Multirater 360 Feedback

- Evaluating Training

- Return-on-Investment

ASTD

LAURIE J. BASSI AND DARLENE RUSS-EFT, EDITORS

Ordering information: Books published by the American Society for Training & Development can be ordered by calling 703.683.8100.

Library of Congress Catalog Card Number: 97-077500
ISBN: 1-56286-049-6

Table of Contents

Introduction

This book and its companion volume, *What Works: Training and Development Practices,* are practical tools for human resource development (HRD) professionals who are seeking to translate the findings of sound research into sound practice within their organizations.

The need for making this translation is obvious. Human resource professionals face an important but daunting task. Creating environments and experiences that enable employees and the organizations for which they work to achieve their full potential is an enormously complicated proposition. Sifting through the huge number of variables that affect human performance, and isolating the effect of any one of them, is next to impossible in the complex, dynamic organizations in which most of us work. And yet, that is precisely what is needed if HRD practices are to be designed and implemented optimally.

Sound research can help make sense of this complexity and provide guidance in the construction of sound practice. But practitioners face at least four problems when they attempt to translate research into practice:

- Although much research contains information that is potentially useful, the findings are often not written in a way that makes them easily accessible.
- The sheer volume of research can be overwhelming. On many topics, there are dozens of books and hundreds of journal articles. The amount of time required to make sense of all of them is prohibitive.
- Not all research is of equal quality. Some research findings merit more weight than others, but making these judgments takes time and requires both a broad and deep understanding of the literature.
- Much research, although relevant and of high quality, is on a relatively narrow aspect of any given topic. Weaving together the insights of many authors takes time and expertise.

These first two volumes in ASTD's *What Works* series solve these problems and, in so doing, facilitate the translation of research into practice. The ASTD Research Committee chose the contributing authors both for their expertise and their commitment to fostering the translation of sound research into sound practice. Committee members asked the authors to critically assess the research evidence on their topics and to provide critical, authoritative, and succinct reviews of the research along with implications for practitioners.

The topics for these first two volumes of the *What Works* series by no means exhaust the issues that are of concern to HRD professionals. Rather, the committee selected these topics both because of their importance to the HRD community and the potential for research to address them meaningfully. The division of topics between the first two volumes of *What Works* is as follows:

What Works: Assessment, Development, and Measurement
1. Competency Assessment Methods, Lyle M. Spencer Jr.
2. Learning Style, Nancy M. Dixon, Doris E. Adams, and Richard Cullins
3. Organizational Learning, Victoria J. Marsick and Karen E. Watkins
4. Multirater 360 Feedback, Gary N. McLean
5. Evaluating Training, Joan Hilbert, Hallie Preskill, and Darlene Russ-Eft
6. Return-on-Investment, Ann P. Bartel

What Works: Training and Development Practices
1. Leadership Development, W. Warner Burke
2. Conflict Management, Keith G. Allred
3. Diversity Training, Robert T. Moran and Janice L. Stockon
4. Technology Training, Rex J. Allen
5. Behavioral Modeling, Darlene Russ-Eft

With the benefit of hindsight, it should come as no surprise that the research on some of these topics is more advanced than on others. We discovered that some topics, although of critical importance, have not yet been sufficiently well researched to provide authoritative, research-based advice on what works and what doesn't. In these cases, the authors have focused on providing guiding principles upon which sound practice can and should be based.

We expect that this will be the first of a series of volumes focusing on translating research into practice. It is our hope and expectation that future volumes will address a wider array of topics, and that this current effort will stimulate the research community to tackle those topics where the need for guidance from research has not yet been met.

Laurie J. Bassi
Series Editor
Vice President, Research
ASTD
November 1997

1996–1997 ASTD Research Committee

ASTD is grateful to the members of the 1996–1997 ASTD Research Committee for their thoughtful guidance during preparation of this book.

Chair
Victoria J. Marsick, Ph.D.
Professor, Adult Education
Department of Organization
   and Leadership
Columbia University Teachers College
New York, New York

Michael F. Cassidy, Ph.D.
Associate Professor
School of Business Administration
Marymount University
Arlington, Virginia

Edward R. Del Gaizo, Ph.D.
Director of Research
Learning International, Inc.
Stamford, Connecticut

John Gumpert
Director, Training and
   Organizational Development
Union Carbide Corporation
Danbury, Connecticut

Timothy R. McClernon, Ph.D.
Saint Paul Group
Minneapolis, Minnesota

Gary N. McLean, Ed.D.
Professor and Coordinator
Human Resource Development
University of Minnesota
St. Paul, Minnesota

Karen L. Medsker, Ph.D.
Chairman, Human Resource Development
School of Business Administration
Marymount University
Arlington, Virginia

Candice L. Phelan, Ph.D.
Manager, Learning Systems and Processes
Lockheed Martin Corporation
Bethesda, Maryland

Jack Phillips, Ph.D.
Performance Resources Organization
Birmingham, Alabama

Hallie Preskill, Ph.D.
Associate Professor
College of Education
University of New Mexico
Albuquerque, New Mexico

John Redding, Ed.D.
Executive Director
Institute for Strategic Learning
Naperville, Illinois

William J. Rothwell, Ph.D.
Associate Professor
Human Resource Development
Pennsylvania State University
University Park, Pennsylvania

Darlene Russ-Eft, Ph.D.
Director, Research Services
Zenger Miller
San Jose, California

Catherine Sleezer, Ph.D.
Assistant Professor
School of Occupational and
    Adult Education
Oklahoma State University
Stillwater, Oklahoma

Richard A. Swanson, Ph.D.
President, Academy of Human
    Resource Development
Professor and Director,
HRD Research Center
University of Minnesota
St. Paul, Minnesota

Meena Wilson, Ph.D.
Center Associate, Global Resources
The Center for Creative Leadership
Greensboro, North Carolina

Lyle Yorks, Ed.D.
Professor of Management and Chair
Department of Business Administration
Eastern Connecticut State University
Willimantic, Connecticut

CHAPTER 1

Competency Assessment Methods

Lyle M. Spencer Jr., Ph.D.
Vice President
Research and Technology
Hay Group

This chapter describes the job competency movement from its history to its current status. The job competency movement is an approach to getting the right person into the right job. It starts with the person in the job, makes no prior assumptions about the characteristics needed to perform the job well, and determines from open-ended behavioral event interviews which human characteristics are associated with job success. The movement emphasizes criterion validity and is context sensitive so that competency-based selection predicts superior job performance and retention—both with significant economic value to organizations—without race, age, gender, or demographic bias. By contrast, earlier approaches in which psychologists and human resource development professionals identified the tasks required for a job and constructed tests to measure those skills, proved inadequate in predicting success on the job.

HISTORY

The modern competency movement in American educational and industrial-organizational psychology dates from the late 1960s and early 1970s. At that time in American psychology, interest in personality traits was largely out of fashion. Such authorities as Ghiselli (1966) and Mischel (1968) argued that testable personality traits rarely showed correlations better than .33 (10 percent of the variance) with job performance, so research on these variables was of questionable value. (Despite changing fashions in psychology, managers and human resource professionals continued to look for such competencies as "initiative" and "communications skills.")

At the same time, an increasing number of studies were published that showed that traditional academic aptitude and knowledge content tests, as well as school grades and credentials, did not predict job performance or success in life (see McClelland, 1973, for a review of this literature) and often showed bias against minorities, women, and persons from lower socioeconomic strata who had not received elite education (Fallows, 1985).

These findings prompted McClelland to specify principles for doing research to identify competency variables that did predict job performance and were not biased (or at least, were less biased) by race, sex, or socioeconomic factors. The following were the most important of these principles:

- Use of **criterion samples** that compare people who are clearly successful in job or other outcomes with persons less successful to identify those characteristics associated with success.
- Identification of **operant thoughts and behaviors** causally related to these successful outcomes. That is, competency measures should involve open-ended situations in which an individual has to *generate* behavior, as distinguished from respondent measures such as self-report and multiple-choice tests that require choosing one of several well-defined alternative responses in highly structured situations. Jobs and other aspects of people's lives rarely present such test conditions. Rather, the best predictor of what a person can and will do is what he or she spontaneously thinks and does in an unstructured situation or has done in similar past situations.

Two case studies—one concerning Foreign Service Information Officers and the other, social workers in Massachusetts—illustrate the competency methodology and the social issues it addressed.

The U.S. State Department: Foreign Service Information Officers

In 1971, the U.S. State Department's Information Service (USIS) approached McClelland when it found that applicants' scores on the Foreign Service information officers' (FSIOs) written exams did not predict success on the job as an FSIO (McClelland & Dailey, 1973). Scores from the General Aptitude Test battery and the General Background Knowledge Test were slightly negatively correlated with job performance ($r=-.22$, $p<.10$): The better an FSIO candidate did on the tests, the worse he or she did as a diplomat. Further, very few minority candidates passed at the high levels required to be hired as an FSIO. Given the lack of validity of the test scores' prediction of on-the-job success, the rejection of minority candidates was illegal discrimination against a protected class under civil rights law (McClelland & Dailey, 1972, 1973; McClelland, 1973).

McClelland's challenge was to answer the question, If traditional aptitude measures don't predict job performance, what does? McClelland response was, first, to ask the State Department for a criterion sample of superior FSIOs (those ranked in the top 10 percent) and a contrasting sample of average or poor performers, or a mix of both. Second, McClelland and Daily (1972) developed a technique called the Behavioral Event Interview (BEI), which combined Flanagan's (1954) critical incident method with the Thematic Apperception Test (TAT) probes that McClelland developed over 30 years of studying motivation (McClelland, 1985).

The BEI differs from the critical incident interview (CII) in that Flanagan was interested in identifying the task elements of jobs, whereas McClelland was interested in the characteristics of the people who did a job well. For example, Flanagan's analysis of CII data found that supervisors spend 42 percent of their time in meetings, and McClelland's analysis of BEI data found that superior diplomats are higher than average performers in nonverbal sensitivity.

The BEI asks people to think of several important on-the-job situations in which things turned out well or poorly and then to describe these situations in "short story" detail, answering such questions as: What led up to the situation? Who was involved? What did you think about, feel, want to happen in the situation? What did you do? What was the outcome?

Third, McClelland and his colleagues "thematically analyzed" BEI transcripts from successful and unsuccessful information officers to identify characteristics that differed between the two samples, generally behaviors shown by superior performers and not shown by average performers. These thematic differences were translated into objective scoring definitions that could be reliably coded by different observers.

BEI transcripts were then scored, or coded, according to these definitions using a method now called CAVE, for *Content Analysis of Verbal Expression* (Zullow et al., 1988), which had been developed to measure motivation (Atkinson, 1958). CAVE coding enables investigators to count (measure empirically) and test statistically differences in the characteristics shown by superior and average performers in various jobs. This method was used extensively in a subsequent study of the competencies characterizing outstanding diplomats in the regular Foreign Service (McClelland, Klemp, & Miron, 1977.)

Competency characteristics that differentiated superior from average information officers included cross-cultural positive regard and interpersonal sensitivity and speed in learning critical networks. Two examples illustrate these competencies:

- Cross-cultural positive regard and interpersonal sensitivity is another way of saying the ability to sit down opposite somebody from a foreign culture and really understand what the person is saying. One diplomat told of maintaining friendships with radical Algerian students who had threatened to burn down her USIS library (words and competencies coded in brackets):

> [D]espite the troubles we had with them, *I'd never stopped liking and respecting the student leaders [positive regard]. They were just becoming conscious of their nationalism [interpersonal understand-*

ing], and that they were going to be the leaders of a greatly changed country. *I could understand that they needed to rebel against us, to stand up to us, throw us out [interpersonal understanding]—even when they wanted to burn my library! [self-control].* So I told them that, *and invited them to use our facilities to hold some of their meetings [initiative, relationship building]. I tried to get resident Americans here to come and listen so more of them would understand [influence].* I've got good contacts with some of the student leaders now. And we haven't been burned down yet!"

- Speed in learning critical networks is evident from one FSIO's description of going to an African country and very rapidly figuring out that it was *"the prime minister's executive assistant's mistress's nephew who called shots on petroleum policy"* and how to get invited to a party to meet and began lobbying this nephew quickly *[organization awareness]*.

These and other nonacademic competencies, such as management skills and the ability to generate a number of promotional ideas, did predict successful performance in FSIO jobs and did not discriminate against candidates by race, sex, or socioeconomic status.

Massachusetts Social Workers

In 1993, U.S. welfare laws (heavily influenced by social workers' professional associations) required states to professionalize social work by mandating that social workers have a master's degree in social work from a university (that is, be credentialed) and pass a government General Aptitude Test Battery (GATB). Social workers who met this standard tended to be upper-middle class white women with graduate degrees from elite universities. However, the superior performers in social work agencies, as rated by supervisors, clients, and client outcomes, were mostly middle-aged black women who had, on average, a sixth-grade education but a deep understanding of the culture and problems of their clients. When the state authorities in Massachusetts realized that the new law would result in wholesale firings of minority employees, they asked McClelland and his colleagues to develop a competency model.

Competencies that predicted success in social work included
- nonverbal empathy
- positive expectations of clients
- an optimum level of administrative skills, including rule-based action (that is, if S service is needed, then complete P paperwork), conscientiousness, and attention to detail. (The competencies underlying administrative skills, which is now called analytic thinking and concern for order and quality, were curvilinear: Too little administrative skill, and clients did not get help, but too much attention to paperwork and not to clients, and service providers were ineffective.) GATB test scores were negatively correlated with job performance. Credentialed social workers from upper-middle-class backgrounds could do admin-

istrative work but were significantly less effective because they literally could not understand what their clients were saying in accented "black English," much less understand or empathize with clients' problems, values, or culture (McClelland, 1994).

McClelland's competency methodology is a radical departure from traditional job analysis. Job analysis methods define work in terms of elements of the *job*: they follow people around with stopwatches or use surveys that find that employees spend 14.3 percent of their time "communicating." Competency analysis defines jobs in terms of the characteristics and behavior of the people who do the job well.

For example, most managerial jobs involve planning and organizing tasks. The interesting question is what leads a person to plan and organize well or efficiently. Competency research shows that two underlying competencies related to effective planning and organizing are *achievement motivation* (a motive concern with increasing efficiency) and *analytic thinking* (the ability to array things in hierarchical or sequential order: to identify what is most important to do first, and what needs to be done at time 1 to be able to do a subsequent task at time 2, to be able to finish the project at time 3).

Growth of Competency Methodology

Use of the competency methodology grew rapidly in the 1970s when it was adopted by

- the U.S. Navy as the basis for all Navy leadership and management programs
- the U.S. Department of Education's Fund for Post-Secondary Education (FIPSE), which sponsored competency-based college admissions and curricula projects at 33 universities
- the American Management Association (AMA), which funded research on supervisory competencies and the development of competency-based assessment centers and an MBA program.

The AMA research and applications were summarized in *The Competent Manager* (Boyatzis, 1982). *The Competent Manager* was the first book-length description of competency research methodology. It included a competency dictionary and reported findings from 2,000 managers in 41 supervisory, management, and executive jobs.

By 1991, more than 100 researchers in 24 countries had contributed to a database of approximately 1,000 competency models (300 were based on BEI, and 700 were generated by expert systems). Competency models for a wide variety of industry, government, military, health care, and education jobs around the world and competency-based applications were meta-analyzed and published in *Competence at Work* (Spencer & Spencer, 1993). That book provided the following:

- an updated description of competency research methodologies
- an expanded generic competency dictionary, with "just noticeable difference" scales for 20 core competencies, which accounted for 85 percent of the variance in most competency models
- generic competency models for many jobs

- so-called best practice case studies of competency-based human resource applications for assessment, selection, development, succession planning, performance management, and compensation
- societal applications.

COMPETENCY METHODOLOGY

Definition of a Competency

A competency is defined as "an *underlying* characteristic of an individual which is *causally* related to *effective* or *superior* (one standard deviation above the mean) performance in a job" (Boyatzis, 1982). The superior performance definition of competence (which comes to the top 14 percent, roughly the top one out of 10 performers in a job) is preferred for two reasons:

1. *Known economic value.* Hunter, Schmidt, and Judiesch (1990) found that, depending on the complexity of the job, performance one standard deviation (S.D.) above the mean is worth between 19 percent and 48 percent economic value-added in nonsales jobs, and from 48 percent to 120 percent increased productivity in sales jobs. Figure 1 illustrates the economic gains from superior performance.

A study of sales in 44 firms by Sloan and Spencer (1991) found that for salespeople earning an average of $41,777 annually, superior performers sold an average $6.7 million, whereas typical performers sold $3 million. Superior salespeople sold 123 percent more than average salespeople. These data suggest the practical economic value of a competency model that enables an organization to find or train even one additional superior salesperson. Hunter, Schmidt, and Judiesch's global estimation methodology and findings provide powerful tools for estimating and evaluating the economic value of competency-based human resource applications (see "Applications" below).

Figure 1. Economic value added by superior performance.

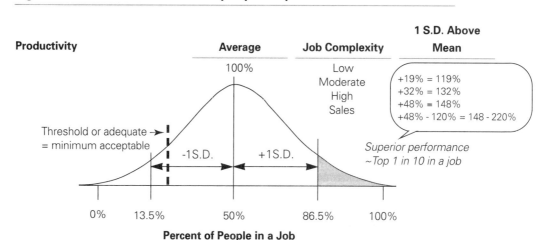

2. *Benchmarks and direction for adding value.* As with any so-called best practice benchmark, when the definition of *competence* is doing a job the best way it can be done, people will be driven to add value, that is, to do better than their present or their firms' present average level of performance. Any human resource approach that does not use an explicit benchmark that is superior to its present performance risks staffing, training, and managing to mediocrity. It will be unlikely to improve on its existing (average) performance level.

A competency is any individual characteristic that can be measured reliably and that distinguishes superior from average performers, or effective from ineffective performers, at statistical levels of significance. "Differentiating" competencies distinguish superior from average performers. "Threshold" or "essential" competencies are required for minimally adequate or average performance. The threshold and differentiating competencies for a given job provide a template for personnel selection, succession planning, performance appraisal, and development.

Competency characteristics are usually classified as (1) operant or respondent traits (for example, motives, self-concepts, attitudes, values, or occupational preference), (2) declarative knowledge (for example, know *that*), or (3) procedural skills (for example, know *how*). Procedural skills may be cognitive or behavioral skills. Content knowledge is declarative knowledge (that is, what one *knows*) of facts or procedures, either technical (such as how to trouble-shoot a defective computer) or interpersonal (such as the five rules of effective feedback), as measured by respondent tests. Skills are procedural knowledge (that is, what one can *do*), either covert (for example, deductive or inductive reasoning) or observable (for example, active listening skills in an interview).

Figure 2 illustrates these levels of competencies. This figure, known as an iceberg diagram, shows the easily visible skill and knowledge competencies above the water line and the less easily seen self-concept and motivation traits below the iceberg's water line.

Traits are general dispositions to attend to certain categories of stimuli or to behave or respond in certain ways, or to do both. Traits can be categorized as operant or respondent. *Operant traits* are intrinsic drives to act in the absence of environmental pressures or rewards. These traits are formed early in life by association of thoughts and behaviors with pleasurable experience, and they are satisfied by the intrinsic pleasure of engaging in the thought or activity itself. *Respondent traits* are conscious beliefs or value drives formed by early social reinforcement. These traits are satisfied by external reinforcement praise or by symbolic or monetary rewards.

The iceberg model (see figure 2) has implications for the design of competency-based human resource applications. Competencies differ in the extent to which they can be taught. Content knowledge and behavioral skills are easiest to teach, and attitudes and values are harder. Although it is possible to change motives and traits (McClelland & Winter, 1971), the process is lengthy, difficult and expensive. From a cost-effectiveness standpoint, the rule is hire for core motivation and traits characteristics,

Figure 2. Iceberg levels of competencies.

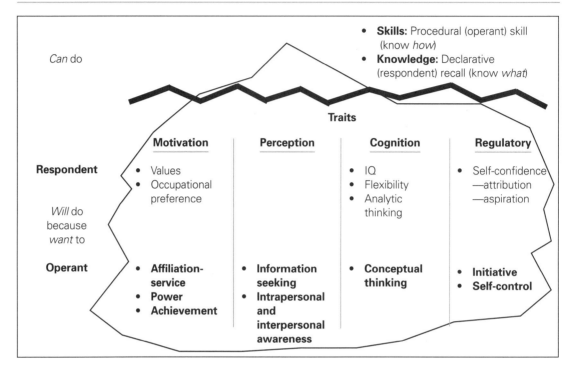

and develop knowledge and skills. Most organizations do the reverse: They hire on the basis of educational credentials and assume that candidates come with the appropriate motives and traits or can be indoctrinated with them. It is more cost-effective to hire people with the right motives and traits and train them in knowledge and skills needed to do specific jobs. Or, in the words of one personnel manager, "You can teach a turkey to climb a tree, but it's easier to hire a squirrel."

Frequency

The strength or "energy" of psychological variables can be measured in different ways. One could use the sum of item scores (for example, Likert 1 = low to 5 = high), or items correctly answered (for example, vocabulary words or analogies on an intelligence test), or the number of times a competency is coded in an interview transcript. These results are usually expressed in deciles on a normal curve, where 50 percent is the norm.

Just-Noticeable-Difference Scales

A second measure of competency strength is known as just different (JND) intervals on a behavioral (indicator) anchored rating scale (BARS; Smith & Kendall, 1963). An important finding of the research reported in *Competence at Work* was the significant variation in the weight or strength of examples of the same competency drawn from different models. Some achievement stories seemed much stronger than others, and some examples of analytical thinking were much more complex than others.

When verbatim examples of each competency were collected from a variety of jobs and Q-sorted by a number of judges according to the extent to which they indicated more or less of the competency in question, competency examples were found to have scaling properties of a clear progression from lower to higher levels on the following four dimensions:

- *Intensity* of the intention (or personal characteristic) involved or completeness of actions taken to carry out an intention
- *Complexity* in taking more things, people, data, concepts or causes into account
- *Time horizon* in seeing further into the future, and planning or taking action based on anticipation of future situations (for example, acting now to head off problems or create future opportunities)
- *Breadth of impact* on the number and position of people affected, (for example, on a scale from a subordinate or a peer to the chief executive officer (CEO) of the organization, to national or international leaders); or the size of the problem addressed (for example, from something affecting part of one person's performance to something affecting the entire organization).

JND scaling of achievement competencies provides new information about the impact of achievement motivation on managerial performance. The traditional finding (McClelland & Boyatzis, 1982) is that the Thematic Apperception Test Exercise measures of achievement motivation do not predict success in higher level managers. Rather, in managerial jobs that require getting others to achieve rather than achieving individually, (socialized) power motivation predicts superior performance. Current competency model data show that more successful executives are qualitatively higher on the achievement scale than either middle managers or less effective executives. That is, they are more likely to take and persist in actions to improve overall organizational quality and productivity or to lead their organizations into new markets, two behaviors that score at a higher JND level on the achievement scale

Another example of the use of JNDs appears with complex thinking. Complex thinking (analytical or conceptual thinking competencies, or both) measures practical or applied intelligence (that is, the degree to which a person does not accept a critical situation or problem at face value or as defined by others' comments but comes to his or her own understanding at a deeper or more complex level). Observation or information seeking, or both, are necessary prerequisites. The basic level of complex thinking (see table 1) that distinguishes superior performance involves recognizing a match or a discrepancy that is not obvious to most other people between the current situation and a known standard (that is, previous experience, learned concepts, or usual expectations).

At higher levels, superior performers use long causal inference chains, see relationships among complex data from unrelated areas, or create concepts or models that explain a complex situation or reconcile discrepant data (see Fisher, Hand, & Russell, 1984; Winter & McClelland, 1978).

For example, self-control predicts superior performance in large, bureaucratic organizations where following the rules is important, but is negatively correlated with success in entrepreneurial and creative jobs. In a reanalysis of a sample of AT&T executives known as Formative Years in Business (Bray, Campbell, & Grant, 1974), Jacobs & McClelland (1994) found that the most competent women left the company to start their own businesses or to move to smaller firms where they would be freer to use their competence, and these women were scored significantly lower in self-control than the executives who remained with AT&T.

Competency Dictionaries

Research reported in *Competence at Work* identified about 360 generic behavioral indicators (plus a greater number of unique indicators that appeared in only a few models, such as the "ability to assess accurately the dye absorption qualities of Pakistani denim" for blue jeans manufacturer fabric buyers). These behavioral indicators describe 20 core competencies (shown in column 3, under Spencer & Spencer) of table 2 that account for 85 percent of the variance in most competency models. Table 2 compares the four principal competency dictionaries developed over the past 25 years:

Table 1. Conceptual thinking (CT) JND scale.

Conceptual thinking: The ability to identify patterns or connections between situations that are not obviously related and to identify key or underlying issues in complex situations. It includes using creative, conceptual, or inductive reasoning.

This person:
1. **Uses basic rules:** Uses simple rules (rules of thumb), common sense, and past experience to identify problems; recognizes when a current situation is exactly the same as a past situation.

2. **Sees patterns:** When looking at information, sees patterns, trends, or missing pieces; notices when a current situation is similar to one from the past and identifies the similarities.

3. **Applies complex concepts:** Uses knowledge of theory or of different past trends or situations to look at current situations; applies and modifies complex learned concepts or methods appropriately; (e.g., statistical process control, TQM demographic analysis, managerial styles, organizational climate); evidence of more sophisticated pattern recognition.

4. **Clarifies complex data or situations:** Makes complex ideas or situations clear, simple, or understandable (or all three); assembles ideas, issues, and observations into a clear and useful explanation; restates existing observations or knowledge in a simpler fashion. (The coder should look for evidence of the ability to see a simpler pattern within complex information.)

5. **Creates new concepts:** Creates concepts that are not obvious to others and not learned from previous education or experience to explain situations or resolve problems. (To score level 5, the coder should be convinced that the concept is new and should be able to cite specific evidence. Do not also score for innovation.)

PROCEDURE FOR CONDUCTING COMPETENCY RESEARCH

Competency-based selection, placement, and succession planning systems are best focused on identification of top candidates for an organization's most important value-added jobs.

The following steps are in a typical competency research project (see table 3 on page 15):

1. **Define performance effectiveness criteria.** The first and very important step is to define the criteria for superior performance: How do you know a "star" when you see one? If the wrong criteria are chosen, all subsequent research will be biased. The best criteria are usually a composite of hard performance data (for example, sales, profits, or productivity measures, where these exist for a job) and nominations by managers, peers, subordinates, and knowledgeable observers (such as clients or human resource professionals who know the job).

    Global estimation of the economic value of superior performance (appendix 1) should always be included in a competency model study. Quick, cheap, and statistically robust estimates of the value of superior performance are invariably useful in cost-justifying competency studies to line managers.

2. **Identify a criterion sample.** The research sample consists of a clear group of superior performers (defined as those performing one standard deviation above the average on the performance effectiveness criteria, or the top 10 percent) and a comparison group of average performers in the target job. The one standard deviation criterion is chosen because of its demonstrable economic value to an organization, as shown in Hunter, Schmidt, and Judiesch (1990).

    A good sample size for simple statistical analysis (t-tests) is 20 job incumbents, 12 superior performers, and eight averages. A rule of competency research is that you always learn most from the stars, so smaller qualitative studies should sample two superior performers for each average (that is, four stars, two averages in an N of six, or six stars, three averages in an N of nine).

3. **Collect data.** Data are collected on superior and average performers in the criterion sample using several methods, such as expert panels, surveys, an expert system database, behavioral event interviews, and observation.

    *   *Expert panel* methods involve asking observers who know the job what competencies they think are required for adequate (average) performance (that is, threshold competencies) and which characteristics distinguish superior performers (that is, differentiating competencies). Experience indicates that about 50 percent of the competencies identified by expert panels are validated by a full competency study.[1]

---

1. Expert panels err in two ways: First, they posit so-called motherhood or folklore items (for example, moral courage) that do not differentiate superior performers. Second, they miss competencies (for example, depressive explanatory style or elicits visual and tactile imagery) for which they lack a psychological vocabulary.

Table 2. Competency dictionaries.

Cluster	Boyatzis (1982); Boyatzis, Cowen, & Kolb (1995)	Spencer & Spencer, *Competence at Work* (1993)	MClelland Dictionary (1996)	Fetzer Consortium (Goleman & Gowing, working papers)
Achievement	Efficiency orientation	Achievement orientation	Achievement orientation	Achievement, motivation, innovativeness
	Initiative	Initiative	Initiative	Initiative (self-direction, self-motivation)
	Attention to detail	Concern for order and quality		Conscientiousness
Affiliation	Empathy	Interpersonal understanding	Interpersonal understanding	Empathy
		Customer service orientation	Customer service orientation	Customer service orientation
		Teamwork and cooperation	Teamwork and cooperation	Team building/teamwork collaboration and cooperation
Power	Persuasiveness	Impact and influence	Impact and influence	Influence
	Written communication			
	Oral communication			Effective (oral) communication
	Organization awareness			Organization awareness
	Networking	Relationship building	Relationship building	Building bonds, handling relationships

Table 2. Competency dictionaries (continued).

Cluster	Boyatzis (1982); Boyatzis, Cowen, & Kolb (1995)	Spencer & Spencer, *Competence at Work* (1993)	MClelland Dictionary (1996)	Fetzer Consortium (Goleman & Gowing, working papers)
Power (continued)	Negotiating			Conflict management/negotiation
Management	Developing others	Directiveness	Directiveness	Coaching and developing teaching others
	Group management	Developing others	Developing others	Leadership
		Team leadership	Team leadership	Change catalyst
				Managing diverse workforce, leveraging diversity
				Managing human resources
Cognitive	Pattern recognition	Conceptual thinking	Information seeking	Information seeking
	Use of concepts		Conceptual thinking	
	Systems thinking (theory building)			
	Quantitative analysis			

Table 2. Competency dictionaries (continued).

Cluster	Boyatzis (1982); Boyatzis, Cowen, & Kolb (1995)	Spencer & Spencer, *Competence at Work* (1993)	McClelland Dictionary (1996)	Fetzer Consortium (Goleman & Gowing, working papers)
Cognitive (continued)	Planning	Analytic thinking	Analytic thinking	
	Using technology	Technical expertise		
Personal effectiveness	Self-confidence	Self-confidence	Self-confidence	Self-confidence (self-esteem), optimism, and hope
	Self-control	Self-control		Self-control (self-management, managing emotions, stress tolerance)
	Flexibility		Flexibility	Flexibility, adaptability
	Social objectivity			
		Organizational commitment	Organizational commitment	
			Integrity	Honesty/integrity, trustworthiness
				Managing diverse workforce, leveraging diversity
				Managing human resources
	Accurate self-assessment			Emotional self-awareness

Table 3. Steps in conducting a competency research project.

1. **Define performance effectiveness criteria**	• Hard data: sales, profits, productivity measures
	• Global estimation: % economic value added by top 1 in 10
	• Multirater 360 feedback nominations and ratings by:
	  —supervisors
	  —peers
	  —subordinates (e.g., managerial style and morale surveys)
	  —customers

2. **Identify criterion sample**	• Superior performers: 4-12 • Average performers: 2-8
3. **Collect data**	• Behavioral Event Interviews (BEI) • Expert panels • 360 feedback • Expert system competency database • Observation
4. **Analyze data (thematic analysis or concept formation)**	• Identify critical/priority job/role task situations. • Identify competencies superior performers use in these situations to get business results. • Develop reliable scales and coding system for competencies. • Code and analyze data to validate competencies that statistically distinguish superior performers. = Competency model for the job/role
5. **Validate competency model**	• Develop assessment instruments to measure competencies identified in step 4 of model (e.g., BEI, tests, rating forms, or assessment center exercises). • Concurrent validity: Assess a second blind criterion sample of superior and average performers and test ability of the competency model to distinguish top performers from the rest. • Predictive validity: select or train a treatment group on the competencies and see if the competency group outperforms a control group.
6. **Develop applications that add economic value**	• Staffing: selection/deselection, succession planning • Development: training, job assignments, career pathing, mentors • Performance management • Human resource asset accounting • Evaluation of human resource programs

- *Surveys* ask observers who know the job to indicate the extent to which average and superior performers exhibit specific behaviors that define competencies. Multirater 360 feedback (that is, superiors, peers, subordinates, and clients who observe job incumbents from different perspectives provide the best data. Morale, as measured by employee satisfaction and organizational climate surveys completed by subordinates, almost always distinguishes superior managers.

- An *expert system database* containing data from some 300 competency models is queried and asked to infer competencies likely to predict superior performance in a job, given certain requirements of the job. For example, the expert system will ask to what extent the job requires continuous efficiency and productivity improvements or the development of products and services. High responses on these items will raise achievement motivation as a competency required for effective performance in this job because previous studies of superior performers in jobs requiring performance improvement and innovation have found achievement motivation to be a differentiating competency.

- *Behavioral Event Interview (BEI)* provides detailed narrative accounts of how superior and average performers have thought and acted in job experiences that were their most critical successes and failures. This method is similar to the debriefing of experts' problem-solving thought processes used for the knowledge acquisition phase of expert-system construction. Transcripts of these interviews can be analyzed for the presence, level, and strength of motive, trait, self-concept, and cognitive and skill competencies that differentiate superior from average performers.

- *Observation* is possible of superior and average performers in actual or simulated (assessment center) work situations, and their behavior may be coded for competencies related to job performance. Observation methods have the disadvantage of being very expensive; properly done BEIs can substitute for observation.

4. **Analyze the data and develop a "competency model" for the job.** Data from the expert panels, surveys, expert system, and BEIs are content-analyzed to identify behaviors and personality characteristics that (a) distinguish superior from average job incumbents, or (b) are demonstrated by all incumbents adequately performing the job.

    BEI transcripts are first coded for known competencies, then subjected to thematic analysis to identify new or unique competencies. Coding criteria for unique competencies are refined until they can be recognized with acceptable interrater reliability. A manual with a detailed competency dictionary and coding is prepared to guide empirical coding of interview, assessment center, or other operant data from job incumbents or candidates. This dictionary and coding manual provides the competency model for the job.

5. **Validation.** Criterion and predictive validity of the competency model is tested by determining the extent to which competencies coded from BEI transcripts or assessed using psychometric tests or assessment center ratings correctly identify known superior versus average performers in a second criterion sample, or correctly predict adequate and superior performance of new hires. It is worth noting that the behavioral event interview, initially used as a hypothesis generation method in constructing the model, can also be used as a psychometric assessment method if properly conducted. BEI transcripts can be coded for competencies with interrater reliability of .8 to .9 (Boyatzis, 1982). Competency scores from BEIs alone have shown criterion validities from .4 to .6 (Spencer, 1978; Winter & Healy, 1982) to as high as .9 for competency "molecules" mapped to specific job situations. For example, the team achievement motive profile, plus one of three internal competencies (such as, self-confidence) and one of three external competencies (such as organizational awareness) predicted economic outcomes over two

years at r=.90 for four types of executives in PepsiCo (strategic, turn-around, developer, and general) (McClelland, 1996).

6. **Develop applications to solve business problems.** Competency models are rarely pure research. Most are conducted to improve organizational performance. Competency-based human resource applications can be classified as follows:

    *   *Staffing:* recruitment, selection, succession and human resource planning, layoffs (during downsizing or strategic change initiatives), and retention
    *   *Development:* formal training, developmental job assignments, mentoring, and evaluation of training and professional development programs
    *   *Performance management:* goal setting and "performance contracting" at the beginning of a performance period, coaching during the performance period, and performance appraisal and reward (or sanctions) at the end of the period
    *   *Compensation:* competency-based pay
    *   Organizational assessment, development, and change.

APPLICATIONS AND IMPLICATIONS

Competency-Based Staffing

Research over the past 10 years shows that competency-based staffing can shift performance .25 to .50 S.D., worth 5 to 25 percent in low- to high-complexity jobs and 30 to 60 percent in sales jobs (Spencer & Morrow, 1996). Competency-based training and performance management shift performance .60 S.D., worth 11 to 30 percent in low- to high-complexity jobs, and 30 to 72 percent in sales jobs (Morrow, Jarrett, & Rupinski, 1997; Burke & Day, 1986, Falcone, Edwards, & Day, 1986).

Cashman and Ott (1966) found that competencies coded from BEIs correlated r=.97 with competencies rated by 360 survey (boss, peer, and subordinate) respondents for a sample of 250 executives.

Jackson (1994) has reported multirater 360 feedback correlations of .21 (self-report), .40 (superiors), .54 (peers), .51 (subordinates), and .84 (combined scores) with senior executive performance. These findings are significant because they demonstrate the construct validity of competencies measured by BEI and 360 survey assessments, and suggest that ratings, which are much less expensive than BEI administration and coding, may be equally valid.

Casio (1982) and Smith (1988) provide methods for calculating the cost-effectiveness of various selection methods, given their costs of administration and criterion validity. The authors' experience is that biodata and paper-and-pencil tests are cheap ways to narrow a selection pool, but past job performance and BEI data are the most cost-effective and most valid assessment methods.

Competency-based staffing is based on many studies that show that the better the fit between the requirements of a job and the competencies of a person, the higher will be the person's job performance and job satisfaction.

High job performance and satisfaction in turn predict retention because good performers need not be fired; and because satisfied employees are less likely to quit (Locke, 1976 ; Mowday, Porter, & Steers, 1982; Caldwell, 1991).

Utility of Competency-Based Selection Systems

Table 4 shows the results of eight competency-based selection systems. Median productivity increases were 24 percent, and median reduction in turnover was 70 percent. In most cases, returns-on-investment exceeded 1,000 percent. Cases include the following:

- Retail sales: 50 percent of 60 new hires were selected on the basis of competencies assessed using a behavioral event interview, and the other 50 percent were selected using traditional biodata criterion (one requirement was 10 years of sales experience, which meant mostly middle-aged white males were hired, an affirmative action concern). In the year following selection, turnover in the competency-selected group was 20 percent (six people), and the average sales were $5,000 per week, compared with 40 percent turnover (12 people) and average sales of $4,200 per week for the traditional group. Benefits of the competency-based selection system were

   —Turnover cost avoidance: six sales people retained at $20,000 per person replacement costs = $120,000

   —Increased revenues (for 30 salespeople): 30 x $40,000 extra sales/year x 50 percent gross margin $600,000/year net increased contribution.

A total one-year benefit of $720,000 return on $30,000 invested in the competency study and selection training was 2,300 percent (Spencer, 1986, pp. 95-96). In addition, the competency-based selection systems resulted in the hiring of more female and minority salespeople (without prior sales experience), solving the affirmative action problem.

Table 4. Meta-analysis of eight competency-based staffing systems.

Industry-Job Family	N	Design	Productivity Increase	Turnover Decrease	Economic Value	Return-on-Investment
Retail sales	60	Control	+19%	-50%	$720,000	2,300%
Wholesale sales	80	Control	+16%	-50%		
Computer-sales trainees	700	Longitudinal	—	-90%	>$3.15 million	>1,000%
Food and beverage executives	47	Longitudinal	+10%	-87%	$3.75 million	>1,000%
Cosmetics sales	74	Control	+33%	-63%	$3.58 million	>1,000%
Computer programmers	100	Longitudinal	—	-99%	$1.43 million	>1,000%
Retail-customer service/telemarketing	320	Longitudinal	+24%	-99%	>$1.6 million	>1,000%
Financial services	120	Control	+24%	—	$750,000	525%
Median			+19-24%	-63%		>1,000%

- Telecommunications firm: reduction in turnover of competency-selected programmers saved 22 professionals costing $65,000 to replace, a $1.43 million return on a $120,000 investment in competency research and selection training.
- At PepsiCo, an 87 percent reduction in executives costing $250,000 to replace saved the firm $4 million.
- In commercial sales, 33 people were hired using the BEI and a competency model; a control group of 41 was selected without behavioral interviews. In the following three years, five of the competency-selected group quit or were fired, compared with a turnover of 17 in the control group. Staff hired through the competency-selected system increased sales an average of 18.7 percent per quarter, compared to a 10.5 percent average increase for salespeople in the control group. On an annual basis, staff chosen through the competency-selected system each sold $91,370 more than control salespeople, a net revenue increase of $2,558,360 ($91,370 x 28 salespeople).
- A large computer firm decided to transfer several thousand senior staff (that it described as "overhead people who cost money" because of their average yearly compensation of $57,000 per person). These staff members were to become "salespeople who make money." Not all staff bureaucrats have the competencies to be effective in sales, so the initial attrition from sales training was 30 percent, or 210 of the 700 staff sent for sales training each year. Sales trainee failures were terminated after four months, when they had failed three consecutive month-end tests. Each failure cost the firm $16,667 in salary costs alone, $3.5 million per year for 210 failures (this figure is conservative because trainee benefits and other costs of training—instructors, materials, and overhead—were also lost.) Using a competency model developed by studying the firm's successful salespeople, the firm cut attrition to 3 percent, 21 dropouts, a 90 percent saving worth $3.15 million (Rondina, 1988).

The benefits of the improved selection system are avoidance of the costs of turnover and increased revenues or productivity from better performing employees hired using competency methods. The costs of turnovers include

- Lost productivity during hiring time (55 to 57 days, or roughly two months' sales or production), acquisition of new staff (roughly one-third of the first-year salary).
- Lower productivity during a new hire's learning curve, which is the time from day hired to day 100 percent productive (defined as the average productivity of average experienced people in the job; learning curve time averages 12 months for technical and professional personnel).
- Out-of-pocket direct costs for relocation and training (Spencer, 1986). The minimum cost of replacing a technical or professional staff member is direct salary for a year (Spencer, 1986; Flamholtz, 1985; Swanson & Gradous, 1988). The actual cost is probably two to three times the direct salary if full-cost accounting for overhead is added to salary and if

lost productivity during replacement (for example, lost sales, loss of a major contract, delay in time to market of a new product) is considered.

Increased revenues and productivity come from better people; as mentioned earlier, superior performers who are one standard deviation above the mean produce 19 percent, 32 percent, 48 percent, and 48 to 120 percent more in low-, moderate-, high-complexity, and sales jobs. The median 24 percent productivity increase from competency-based selection means the same amount of work can be done with 20.5 percent fewer staff:

$$100\% - (100\% / (1 + \% \text{ productivity improvement}))] =$$
$$20.5\% \text{ fewer staff}$$

Appendix 2 provides a worksheet for calculating the benefits of competency-based staffing programs.

Self-Directed Change Based MBA Program

Boyatzis, Cowen, and Kolb (1995) and Boyatzis et al. (in press) have recently shown that M.B.A students' competencies on all 18 competencies developed in the Case Western Reserve Weatherhead School of Management significantly increased during the two-year program using a self-directed change approach in which the students

- get a baseline measure of their competencies in an intensive assessment center conducted during the first two weeks of their first year of study
- identify, set goals, and develop detailed personal learning plans to develop competencies that *they* feel deficient in and *they* commit to improving
- take formal courses, participate in development activities, work with mentors, and receive frequent feedback on their development of target competencies
- are reassessed at the end of their second year of study and "certified" on competencies they have developed successfully, as demonstrated on operant tests, in behavioral simulations, in a so-called document of performance project in an internship assignment, and by 360 feedback from professors, peers, and internship mentor or supervisors who have observed students behavior on the job.

This program was among the first to measure and credential the actual value added by higher education to students on competencies known to predict successful careers and life.

Value of "Unique" Competencies

In studies of superior leaders of Catholic religious orders, McClelland (1996) found that 12 competencies—eight in the standard dictionary and four unique to this study—correctly classified 71 percent of superior and 85 percent of average performers ($r = .49$, $p < .001$, 25 percent of variance). If the unique competencies are dropped, the criterion validity falls to 60 percent ($r = .29$, $p < .01$, 10 percent of variance). Competency scores are not highly correlated (median +.10; Nygren & Ukeritis, 1993). These and similar studies show that the team achievement motive profile is replacing the leadership profile. Such results suggest that it may not be possible to have a reliable definition of generic competency models for jobs. Custom competency research will continue to be needed and cost-justifiable because of increased reliability and validity.

Cross-Cultural Similarities and Differences

Comparison of competency models for similar jobs in different parts of the world reveals surprisingly few differences among superior performers. A major study funded by the U.S. Agency for International Development (USAID) found that superior entrepreneurs in Asia, Latin America, and Africa showed the same 20 competencies as their counterparts in similar jobs in Europe and the United States, and only one competency has differed statistically significantly among the three cultures (Mansfield, McClelland, Spencer, & Santiago, 1987; Spencer & Spencer, 1993, chapter 17). Confrontational messages may be given more bluntly in Australia than in Hong Kong, but superior performers in both cultures are higher in behavioral indicators of impact and influence. Cross-cultural differences exist in the nuances of how competencies are expressed, not in the underlying competencies themselves. Superior expatriates and country nationals and multinational jobs show higher levels of cross-cultural interpersonal understanding. They are better able to understand the meaning of others' words, gestures, and actions and to adapt their own behavior to communicate effectively and build positive working relationships with people from different backgrounds.

A major study (Hay/McBer 1996) of high-performing Asian (Japan, China, Philippines), Americas (Canada, United States, Mexico, Venezuela), and European CEOs (United Kingdom, Belgium, France, Germany, Spain, Italy) found that all had 12 competencies in three clusters:

- Strategic thinking: broad scanning (information seeking), analytic thinking, conceptual thinking and decisiveness
- Drive for success: Self-confidence, achievement motivation, social responsibility, and initiative
- Building commitment: Organization awareness, good judgment of people, leadership, and impact and influence

Significant differences were found for three competency variables:

- Building business relationships: personal versus contractual. Personal relationship building was most important in Asia ("we establish relationships so we don't need written contracts") and least in the Americas where "the (written) deal's the thing: didn't like (supplier personnel), but they had the best price."
- Action orientation: Planning versus implementation. Planners believe "a good plan enables anyone to carry it out," whereas implementers believe "good people will carry us though any situations." Planning is most important in Europe and Asia, especially Japan, whereas the "just damn it, do it" bias for action distinguishes American CEOs.

- Authority: centralized versus participatory leadership. Centralized authority distinguishes superior CEOs in Europe, Canada, and Asia. U.S. and Mexican CEOs use more participatory leadership.

Return-on-Investment

Reanalysis of Morrow et al.'s (1997) data on effect size shifts and return-on-investment from 18 training programs (Spencer & Morrow, 1996) found that

- Traditional theory and knowledge training shifted the performance curve .41 standard deviation and returned an average 87 percent return-on-investment.
- Competency-based training, defined as those programs that taught trainees practice motivation and behavioral skills and had them practice these skills shifted the performance curve .70 standard deviation and effected an average 700 percent return-on-investment.

Both traditional and competency-based training were effective and economically cost-justified, but competency-based training produced almost twice the improvement in performance, and eight times the return-on-investment. Appendix 2 provides a worksheet for calculating the benefits of competency-based development programs.

An "organization" competency study in a pharmaceutical firm found significant work process, organization, leadership, and individual competency differences between high-performing drug-development teams, which took a new drug from discovery to government approval in 2.5 years, and average drug development teams' 12-year development cycle time. Reduction in drug-development cycle time is hugely valuable: Each additional year under patent protection is worth $100 million. The firm reorganized all of its drug-development efforts to the rapid application "venture team" process and structure found by the competency model. This intervention reduced cycle time an average of four years, worth $800 million to the firm, a return on a $100,000 investment in the competency research of 8,000 percent (Boyatzis, Esteves, & Spencer, 1992).

THE FUTURE OF COMPETENCY RESEARCH

Six developments will accelerate research in competency in the future:

1. **Rapid growth of the worldwide competency database** will produce more precise generic models for superior performance in more economically important jobs and more detail about cultural differences in competency expression.
2. **Advances in measurement,** with more precise scaling of competencies and more operant tests of nontraditional abilities, should produce more and better methods of assessing and credentialing competencies. Also more utility studies of the economic value added by competency-based human resources applications—staffing, development, and performance management—would make a conclusive business case for competency methodology.

3. **Increased use of competency-based selection with diverse populations,** with better competency assessment methods will better discover what people *can* do—irrespective of their race, age, sex, formal education, credentials, or previous work histories. For example, a 15-year experiment funded by the Fund for the Improvement of Post-Secondary Education (FIPSE) and conducted by the Center for Adult Experiential Education (CAEL) has tested the use of competencies to select nontraditional students (poor minorities, older women returning to education after raising families) on the basis of competencies assessed using the Behavioral Event Interview. Competencies predict success in college, account for variance in performance not predicted by traditional college admissions tests, do not discriminate on the basis of age or sex, and cause less adverse impact on the basis of race (Austin, Inouye, & Korn, 1986).

    CAEL is now experimenting with an Employee Potential Program, using competencies to select "underclass" youth with few formal work or educational qualifications for jobs and remedial education programs to prepare for employment.

4. **Use of computers and artificial intelligence programs** will evolve into integrated human resource information systems that can aid in determining the competency requirements of jobs, assessing individuals' competencies, making optimum job-person matches using increasingly sophisticated pattern-matching algorithms, and providing development advice or actual training based on assessed gaps between competencies people have and those needed to perform their jobs well.

5. **Neuroscience,** with its rapid advances in the neuroanatomy and neurochemistry of cognition and emotion, personality, and competence, will transform psychology, education, and human resources management. New 3-D imaging methods (for example, PET, NMR, BEAM) enable researchers to watch a competency develop and flow through the brain in real time, from unconscious intent to cognitive planning to programming and execution of motor sequences in speech and behavior. Practical assessment and development implications can only be imagined. PET scans may become as common as BEIs in making assessment decisions. If, as has been speculated (see Restack, 1994, pp. 57-58), managers assessed as "interpersonally insensitive" (the number one reason for executive "derailment" and failure; Lombardo & McCauley, 1988) have right prefrontal lobe deficits, they may be offered cognitive therapy or training—or drugs—which enhance brain metabolism responsible for social perception and behavior. Cognitive methods that effectively change the brain (one definition of "education") will invariably be adopted by corporate training and development.

6. **Societal standards for competency applications** will be set. As noted above, competencies have become the official labor policy of the United States and the United Kingdom and are increasingly used by major business, government, military, educational, health care, and religious organizations (Spencer & Spencer, 1993, chapter 24). Two consor-

tia of academic, government, industry, and education experts, the Fetzer Consortium in the United States and the British Higher Education Council (HEC)/York Conference, have been established to identify best practices and recommend standards for labor law, development of educational curricula, and credentialing of competencies. As this is written, these efforts are just beginning. The first standard recommendation of the Fetzer Consortium is that competency research and measures "used to make decisions about human lives" (such as hiring, firing, promotion, compensation, development opportunities) meet American Psychological Association standards of statistical reliability and validity.

The job competency approach provides a human resource method broadly applicable to staffing, performance management, and individual and organizational development in the challenging years ahead.

APPENDIX 1
Economic Value of Competence Survey

This survey collects data you can use to cost-justify competency-based human resources applications.

Please answer the following questions for an economically valuable job you want to analyze (a sales job is ideal) and return the form to [the Conference Coordinator].

The survey can be answered anonymously, if you wish. Alternatively, if you would like feedback on how your firm's job compares to industry averages and potential returns-on-investment in competency-based selection, training and performance management, you can fill in your name and address at the bottom of the last page, and we will send you a "benchmarking" report. *Individual firm data will be held in strict confidence*—we will report only conference and industry averages.

Thank you for your participation!

I. Your firm's INDUSTRY (product/service): _____

II. The JOB or ROLE you are analyzing: _____

1. The average annual SALARY for this job: $ _____(A1)
2. The BENEFITS RATE for this job:_____% (A2)
3. The BUDGET, financial resources, or payroll a person in this job controls: $ _____(A3)

III. PRODUCTIVITY of Average and SUPERIOR (defined as the **top 1 out of 10**) employee in this job.

4. How much **more** does a SUPERIOR performer produce compared to an experienced Average employee in the job, whose productivity is defined as 100%?

_____100%_____   _____$ (A4)
Average employee   **SUPERIOR** (top 1 out of 10) employee

5. Actual DOLLAR figures for yearly sales or other economic outcomes?

$_____(A5) $_____(B5)
Average employee   **SUPERIOR** (top 1 out of 10)
(e.g., salesperson)   employee (e.g., salesperson)

IV. STAFFING

6. How many employees are there in this job? _____(A6)

7. What is the annual turnover rate for employees in this job?_____%(A7)

V. TRAINING, DEVELOPMENT, PERFORMANCE MANAGEMENT

8. LEARNING CURVE: How many MONTHS does it take for a new hire to become fully productive (equal to the average productivity of an experienced person in the job)? _____(A8)

Please provide the following data for a training program you have attended, sent a colleague to, or evaluated:

9. Please enter the number that best describes the TYPE OF TRAINING: _____(A9)

        (1) Sales (2) Executive (3) Management (4) Supervisory (5) Technical (6) Interpersonal
        Skills/Communications (7) Other _____

10. Please fill in the RELATIVE PERCENTAGES OF TIME (adding to 100%) in training spent:

        a. Learning facts, theories, or ideas   _____%
        b. Practicing motivation or behavioral skills   _____%(A10)
                                                        100%

11. PERCENTAGE OF TOTAL JOB tasks addressed by training:_____% (A11)

APPENDIX 1
Economic Value of Competence Survey (continued)

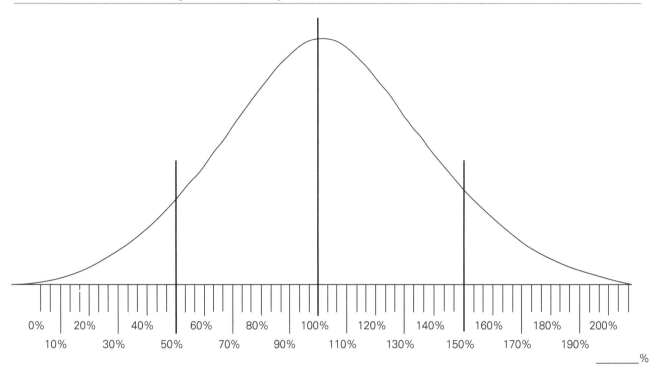

0% 10% 20% 30% 40% 50% 60% 70% 80% 90% 100% 110% 120% 130% 140% 150% 160% 170% 180% 190% 200%

_____%

12. The % Productivity of the average trainee BEFORE training, on the 0–200% scale below the curve; where 100% = the *average* performance of an experienced person in the job: _____% (A12)

13. The % productivity of the trainee AFTER training, on the scale below the curve, where 100% = the *average* performance of an experienced person in the job (fill in a % productivity if *greater* than 200% after training): _____%(A13)

14. How many MONTHS AFTER TRAINING does a trainee reach 100% productivity? _____(A14)

15. For how many months after training is this INCREASED PRODUCTIVITY MAINTAINED? _____(A15)

APPENDIX 2

Competency-Based Human Resource Applications Cost-Benefit and Return-on-Investment Analysis Worksheet

Data Input From Economic Value of Competence Survey

	A	B
I. INDUSTRY		
II. JOB/ROLE		
1. Salary/year	$40,000	
2. Benefits % rate	0.35	
3. Budget, resources controlled	$100,000	
III. PRODUCTIVITY	AVERAGE	**SUPERIOR**
4. Average versus superior %	100%	**148%**
5. Revenue	$300,000	**$444,000**
IV. STAFFING		
6. # employees in job	100	
7. Turnover rate/year	20%	
V. DEVELOPMENT/PERFORMANCE MANAGEMENT		
8. Learning curve in months	12	
9. Type of training	1	
10. % competency based	30%	
11. % job tasks addressed by training	50%	
12. Productivity BEFORE training	80%	
13. Productivity AFTER training	120%	
14. Months to 100% productivity	8	
15. Months training gains persist	24	

APPENDIX 2

Competency-Based Human Resource Applications Cost-Benefit and Return-on-Investment Analysis Worksheet (continued)

CALCULATIONS	BASELINE OR CONTROL		COMPETENCY BASED	
III. LABOR COST DATA				
16. Salary/year	$40,000	=A1		
17. Benefits % rate	0.35	=A2		
18. Total cost/year	$54,000	=A4*A5	$—	
IV. STAFFING				
A. BENEFITS FROM REDUCED TURNOVER				
19. REPLACEMENT COST	$40,000	=A1 OR NOTE 1	$40,000	
20. # I in JOB	100	=A6	100	
21. % turnover/year	20%	=A7	10%	
22. # leave/year	20	=A20*A21	10	B20*B21
23. Turnover cost/year	$800,000	=A19*A22	$400,000	=B19*B22
24. Net benefits from reduced turnover			$400,000	=A23-B23
B. BENEFITS FROM INCREASED PRODUCTIVITY				
25. S.D. effect size shift			.25	
26. % gain from improved selection			12%	=(B4-1)*B25
B1. BENEFITS FROM INCREASED REVENUES				
27. Net revenue/person	$300,000	=A5	$336,000	=A27+(A27*B26)
28. Total revenues—all employees	$30,000,000	=A5*A27	$33,600,000	=A5*B27
29. Net benefits from increased revenues			$3,600,000	+B28-A28
OR B2. BENEFITS FROM COST SAVINGS				
30. Costs managed/person	$100,000	=A3	$100,000	=A3
31. Savings/person	0		$12,000	=B30*B26
32. Total savings—all employees	$—	=A6*A31	$1,200,000	=A6*B31
33. Total benefits from cost savings			$1,200,000	=B32-A32
OR B3. BENEFITS FROM REDUCED STAFF				
34. Total staff required with turnover and productivity %	$100	=A6	89.29	=A7/(1+A26)
35. Total staff costs	$5,400,000	=A18*A34	$4,821,429	=A18*B34
36. Total benefit from reduced staff			$578,571	=A22-B22

APPENDIX 2

Competency-Based Human Resource Applications Cost-Benefit and Return-on-Investment Analysis Worksheet (continued)

CALCULATIONS	BASELINE OR CONTROL		COMPETENCY BASED	
OR				
B4. BENEFITS FROM SHORTER LEARNING CURVE				
37. Learning curve time saved by training in months		4	=A8-A13	
38. Value time/employee		$9,000	=A37*(A18/12)*.5	
39. Total benefit for all employees trained		$900,000	=A6*B66	
V. DEVELOPMENT AND PERFORMANCE MANAGEMENT—QUICK ESTIMATE PRODUCTIVITY	AVERAGE		SUPERIOR	
40. Average vs. superior %	100%		148%	=B4
41. S.D. effect size shift			0.6	
42. $ gain from development			29%	=(B40-1)*B41
43. BENEFITS FROM INCREASED REVENUES			$86,400	=A5*B42
44. Increased revenues— all employees			$8,640,000	=B20*B43
OR				
45. BENEFITS FROM REDUCED COSTS			$28,800	=A3*B42
46. Reduced costs— all employees			$2,880,000	=B20*B45
OR				
47. BENEFITS FROM REDUCED STAFF			22.36	=B20-(B20/(1+B42))
48. Total benefits from reduced staff costs			$1,207,453	=B47*A18
B. EVALUATION	Before Development		After Development	
49. % job time on tasks having training impact	50%	=A11	50%	=A11
50. % productivity on tasks	80%	=A12	120%	=A13
51. Economic value	$21,600	=A18*A49*A50	$32,400	=A18*B49*B50
52. Economic value added/ trainee/year			$10,800	=B51-A51
53. Duration of benefits/years			2	=A14/12
54. Benefit from training— all employees			$2,160,000	=A6*B52*B53

APPENDIX 2

Competency-Based Human Resource Applications Cost-Benefit and Return-on-Investment Analysis Worksheet (continued)

RETURN-ON-INVESTMENT ANALYSIS					
IV. INVESTMENT	A	B	C	D	
Labor costs		Per Diem/Unit	# Days/Units	Total	
1. Benefits rate	35%				
2. Paid days off/year	40				
>Internal staff	Salary	=(A+(A*A1))/260-A2		=B*C	
3. HR professionals	$50,000	$306.82	30	$9,205	
4. Line managers	$65,000	$398.86	8	$3,191	
5. Participant employees	$50,000	$306.82	20	$6,136	
6. Support	$28,000	$171.82	3	$515	
Vendors					
7. Consultants		$2,000	20	$40,000	
8. Travel and expenses		$500	4	$2,000	
9. Materials		$125	6	$750	
10. Equipment					
11. TOTAL INVESTMENT				$61,797	=SUM(A3:A10)
RETURN					
12. Reduced turnover				$400,000	From benefits WS A24
13. Reduced staff				$578,571	From benefits WS A26
14. TOTAL RETURN				$978,571	=SUM(A12:A13)
15. RETURN ON INVESTMENT				1484%	=(A14-A11)/A11

NOTES

The worksheet uses data from appendix 1, "Economic Value of Competence Survey" and spreadsheet references (for example, A1:A15 are the input fields on survey). It gives formulas opposite calculated fields and highlights input fields in gray; and unused fields are shown in diagonal cross hatching.

IV. STAFFING BENEFITS come from reduced replacement costs and increased productivity—increased revenues, cost savings, or reduced staff because fewer more productive people can do the same amount of work:

> #more productive staff
> =previous staff
> /(1+%productivity increase)

Effect size shift from competency-based training is conservatively assumed to be .25 standard deviation (B25). Note that these benefits may "double (or triple) count" the true benefits from the effect size shift. Researchers should be careful to count only benefits they can justify.

A minimum estimate of the cost of turnover is the direct salary of a person who leaves. A full-replacement accounting that assumes a hiring cost (A3) of one-third salary (whether paid to a search firm or incurred internally); lost productivity at salary value of time (A6) for the number of days it takes to fill the job divided by 365 days in a year; learning curve time of 12 months, and new-hire productivity averaging 50 percent during this time, hence a learning curve cost of A3*A8; and out-of-pocket direct costs of $3,000 (A10) = 129 percent direct salary (see spreadsheet in figure 1A).

Figure 1A. Full replacement accounting spreadsheet.

FULL-REPLACEMENT COST	A	FORMULA
1. Salary/year	$40,000	=A1
2. Benefits % rate	0.35	=A2
3. Total cost/year	$54,000	=A4*A5
4. Hiring cost	$13,333	=A1/3
5. Days to fill job	55	
6. Cost of lost productivity during time to fill job	$8,137	=A3*(A6/365)
7. Learning curve time in months	12	
8. Average productivity during learning curve period	0.5	
9. Cost of lost productivity during learning curve	$27,000	=A3*(A7/12)*A8
10. Direct costs of relocation, training, etc.	$3,000	
11. TOTAL COST OF TURNOVER/PERSON	$51,470	=A4+A6+A9+A10

V. DEVELOPMENT: TRAINING, AND PERFORMANCE MANAGE-MENT BENEFITS similarly come from increased revenues, cost savings, and reduced staff due to greater productivity. The "quick estimate" of development benefits uses the .60 (B41) standard deviation effect size shift for training and performance management found by several studies (for example, Burke & Day, 1986). Again note the caution against double or triple counting for productivity increase benefits. The "evaluation " benefits calculation uses the difference between before- and after-development productivity x the salary + benefits cost of employee time spent on tasks affected by training. This is a *minimum* estimate—most employees leverage three times their salary plus benefits costs. A3:Budget or resources controlled or A5: Revenues produced by an employee in a job should be substituted for A18: Salary + Benefits cost in economic value (A51), if these figures are known.

VI. RETURN-ON-INVESTMENT

An ROI analysis is shown for a typical competency-based human resources application. Internal firm labor costs are valued at salary plus benefits divided by days worked per year (average = 220). Vendor costs are at per diem or per unit cost multiplied by units expended. Costs should include both the competency study and its implementation—in this case, training line managers to use competency methods to hire new employees. The case return is based on IV. STAFFING benefits of B1. Reduced Turnover ($400,000) and B3. Reduced Staffing Needs ($578,571). The return on a $61,797 investment in the competency project is $978,571, 1,484 percent.

REFERENCES

Atkinson, J.W., editor. (1958). *Motives in Fantasy, Action and Society*. Princeton, NJ: Van Nostrand.

Austin, A.W., C.J. Inouye, & W.S. Korn. (1986). *Evaluation of the CAEL Student Potential Program*. Los Angeles: University of California, Los Angeles.

Boyatzis, R.E. (1972). "A Two Factor Theory of Affiliation Motivation." Unpublished doctoral dissertation. Harvard University.

Boyatzis, R.E. (1982). *The Competent Manager: A Model for Effective Performance*. New York: Wiley-Interscience.

Boyatzis, R.E., & J. Burruss. (1977). *Validation of a Competency Model for Alcohol Counselors in the U.S. Navy*. Boston: McBer.

Boyatzis, R.E., S.S. Cowen, & D.A. Kolb. (1995). *Innovation in Higher Education*. San Francisco: Jossey-Bass.

Boyatzis, R.E., M. Esteves, & L. Spencer. (1992). "Entrepreneurial Innovation in Pharmaceutical Research and Development." *Human Resource Planning*, volume 15, number 4, 15–29.

Boyatzis, R.E., D. Leonard, K. Rhee, & J.V. Wheeler. (in press). "Competencies Can Be Developed, But Not in the Way We Thought." *Capability*. UK: Leeds University.

Boyle, S. (1988). "Can Behavioral Interviews Produce Results?" *GA*, volume 4, number 1. Leicester, UK: British Psychological Society.

Bray, D.W., R.J. Campbell, & D.L. Grant. (1974). *Formative Years in Business: A Long Term Study of Managerial Lives*. New York: Wiley.

Buchnorn, D. (1991). *Behavioral Event Interview Quantitative Results*. New York: L'Oreal Corporation.

Burke, M., & R. Day. (April-May 1986). "A Cumulative Study of the Effectiveness of Managerial Training," *Journal of Applied Psychology*.

Caldwell, D.F. (April 1991). "Soft Skills, Hard Numbers: Issues in Person-Job/Person-Organization Fit." Paper presented at the Personnel Testing Conference of Southern California Spring Conference, Ontario, CA.

Caldwell, D.F., & C.A. O'Reilly. (1990). "Measuring Person-Job Fit with a Profile-Comparison Process." *Journal of Applied Psychology*, volume 75, number 6, 648–657.

Carkuff, R.R. (1969). *Helping and Human Relations* volumes 1 and 2. New York: Holt, Rinehart, & Winston.

Cascio, W.F. (1982). *Costing Human Resources: The Financial Impact of Behavior in Organizations*. Boston: Kent.

Cashman, D., & C. Ott. (Nov. 6, 1966). "The CIGNA High Performance Leadership Model." Paper presented at the Connecticut ASTD Conference on Competencies.

Costa, P.T., & R.R. McCrae. (1992). *Professional Manual for the Revised NEO Personality Inventory and NEO Five-Factor Inventory*. Odessa, FL: Psychological Assessment Resources.

Everett, N.B. (1965). *Functional Anatomy*. Philadelphia: Lea & Febiger.

Falcone, A.J., J.E. Edwards, & R.R. Day. (1986). "Meta-analysis of Personnel Training Techniques for Three Populations." Paper presented at the Annual Meeting of the Academy of Management, Chicago.

Fallows, J. (December 1985). "The Case Against Credentialism." *The Atlantic Monthly*, 49–67.

Fisher, K.W., H.H. Hand, & F. Russell. (1984). "The Development of Abstractions in Adolescence and Adulthood." *Beyond Formal Operations: Late Adolescent and Adult Cognitive Development*, M.L. Commons, et al., editors. New York: Praeger.

Flanagan, J.C. (1954). "The Critical Incident Technique." *Psychological Bulletin*, volume 51, 327–358.

Gendlin, E.T. (1981). *Focusing*. New York: Bantam.

Goleman, D. (1995). *Emotional Intelligence*. New York: Bantam.

Goleman, D. (1997). *Generic Emotional Intelligence Competence Framework*. Trenton, NJ: Rutgers University Press Fetzer Consortium.

Ghiselli, E.F. (1966). *The Validity of Occupational Aptitude Tests*. New York: John Wiley.

Hay/McBer. (1966). *Mastering Global Leadership: H/B International CEO Leadership Study*. Boston: Author.

Hunter, J.E., F.L. Schmidt, & M.K. Judiesch. (1990). "Individual Differences in Output Variability as a Function of Job Complexity." *Journal of Applied Psychology*, volume 75, number 1, 28–42.

Jackson, D. (May 24, 1994). "Personality and Performance in Senior Executives." (Unpublished paper.) London, Ontario: University of Western Ontario.

Jacobs, R.L., & D.C. McClelland. (Winter 1994). "Moving up the Corporate Ladder: A Longitudinal Study of the Leadership Motive Pattern and Managerial Success in Women and Men." *Consulting Psychology Journal*, volume 46, number 1, 1061–4087.

Locke, E.A. (1976). "The Nature and Causes of Job Satisfaction." *Handbook of Industrial and Organizational Psychology*, (pp. 1328–1330), Marvin Dunnette, editor. Chicago: Rand McNally.

Lombardo, M.M., & C.D. McCauley. (1988). "The Dynamics of Management Derailment." *Technical Report #34*. Greensboro, NC: Center for Creative Leadership.

Mansfield, R.S., D.C. McClelland, L.M. Spencer, & J. Santiago. (1987). *The Identification and Assessment of Competencies and Other Personal Characteristics of Entrepreneurs in Developing Countries*. Final Report: Project No. 936-5314 Entrepreneurship and Small Enterprise Development. Contract No. DAN-5314-C-00-3065-00. Washington, DC: United States Agency for International Development; Boston: McBer.

McClelland, D. (1996). *Assessing Competencies: Use of Behavioral Event Interviews to Assess Competencies Associated with Executive Success*. Boston: Hay/McBer.

McClelland, D.C. (1965). "Toward a Theory of Motive Acquisition." *American Psychologist*, volume 20, 321–333.

McClelland, D.C. (1973). "Testing for Competence Rather Than for Intelligence." *American Psychologist*, volume 28, 1–14.

McClelland, D.C. (1975). *Power: The Inner Experience*. New York: Irvington.

McClelland, D.C. (1984). "Entrepreneurship and Management in the Years Ahead." *The Individual and the Future of Organizations*, volume 7, C.A. Bramlette & M.H. Mecon, editors. Atlanta: Georgia State College of Business Administration. (Also reprinted in McClelland, D.C. (1978). *Motives, Personality and Society*. New York: Praeger.

McClelland, D.C. (1985). *Human Motivation*. Glenview, IL: Scott Foresman.

McClelland, D.C. (January 1994). "The Knowledge-Testing-Educational Complex Strikes Back." *American Psychologist*, , 66–69.

McClelland, D.C., J.W. Atkinson, R.A. Clark, & E.L. Lowell. (1953). *The Achievement Motive.* New York: Appleton-Century-Crofts.

McClelland, D.C., & R.E. Boyatzis. (1982). "The Leadership Motive Pattern and Long Term Success in Management." *Journal of Applied Psychology* volume 67, number 6, 737–743.

McClelland, D.C., & C. Dailey. (1972). *Improving Officer Selection for the Foreign Service.* Boston: McBer.

McClelland, D.C., & C. Dailey. (1973). *Evaluating New Methods of Measuring the Qualities Needed in Superior Foreign Service Information Officers.* Boston: McBer.

McClelland, D.C., W.B. Davis, R. Kalin, & E. Wanner. (1972). *The Drinking Man: Alcohol and Human Motivation.* New York: Free Press.

McClelland, D.C., G.O. KIemp Jr., & D. Miron. (1977). *Competency Requirements of Senior and Mid-Level Positions in the Department of State.* Boston: McBer.

McClelland, D.C., & D. Winter. (1971). *Motivating Economic Achievement.* New York: Free Press.

Mischel, W. (1968). *Personality and Assessment.* New York: Wiley.

Morrow, C.Q. Jarrett, & N.T. Rupinski. (1997). "An Investigation of the Effects and Economic Utility of Corporate-wide Training." *Personnel Psychology,* volume 50, number 1, 91–119.

Mowday, R.T., L.W. Porter, & R.M. Steers. (1982). *Employee Organization Linkages: The Psychology of Commitment, Absenteeism and Turnover.* New York: Academic Press.

Nygren, D., & M. Ukeritis. (1993). *Competencies of Outstanding Leaders: A Model for Leaders of Roman Catholic Religious Orders in the United States.* Chicago: DePaul University Center for Applied Social Research.

Restack, R.M. (1994). *The Modular Brain.* New York: Simon & Schuster.

Rondina, P.(October 1988). "Impact of Competency-Based Recruiting Techniques on Dropout Rates in Sales Training Programs." Paper presented at the McBer 25th Anniversary Symposium, Boston.

Sloan, S., & L.M. Spencer. (February 1991). "Participant Survey Results: Hay Salesforce Effectiveness Seminar." Atlanta: Hay Management Consultants.

Smith, M. (1988). "Calculating the Sterling Value of Selection." *GA,* volume 4, number 1. Leicester, UK: British Psychological Society.

Smith, P.C., & L.M. Kendall. (1963). "Retranslation of Expectations: An Approach to the Construction of Unambiguous Anchors for Rating Scales." *Journal of Applied Psychology,* volume 47, 149–155.

Spencer, L.M. (1978). "The Navy Leadership and Management Training Program: A Competency-Based Approach." Proceedings for the Sixth Symposium: Psychology in the Department of Defense. Colorado Springs: U.S. Air Force Academy Department of Behavioral Sciences and Leadership.

Spencer, L.M. (1986). *Calculating Human Resource Costs and Benefits.* New York: John Wiley.

Spencer, L.M., & C. Morrow. (September 6, 1966). "The Economic Value of Competence: Measuring the ROI." Boston: Linkage Corp. conference *Using Competency-based Tools to Enhance Organizational Performance.*

Spencer, L.M., & S. Spencer. (1993). *Competence at Work.* New York: John Wiley.

Stahl, S.M. (1996). *Essential Psychopharmacology*. New York: Cambridge University Press.

Stamp, G. (1990). *A Matrix of Working Relationships*. Brunel, UK: Brunel University Institute of Organization and Social Studies.

Swanson, R.A., & D.B. Gradous. (1988). *Forecasting Financial Benefits of Human Resource Development*. San Francisco: Jossey-Bass.

Winter, D.G., & J.M. Healy. (1981). "An Integrated System for Scoring Motives in Running Text: Reliability, Validity, and Convergence." Paper presented at the American Psychological Association, Los Angeles. (Published by the Department of Psychology, Wesleyan University, 1982.)

Winter, D.G., & D.C. McClelland. (1978). "Thematic Analysis: An Empirically Derived Measure of the Effects of Liberal Arts Education." *Journal of Educational Psychology*, volume 70, number 1, 8–16.

Zullow, H.M., C. Oettingen, C. Peterson, & M.E. Seligman. (1988). "Pessimistic Explanatory Style in the Historical Record." *American Psychologist*, volume 43, number 9, 673–682.

CHAPTER 2

Learning Style

Nancy M. Dixon, Ph.D.
Associate Professor
Administrative Sciences Department
George Washington University

Doris E. Adams, Ph.D.
Associate Professor
Business and Economics Department
Trinity College of Vermont

Richard Cullins, Ed.D.
Program Manager
Training and Development
Federal Aviation Administration

This chapter reviews the key research and practice literature on individual learning style and identifies its potential usefulness for HRD practitioners. The authors describe the various approaches to the assessment of learning style and review some of the available instrumentation. They address the questions, How are instruments that measure learning style best used to promote effective learning outcomes, performance, and career development? and How does learning style relate to the constructs of cognitive style, individual differences, and personality? They conclude that research provides indications but no clear direction for the application of learning-style information to practice.

> "Everything, men, animals, trees, stars, we are all one substance involved in the same terrible struggle. What struggle?…Turning matter into spirit."
> …Zorba scratched his head [and said] "I've got a thick skull boss, I don't grasp these things easily. Ah, if only you could dance all that you've just said, then I'd understand…Or if you could tell me all that in a story, boss."
>
> Nikos Kazantzakis
> *Zorba the Greek*

INTRODUCTION

Marissa is an ENTP, a converger, a high activist and pragmatist, global, field dependent, and impulsive; she has PEPS scores high in design, persistence, pair, team, and mobility; and she is not self-directed. By the end of this chapter, the reader will know what each learning-style label means and have some idea of the use that might be made of this information.

Observers of the learning process note that people choose different settings, learning activities, teaching methods, and media through which to learn. They also show differences in their readiness to direct their own learning process. For example, when attending a lecture, some people fully attend to the speaker, others doze, while others may be gazing out the window thinking of something far removed from the content of the lecture. Several researchers interested in categorizing and labeling the differences in style have developed a variety of typologies and related instruments to describe and identify these differences in what they label as a person's learning style. These frameworks do not say that one style is better than another, but describe each style type.

The interest in studying learning style in adults arose out of an awareness of differences in how people learn and a hypothesis that somehow learning outcomes could be better if these differences were planned for in designing instruction. The research on learning style began in the early 1970s with Hill's (1972) educational sciences work, Kolb's (1976a) publication of the *Learning-Style Inventory Technical Manual*, the development of the Productivity Environmental Preference Survey (PEPS) from earlier work on an instrument for children (Dunn, Dunn, & Price, 1979; Price, Dunn, & Dunn, 1982) and the *Canfield Learning Styles Inventory* (1983). In the 1970s and 1980s, a synthesis of the research on learning styles was presented by Kirby (1979) and Knaak (1983), which reflected an increased interest in this emergent construct. Simpson (1980) called for more research on this construct.

Since that time, numerous instruments measuring often unrelated style components have emerged. Once scored, these instruments categorize some people as more abstract, others more concrete; some with preferences for detail, others who prefer a holistic view; some who want to listen, others who learn best through visual stimuli; some who are more self-directed than others, and so on. No single theory has emerged to define the construct. In fact, many of the instruments lack a theoretical basis for their design.

Curry (1987) examined the psychometric profiles of 21 separate learning-style instruments. After studying the documentation behind these instruments, she believed it possible to place all the instruments into one of three categories. She created a three-tier typology of learning-style instrumentation and measurement. On the first tier are those models that tend to focus on personality and psychological type. The second tier focuses on information processing or how one best acquires new information. The third focuses on instructional preferences, the array of environmental preferences (lighting, temperature, visual versus tactile, learning through doing, reading, reflecting, and the like) that influence the teaching-learning process. The third tier is the most directly observable. Curry's typology will be used later in the discussion of several learning-styles instruments.

GENERAL PSYCHOMETRICS OF LEARNING-STYLE INSTRUMENTATION

Because there are different approaches to the assessment of learning style, there are different aspects to the design of available instrumentation. Each tool should be assessed by potential users for its psychometric strength. Several studies review many of these instruments in depth (Keefe, 1982; Messick, 1976; Sewall, 1986; Sims & Sims, 1995). Hickcox (1995) notes that learning-style assessments make use of five identifiable methods: inventories, tests, interviews, and analysis of products of learning. In recent years, several tools have received perhaps more attention than others, among them: Dunn, Dunn, and Price's Learning Styles Inventory (1979)/ Productivity Environmental Preference Survey (Price, Dunn, & Dunn,1982); Kolb's Learning-Style Inventory (1985); Honey and Mumford's Learning Styles Questionnaire (1989); the Myers-Briggs Type Indicator (Briggs & Myers, 1977); and Guglielmino's (1977) Self-Directed Learning Readiness Scale, and Guglielmino and Guglielmino's (1991) Learning Preference Assessment. Sewall (1986), Curry (1987), Allinson and Hayes (1988, 1990), and Candy (1991) have assessed the psychometrics of the most well-known instrumentation. These five tools will be described in the next section with comments about their reliability and validity from these reviews. As will be noted, the reviewers do not always agree on the reliability and validity of the tools.

Of the psychometrics that help determine the relative strength of a test or research instrument, reliability and validity are perhaps the most useful. Reliability is the consistency of an instrument in measuring whatever it purports to measure over time and multiple administrations. The scale for a reliability coefficient is from 0.00 to 0.99. An acceptable coefficient is 0.70 or higher. There are several types of reliability: coefficient of stability or test-retest, equivalence, and internal consistency or split-half. A coefficient of stability is determined when scores can be correlated from the same test of a group of people on two separate occasions (test-retest). Equivalence is determined when parallel, but different, versions of a test are administered to a group, and the results can be correlated. Typically, the different tests use the same items in different order. Internal consistency, or split-half, is a measure of how much error there is in the construction of the test between two items on the test or among several test items.

Validity is the extent to which an instrument actually measures what it is supposed to measure. Validity tells us how useful the instrument is. There are different types of validity: face validity, content validity, criterion-related validity, and construct validity. *Face validity* is simply superficial. It is the degree to which, without measurement, the test appears to measure what it is designed to measure. *Content validity* is a more systematic examination of the content by a group of experts who can agree that the test measures what it is supposed to measure. An example might be agreement by a group of journalism teachers that a test properly covers the main parts of the construction of a news story. *Criterion-related validity* can be either concurrent or predictive. *Concurrent validity* helps determine whether different items or tests measure something similar, like spatial ability, and can be correlated. *Predictive validity* is the degree to which items can predict behavior or performance. College Board (SAT) scores are an example. Finally, *construct validity* is an assessment of the degree to which an item or test actually measures a behavior, theory, or trait (for example, intelligence, or more appropriate to this discussion, learning style). Does the instrument measure the construct of learning style?

REVIEW OF SPECIFIC LEARNING-STYLE INSTRUMENTATION

Five different instruments are described below. Each purports to measure learning style, though each examines somewhat different constructs. Each instrument will be described in terms of what it measures according to the developers, the nature of the instrument, how the style gets derived, sample questions, its reliability and validity, and specific criticisms of the instrument that have arisen in the literature. Each will be placed in the context of Curry's (1987) typology.

Dunn, Dunn, and Price's LSI and PEPS

Dunn, Dunn, and Price's Learning Styles Inventory (LSI) (1979) and Productivity Environmental Preference Survey (Price, Dunn, & Dunn, 1982) take a holistic view of learning style. Given Curry's (1987) three-tier typology, the LSI/PEPS assesses both information processing and instructional preference. The developers view learning style as a collection of learner attributes including emotional, sociological, psychological, and environmental considerations (see figure 1). People are assessed on each of these attributes, and the results present a profile of the individual learner. According to Dunn, Dunn, and Price, such a profile assists adults in more effectively designing their learning and helps teachers and managers address individual differences.

Curry (1987) notes that there are several versions of the questionnaire. The LSI (Dunn, Dunn, & Price, 1979) was developed for children, but a separate instrument, based on the LSI, called the Productivity Environmental Preference Survey (PEPS), (Price, Dunn, & Dunn, 1982) was developed specifically for adult employees in organizations. This is a 100-

Figure 1. Learner attributes that Dunn, Dunn, and Price's LSI assesses.

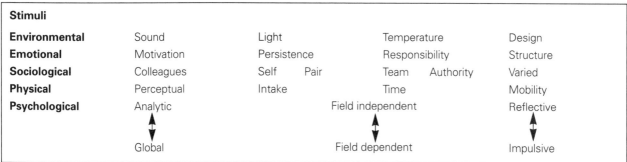

item self-report questionnaire. Respondents are asked to respond to each item as true or false in relation to their own learning. PEPS items include the following:

- "I prefer working in bright light."
- "I often have to be reminded to complete tasks or assignments."
- "I can block out sound when I work."

A computerized, individual profile of the respondent is provided by the instrument developers. A graph shows the relative location of each person's standard score in each area measured by the instrument. The standard score scale ranges from 20 to 80 with a mean of 50 and standard deviation of 10. Individuals having a standard score of 60 or more strongly prefer the measured area as a factor when they study or work, and those with a standard score of 40 or less do not. Examination of the composite results for both instruments yields data on how learners differ and provides information useful in making children and adults more productive. Curry (1987) concludes that Dunn, Dunn, and Price's LSI has good reliability and validity.

Kolb's Learning-Style Inventory

Kolb's Learning-Style Inventory (LSI) (rev. 1985) may be the most used and studied tool available today. Given Curry's (1987) three-tier model, the LSI deals specifically with instructional preferences but uses information processing as a basis for determining learning style. The LSI was designed by David Kolb to measure an individual's preferred way of taking in information from the environment and transforming that information to make sense of it. The four styles provide learners with information regarding the characteristics of their learning approach that may help or hinder their learning process. Kolb (1984) developed the LSI to give people information about their learning preferences in order that they might learn more effectively.

Kolb's (1985) inventory is one of the few that are guided by a theoretical framework, experiential learning theory, that describes the learning process. In developing this theory Kolb (1984) drew from the work of Dewey, Piaget, and Lewin. Kolb depicts an experiential learning cycle with four learning orientations beginning with an immediate, concrete experience that is reinforced through reflective observation of that experience. Out of reflection, an individual develops abstract concepts about his or her experience and is able to generalize those concepts to other experiences and situations. Concepts are then "tested" in actual situations to validate or reframe the learning. Finally, concrete experience of the test begins the cycle anew. As people develop, they often will specialize by developing a preferred approach to learning that may limit their ability to learn especially in complex situations requiring increased flexibility. As Kolb developed the LSI, he also drew on the Jungian concept of types.

Kolb's LSI (1985) is a 12-item self-administered, self-report inventory that measures the relative emphasis a learner places on each of the four learning orientations described above. The person completing the tool is asked to rank-order the four sentence endings for each item according to how well each one fits with how he or she would go about learning something. For example,

- "I learn best from: ____personal relationships, ____observation, ____rational theories, ____a chance to try out and practice."
- "When I learn: ____I get involved, ____I like to observe, ____I evaluate things, ____I like to be active."

A scoring process reduces the person's ranking on each item to four scores on each of the learning orientations included in the experiential learning cycle: concrete experience (CE; "feeling"), reflective observation (RO; "watching"), abstract conceptualization (AC; "thinking"), and active experimentation (AE; "doing"). These scores measure the respondent's relative emphasis on each of the four learning orientations. One's style is determined by creating two scores from the four above that indicate the preference the learner has for combining a mode of apprehending information (the concrete-abstract dimension) and transforming that information to make it useful (the reflective-active dimension). The scores are placed on an *x/y* axis. Coordinates are arrived at through the following calculations:

$$x\text{axis} =$$
$$\text{AE-RO}$$
$$y\text{axis} =$$
$$\text{CE-AC}.$$

These scores are plotted on a graphic representation of the learning cycle and locate the person's style (namely, Diverger, Assimilator, Converger, and Accommodator (see figure 2).

Figure 2. Kolb's learning-style type grid.

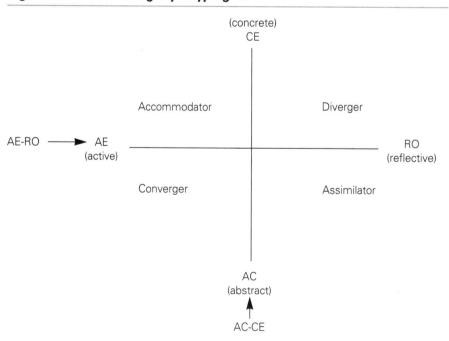

According to Kolb (1984; Kolb & Smith, 1986), Convergers' dominant learning abilities are Abstract Conceptualization (AC) and Active Experimentation (AE). Their knowledge is organized, so that through deductive reasoning, they can focus on specific problems. A strength is the ability to find solutions to problems and make decisions to act on those solutions. Convergers would rather have their solution implemented than wait for significant amounts of data to support the validity of the idea. They are relatively unemotional, preferring to deal with things rather than people. Divergers have the opposite strengths of the Converger. Their dominant learning abilities are Concrete Experience (CE) and Reflective Observation (RO). This learning style is called Diverger because these people perform better in situations that call for seeing the situation from diverse perspectives and generating new ideas. Divergers are interested in people and inclined to be imaginative and emotional. They prefer to deal with people rather than things, observe rather than take action, and generate possibilities rather than draw conclusions. Assimilators' dominant learning abilities are Abstract Conceptualization and Reflective Observation. They excel at inductive reasoning and assimilating different perspectives into an integrated explanation. They are interested in abstract concepts, less interested in people, and less concerned with practical application. For Assimilators, it is important for a theory to be logical and precise. Accommodators, are opposites of Assimilators. Their learning abilities are Concrete Experience and Active Experimentation. Accommodators' primary interest is in "doing" and in new experiences. They are risk takers and excel in situations that require immediate adaptation. Accommodators like to deal with people but can be impatient. They tend to solve problems in an intuitive and trial-and-error fashion. Where conditions require, Accommodators will rely heavily on others' analytic abilities.

Kolb (1984) reports gender differences in his measure of learning style. Males and females are similar on the Active-Reflective dimension, but they differ on the Abstract-Concrete dimension. Kolb found that 59 percent of males studied were oriented toward the abstract, but 59 percent of women studied were oriented toward the concrete. Kolb attributes the differences to social adaptation, noting that men are socially rewarded for developing a more impersonal, logical orientation. Kolb also suggested that, over time, he expected the expansion of career choices for women to begin to strengthen other sets of skills, and thus women may begin to evidence less concrete and more abstract perceptual skills.

Kolb's LSI (1985) continues to enjoy wide use despite critical scrutiny in the literature (Wunderlick & Gjerde, 1978; Freedman & Stumpf, 1978, 1980; Certo & Lamb, 1980; Sewall, 1986; Sims, Watson, & Buchner, 1986). Sewall suggests that the LSI has relatively low reliability and validity. Curry (1987) rates the LSI reliability as strong and validity as fair. Kolb's LSI (and other instruments that ask individuals to rank options) is criticized because its construction prevents the modes of learning from being independent. Ranking one option for an item first does not allow any other choice to be equally valued. Thus, the LSI does not measure the ability of a learner to adopt a flexible style to best learn in any situation.

Honey and Mumford's Learning Styles Questionnaire

Honey and Mumford's Learning Styles Questionnaire (LSQ) (rev. 1989) is based on Kolb's (1984) experiential learning theory. It is an assessment of instructional preferences in Curry's (1987) typology. The LSQ improves upon Kolb's LSI (1985) in several fundamental areas: its basis in potentially observable data, rather than self-reported data; its reliability and validity; and its ease of use and interpretation. The use of items that are observable behaviors that can be validated by a teacher or instructor has afforded the LSQ more positive acceptance in the literature.

Honey and Mumford (1989) have fully acknowledged Kolb's (1984) work as the foundation for their LSQ. They agree with Kolb's four primary typologies of learning style but found Kolb's nominal descriptors—Converger, Diverger, Assimilator, and Accommodator—semantically imprecise, preferring instead Activist, Reflector, Theorist, and Pragmatist.

The Learning Styles Questionnaire (LSQ) (1989) is an 80-item agree/disagree inventory that measures the relative emphasis a learner places on four learning orientations. Sample questions include

- "It is best to think carefully before taking action."
- "I enjoy the drama and excitement of a crisis situation."
- "I regularly question people about their basic assumptions."
- "In discussions, I usually produce a lot of spontaneous ideas."

Honey and Mumford (1989) have taken a different approach to the identification and determination of learning style. Unlike Kolb (Kolb & Smith, 1986), they have weighted each of their four scales equally. A maximum of 20 points can be scored on each scale. Once scores have been calculated, they are plotted on an *x/y* axis, roughly parallel in concept to Kolb's Cycle of Learning. The difference is that the respondents plot each of the four preferences, yielding a comparative picture of their relative preference for each of the four style types.

Honey and Mumford (1989) describe the four style types as follows:

> Activists involve themselves fully and without bias in new experiences. They enjoy the here and now and are happy to be dominated by immediate experiences. They are open minded, not skeptical, and this tends to make them enthusiastic about anything new. Their philosophy is: "I'll try anything once." They tend to act first and consider the consequences later. Their days are filled with activity. They tackle problems by brainstorming. As soon as the excitement from one activity has died down, they are busy looking for the next. They tend to thrive on the challenge of new experience, but are bored with implementation and longer term consolidation. They are gregarious people constantly involving themselves with others, but in doing so they seek to center all activities around themselves.
>
> Reflectors like to stand back and ponder experiences and observe them from many different perspectives. They collect data, both firsthand and from others, and prefer to think about it thoroughly before coming to any conclusion. The thorough collection of data about experience and events is what counts, so they tend to postpone reaching definitive conclusion for as long as possible.

Their philosophy is to be cautious. They are thoughtful people who like to consider all possible angles and implications before making a move. They prefer to take a back seat in meetings and discussions. They enjoy observing other people in action. They listen to others and get the drift of the discussion before making their own points. They tend to adopt a low profile and have a slightly distant, tolerant, unruffled air about them. When they act, it is part of a larger picture that includes the past as well as the present, and others' observations as well as their own.

Theorists adapt and integrate observations in complex but logically sound theories. They think problems through in a vertical, step-by-step, logical way. They assimilate disparate facts into coherent theories. They tend to be perfectionists who will not rest easily until things are tidy and fit into a rational scheme. They like to analyze and synthesize. They are interested in basic assumptions, principles, theories, models and systems thinking. Their philosophy prizes rationality and logic. "If it's logical, it's good." Questions they frequently ask are: "Does it make sense?" "How does it fit with that?" "What are the basic assumptions?" They tend to be detached, analytical, and dedicated to rational objectivity, rather than anything subjective or ambiguous. Their approach to problems is consistently logical. This is their "mental set" and they rigidly reject anything that does not fit with it. They prefer to maximize certainty and feel uncomfortable with subjective judgments, lateral thinking, and anything flippant.

Pragmatists are interested in trying out ideas, theories, and techniques to see if they work in practice. They positively search out new ideas and take the first opportunity to experiment with applications. They are the type of people who return from management courses brimming with new ideas they want to try out in practice. They like to get on with things and act quickly and confidently on ideas that attract them. They tend to be impatient with ruminating and open-ended discussions. They are essentially practical down-to-earth people who like making practical decisions and solving problems. They respond to problems and opportunities as a challenge. Their philosophy is "There is always a better way," and "If it works, it's good." (p. 5)

Honey and Mumford's (1989) learning-styles research demonstrates that women are higher activists than their male counterparts. They also offer that women perhaps have had to be more active in the contemporary workforce to be successful. Cullins (1996) replicated this finding in air traffic control selectee training. He noted that, at the time, the instructor population was 98 percent male (and low activists). Female trainees were found, as a group, to be high activists. Cullins reflected on the implications for controller training. Air traffic controllers rely on analytical precision and are not given to experimentation. Thus, one might expect to see low scores on the activist scale. Women activists were still successful in the training program (fewer than male counterparts), perhaps because of other intervening variables related to how they process and use knowledge.

Allinson and Hayes (1988, 1990) have provided the only independent evaluation of the Honey and Mumford's LSQ's (1989) validity and reliability. They report acceptable reliability and note that the LSQ appears to be stable and internally consistent. They report mixed results on validity. They found the LSQ to possess good construct and content validity but little predictive validity.

Myers-Briggs Type Indicator

Another well-known instrument is the Myers-Briggs Type Indicator (MBTI) (Briggs & Myers, 1977). According to Curry's (1987) typology, the MBTI falls in the first tier, a measure of personality and psychological type. The MBTI Technical Manual (Myers & McCaulley, 1989) notes that the MBTI identifies individual styles of information gathering and decision making that might put the tool in the category of information processing. The MBTI has been available for over 40 years. It is based on Carl Jung's theory of psychological types and his seminal research describing the introversion-extraversion dichotomy and the ways perception and judgment are used by different people. Katherine C. Briggs used Jung's theories to develop her own classification of type and with her daughter Isabelle Briggs-Myers developed tools to assess differences in individuals. The first edition of the MBTI was published in 1962 (Myers & McCaulley). It was designed to assess personality type and interpersonal functioning but has been used to assess learning-style patterns as well (Golay, 1982).

The MBTI (Briggs & Myers, 1977; Myers & McCaulley, 1989) assesses four different bipolar indices: extraversion-introversion (EI); sensing-intuition (SN); thinking-feeling (TF); and judgment-perception (JP). The MBTI postulates that opposite poles are mutually compatible (that is, that a preference for one pole is neither positive or negative, simply a difference). The EI index is the most intuitively obvious. It measures preference for either extraversion or introversion. *Extraverts* are gregarious, effusive, expressive, and auditory, preferring to focus on the outer world of people and things. *Introverts* are quiet, inward, intimate, contained, and visual, preferring to focus on the inner world of ideas and impressions. The SI index reflects an individual's preference for *sensing* (relies on reportable facts and events and concrete information gained from the senses) or *intuition* (relies on meaning, relationships, or possibilities, or a combination). The TF index reflects an individual's preference for *thinking* (logical, impersonal decisions, based on objective analysis or cause and effect) or *feeling* (reliance on personal or social values, a more subjective evaluation of person-centered concerns). Finally, the JP index reflects a person's reliance on *judgment* (using a planned and organized approach to evaluate the outer world, a preference for having things settled) or *perception* (using a perceptive process to evaluate the outer world, a spontaneous approach that prefers to keep options open).

MBTI is a 126-item (Form G), self-administered, self-report instrument (Myers & McCaulley, 1989). Also available are an abbreviated version (Form AV), which is self-scoring, Form F for formal research as well as the Expanded Analysis Report (Form K). The items demand a forced-choice response between the poles of the preference being addressed. Parts 1 and 3 include questions like: "Do you usually get along better with (A) imaginative people, or (B) realistic people?" and "Among your friends, are you (A) one of the last to hear what is going on, or (B) full of news about everybody?" Respondents are asked to identify which answer comes closer to telling how they usually feel or act. Part 2 asks respondents to select the word in each pair that appeals to them most. Examples are: "(A) compassion [or] (B) foresight " and "(A) quick [or] (B) careful."

A type is identified through a hand or computer calculation of points that are the weighted totals of answers for each pole of the four indices (Myers & McCaulley, 1989). The points are converted into preference scores and then into continuous scores and plotted on a report form for the respondent (see figure 3). The assessment classifies the subject as one of 16 MBTI types, which are measures of their relative preference for one pole of the index over the other. Thus, if one preferred extraversion over introversion, sensing over intuition, thinking over feeling, and judgment over perception, that person would be classified as an ESTJ, denoted by the first letter of the preference. As there are 16 possible combinations, there are 16 types. Each of the 16 types are different approaches to life and have implication for how one interacts with people and organizations. The 16 types have not been found to be distributed evenly across populations studied. Consistently, samples have also demonstrated gender difference. Women have relatively more feeling types and men have more thinking types (Myers & McCaulley, 1989).

Sewall (1986) found that the MBTI's reliability was on a par with other self-report instruments. He reports the MBTI's validity as moderate. Curry (1987) found good reliability and strong validity for the MBTI.

Guglielmino's Self-Directed Learning Readiness Scale and Learning Preference Assessment

The final instrument to be reviewed is Guglielmino's Self-Directed Learning Readiness Scale (SDLRS) (1977) and the Learning Preference Assessment (LPA) (Guglielmino & Guglielmino, 1991). The SDLRS was designed to measure a complex of attitudes, abilities, and characteristics that make up readiness to engage in self-directed learning. Curry (1987) would position the SDLRS/LPA as an assessment of instructional preference. Guglielmino describes the questionnaire as providing data on learning preferences and attitudes toward learning. Currently, the SDLRS is the most widely used measurement of an individual's readiness for self-directed learning. It has been used in numerous doctoral dissertations and as the basis of a number of other research studies (Candy, 1991). This char-

Figure 3. Profile of an ENTP on the MBTI Report Form.

EXTRAVERSION	E		X											I	INTROVERSION
SENSING	S										X			N	INTUITION
THINKING	T			X										F	FEELING
JUDGING	J											X		P	PERCEIVING
		60	50	40	30	20	10	0	10	20	30	40	50	60	

acteristic or preference for self-directed learning in an individual has been of interest to adult educators and trainers. Self-direction is increasingly valued in workers in today's ever-changing work environment. Organizations are calling for people who are capable of continuous learning and are self-motivated.

The SDLRS was developed and refined in 1977 by Lucy Guglielmino (1978) through the use of a Delphi technique. Fourteen experts in the field of adult education participated in the study to generate characteristics of self-directed learners. Factor analysis of the instrument led Guglielmino to identify eight factors (namely, openness to learning opportunities, self-concept as an effective learner, initiative and independence in learning, informed acceptance of responsibility for one's own learning, love of learning, creativity, future orientation, and ability to use basic study and problem-solving skills). Several forms of the instrument are available, a translation of the SDLRS in several languages, a form for adults with low reading level or who are not native English speakers, and a children's version. These forms are scored by Guglielmino and Associates who provide a computer printout of individual and aggregate statistics related to the test and the demographics of the group who completed the questionnaire. Guglielmino and her husband, Paul (1991), developed a self-scoring version of the SDLRS, called the Learning Preference Assessment (LPA).

The SDLRS (Guglielmino, 1977) is a self-report instrument with 58 items, both negatively and positively phrased, which the respondent ranks on a Likert-type scale. Following are some examples of the items:

- "If there is something I want to learn, I can figure out a way to learn it."
- "I don't work very well on my own."
- "I'll be glad when I'm finished learning."
- "Learning is fun."

After reading each item, the respondent would choose the response that best represents the degree to which the statement is true. Choices are

1 = Almost never true of me; I hardly ever feel this way.

2 = Not often true of me; I feel this way less than half the time.

3 = Sometimes true of me; I feel this way about half the time.

4 = Usually true of me; I feel this way more than half the time.

5 = Almost always true of me; there are very few times when I don't feel this way.

A total score is determined by adding up all the responses. The higher the score, the more ready the respondent is for self-directed learning. The adult norm from the national norming of the scale is 214. A mean score of 227.7 was derived from a metanalysis of 29 different studies using the SDLRS with adult populations (McCune, Guglielmino, & Garcia, 1990). Level of education tends to correlate positively with SDLRS scores (Guglielmino & Guglielmino, 1991). Level of management (Durr, 1992) and job performance (Roberts, 1986; Durr, Guglielmino, & Guglielmino, 1994) are also positively associated with readiness for self-direction in learning. No significant gender differences have been found in the results from the SDLRS.

The SDLRS (Guglielmino, 1977) has been used extensively and contributed to an expanding body of knowledge about self-direction in learning. Most reliability estimates for the SDLRS have been high (Guglielmino, 1977, 1989; Brockett, 1985; Graeve, 1987). However, the instrument also has been criticized on the basis of its reliability and validity. Field (1989; 1991) and Brockett (1985) identified low item-test correlations of the reverse-scored items (those for which a positive score indicates a low level of self-direction). Guglielmino included these items to avoid the development of a response set. Brockett was also concerned that the educational level of respondents affected their ability to respond adequately to the SDLRS. Guglielmino responded to this concern by developing a form of the SDLRS that contains fewer items and has a lower reading level.

The most lively debate related to the SDLRS (Guglielmino, 1977) has been about its validity. Although Field (1989) questioned the development of the SDLRS and the resultant items on the scale, the instrument is usually thought to have high content validity because of the method used in its development. Construct validity has been noted as good in several studies (Hall-Johnson, 1981; Graeve, 1987; Finestone, 1984; Jones, 1990; Delahaye & Smith, 1995). In these studies positive correlations are demonstrated between SDLRS scores and variables such as number of learning projects conducted, hours spent on self-planned learning, autonomy, and observer ratings of characteristics or behaviors related to self-direction in learning. Field (1989) suggests, as a result of his study of the validity of the SDLRS, that there are not different factors measured by the scale and that what is measured is not an indicator of readiness for self-directed learning but perhaps is more related to love of learning and enthusiasm for it. Bonham (1991) agrees with this latter assertion. Field's critique of the SDLRS created lively debate and generated counterclaims from proponents of the validity of the instrument (Guglielmino, 1989; McCune, 1989; Long, 1989).

Some confusion exists in the literature related to precisely what is being measured by the instrument (Candy, 1991). Descriptors used for the characteristic that is being assessed are attitude, preference, learning style, readiness, skill, ability, and characteristic. Candy suggests that users of the SDLRS have moved beyond the initial target population for the instrument, people within organizations. He argues that self-directed learning readiness is not a context-free construct.

Summary of Reliability and Validity of Learning-Style Instruments Reviewed

From the various psychometric reviews, the authors have compiled a summary of the reliability and validity of the learning-style instruments, which appears in table 1.

Each of these instruments differs from the others in what it assesses and how it assesses it. Although the MBTI appears the stronger tool psy-

Table 1. Summary of the reliability and validity of learning-style instruments the authors reviewed.

Instrument	Dunn, Dunn, and Price	Kolb	Honey and Mumford	Myers-Briggs	SDLRS
Reliability					
Test-retest	good	very good	very good	very good	very good
Split-half	good	good	good	good	good
Validity					
Content	good	good	good	good	very good
Construct	good	good	good	very good	good/poor
Predictive	good	fair	fair	good	good

chometrically, arguably it addresses instructional preference less than the others and perhaps has more limited value in the development of instruction and instructional environments. Each instrument must be examined discreetly for its own strengths and weaknesses. All are within acceptable psychometric limits.

It should be noted that the issue of self-reported data is always a concern in determining reliability and validity. Self-reported data do not provide an objective assessment of the subject under measurement and therefore are not considered to be as accurate as data gathered through direct observation or measurement.

The previous section of the chapter focused on the review of five instruments that represent each of the three tiers of Curry's (1987) typology for categorizing learning-style instrumentation. With an understanding of some of the more well-known instruments for measuring the variable construct of learning style and some exposure into how these instruments compare in terms of reliability and validity, the practitioner is likely to have some questions about use of these instruments and how learning style relates to other similar constructs. The remaining sections of this chapter will address these two areas.

APPLICATION OF LEARNING-STYLE CONSTRUCT TO PRACTICE

Use in Modifying Instruction

The idea of matching learning style to instructional style or approach in order to improve learning is a very attractive one. And it would appear reasonable given the acknowledged differences in the way people approach learning; if the book is too theoretical for me, give me one that is more practical and I will learn more; instead of making me do the role play, just tell me what I need to know about the subject, and I will understand it more fully.

As much as this idea seems to be common sense, research does not bear it out. Studies have not demonstrated that matching instruction with learning style increases or improves learning. Except in laboratory settings, it would be difficult to even design ways to test this theory because each individual has not one but many styles. A single individual may prefer group instruction to individual instruction, theory over concrete experience, listening over reading, and bright light to soft light. Instruction that matches any one style is at the same time likely to mismatch on four or five of the person's other styles. It would not seem possible to create an instructional process that influenced only one style.

At a minimum, it may be important to assess multiple variables in tandem for the results of learning-style instruments to be more useful in designing instruction. For example, Cullins (1996) examined the interaction between measures of student motivation, instructor learning style, and student learning style in air traffic controller pretraining. He found that motivation was a positive intervening variable in cases in which students did not share the learning-style preferences of the instructor cadre.

Motorola instituted a process to implement self-directed learning at its facility in Boynton Beach, Florida (Durr, 1995). The company used the SDLRS (Guglielmino, 1977) to determine the readiness of employees to participate in the program. This suggests that more effective outcomes could result from matching someone who is ready or motivated for self-directed learning with an opportunity to design his or her own learning.

To complicate the matching task even further, most learning-style instruments measure preference, not ability. People can often learn in other ways than the ones they prefer. This is an important distinction. For example, an individual might prefer to learn communication skills by reading the theory, but because of the nature of the subject matter, would actually learn communication skills more effectively by role playing. Preference is important, but so is the nature of the discipline and how one would best learn, given a particular content area.

Kolb (1984) has studied the relationship of disciplines to the four poles of his learning orientation framework and has found that the disciplines of humanities and social science are based in concrete experience and reflective observation. Therefore, he would expect learning in these disciplines to be facilitated by simulations, fieldwork, and reflective journal writing. The natural sciences and mathematics were found to be primarily reflective and abstract, however. Here, according to the theory, simulations or fieldwork would be of little help. Learners would need theory and thought questions to master the discipline. The MBTI data bank (Myers & McCaulley, 1989) also relates discipline to type.

A branch of research that bears upon the question of matching learners to instructional strategy is Aptitude-Treatment-Interaction (ATI). Tobias (1987) reports that ATI research of the last several decades investigated whether matching learners with different methods of instruction based on individual characteristics would yield improved performance. Researchers were unable to predict conclusively that learners at one end of an individual difference continuum would perform better than individuals at the other end of the continuum. It should be noted that the learner characteristics investigated in these studies were cognitive styles, rather than the more familiar learning styles, but the outcomes of this extensive and rigorous research gives faint hope that matching is either feasible or productive.

Finally, some researchers have questioned whether matching is an appropriate goal even if it were feasible. If instruction were consistently matched to style preference, learners might not have the opportunity to expand their learning repertoires and would become over time increasingly specialized in their ability to learn. Dixon and Adams (unpublished manuscript) identified the patterns in thinking that lead people to maintain a specialized learning style, especially in threatening or complex situations. People are likely to feel threatened, especially in a new situation, and hold more tightly to a familiar learning approach to protect themselves from looking stupid or being embarrassed. These responses often become obstacles to deriving a positive learning outcome from the situation.

Kolb (1976b;1984) suggests that a more appropriate goal would be for learners to be able to broaden their experience with various learning methodologies and increasingly expand their use of less preferential styles. The assumption underlying the learning-style measurements of information processing and instructional preference is that style can be altered and a more flexible style is the desired goal. Kolb (1984) and Dunn, Dunn and Price (1979) find that learning style is adaptive and may change gradually over time depending on the adaptational demands on the learner. In particular the experience of the learner can influence style over time. For example, engineers, who are typically abstract and active, tend to become more concrete as they move into management positions.

Thus, Kolb's (1984) suggestion seems to call for using a variety of approaches to instruction in any learning environment. Kolb encourages teachers to construct instructional activities that address each component of the learning cycle. In doing this, each learner's preferences for learning or style would be included in the learning experience. This approach avoids the problems associated with matching learners with learning activities and calls for learners to have information about their own learning style so they can manage their own learning. This self-management process might include asking for guidance and support in creating optimal conditions for learning and in stretching beyond one's comfort zone, requesting an alternative learning activity for understanding a particular concept, or discovering new resources for learning. In the case of self-directed learning, it would be helpful to create approaches to assist someone with a lower SDLRS score to become more skilled at designing and managing his or her own learning (Guglielmino, 1977).

Bernice McCarthy (Excel, 1996b) used Kolb's (1984) model and his LSI (1985) together with an assessment of hemispheric dominance (right brain/left brain) to create an instructional framework called the 4MAT system. This system aids teachers in designing instruction that attends to each learner's needs by systematically addressing all learning-style preferences found in Kolb's cycle of learning in any given lesson or module of instruction. In the 4MAT system, McCarthy creates designs intended to meet the individual needs of all the learners in a given class. She recognized the limits of matching and that individuals may need to be challenged to use other than dominate modes of learning to optimize their learning. McCarthy's work may be the best example of the application of learning-styles information. In The 4MAT Research Guide (Excel, 1996a), the authors cite numerous research and empirical studies that show evidence that application of the 4MAT system measurably improves student learning and attitudes toward learning. Her work is also impressive in that she has applied 4MAT in all levels of education. McCarthy (Excel, 1996a) provides examples of designs for instruction for primary school, middle school, high school, community college, and law school students.

The Center for Creative Leadership (CCL) uses the mnemonic GAG (Going Against the Grain) to reference the learning activities in their programs that are outside the comfort zone of participants. By using the GAG mnemonic, instructors acknowledge participant discomfort and frame the experience as a "stretch" rather than a program deficiency. In an extensive evaluation of LeaderLab®, a CCL program that involves many nontraditional activities, Young and Dixon (1996) found that the perceived value of these GAG activities increased over time. This finding is particularly significant because program ratings typically decrease over time. However, the uncomfortable activities that were rated low immediately after the program were rated higher several months later as the discomfort of the experience faded, but the lessons learned from the experience were remembered and valued.

The personality-type learning style measured by the MBTI is thought to remain static over time (Myers & McCaulley, 1989). People can alter the strategies they use to interact with the learning context, but their basic preference would not change. Myers and McCaulley suggest that the information from the MBTI is useful in instruction in order to develop different teaching methods to meet the needs of different types; understand different motivations for learning; analyze curricula, methods, media, and materials in light of the needs of different types; and provide help to teachers, administrators and parents to work more constructively together. This information is viewed as helpful, not prescriptive.

Use in Career Counseling

There are correlations between learning style and career choice (Kolb, 1984; Brown & Burke, 1987; Baker, Simon, & Bazeli, 1987). Academic disciplines and thus related career paths differ in the extent to which they favor one learning style over another. Kolb suggests that students may select a specialization based on their learning style. For example, Kolb's studies have shown that engineering programs favor abstract and active orientations over concrete and reflective orientations. Social work programs favor concrete and reflective orientations. In one study, students in undergraduate programs whose learning style fit the discipline demands had higher grades. Kolb reports on another study in which students whose learning style did not fit the discipline felt more political and social alienation. They were less highly involved with their peers. Thus, learning style may influence the comfort that individuals feel within a given professional environment.

Honey and Mumford (1989) report mean scores for eight different job classifications (see table 2), suggesting that people with certain learning-style profiles may gravitate toward similar employment options or that once employed in a given occupation individuals develop similar stylistic preferences.

Table 2. Mean scores for eight different occupations. [All scores on 20-point scales: 1-low, 20-high.]

	Activist	Reflector	Theorist	Pragmatist
Salespeople (N=89)	13.3	11.5	11.4	14.1
Trainers (N=96)	11.2	12.9	11.4	12.4
Marketing managers (N=93)	9.3	13.8	12.5	13.6
Engineering/science (N=73)	8.6	14.2	12.2	12.7
Research/development managers (N= 262)	8.0	14.5	13.1	13.4
Production managers (N=78)	7.4	12.7	15.2	16.0
Finance managers (N=60)	7.0	14.9	14.5	15.3
Female British managers (N=174)	10.3	13.4	12.7	12.6

The MBTI (Myers & McCaulley, 1989) is often used by career counselors to assist people in choosing a career or position and work environment that best suits their personality type. The Center for Applications of Psychological Type has collected data on occupations related to personality type. Individuals from all 16 types are employed in all the selected occupations, but each occupation attracts some types more than others. Myers and McCaulley note that the SN preference seems to be the most important in identifying choice of occupation. The EI preference relates to finding an appropriate work setting to carry out the occupation.

The results of learning-style assessments are most appropriate as sources of information for respondents to choose to use in whatever way they find most helpful. The researchers and instrument developers provide some specific suggestions to professionals who are likely to guide adults in learning and counseling environments. Little support is given to matching instruction to individual learning styles because of the difficulty of controlling for all the various styles or differences in a group situation as well as for other reasons already discussed. Matching might be more feasible in individualized instruction. Instructional environments that provide support and opportunity for learners to experience a variety of modes of learning are suggested. Similarly, people would profit by being given information on style differences in academic and career choices.

RELATIONSHIP OF LEARNING STYLE TO OTHER SIMILAR CONSTRUCTS

There are many overlapping fields of research that are all directed to creating a better understanding of how people differ. Although quite varied in their individual inquiry, research agendas have explored the possibilities and limits in improving human performance. Education and psychology have long shared in this quest. For example, research on learning style has identified differences in the way people prefer to learn, research on cognitive style has examined more fixed cognitive differences or abilities that frame an individual's way of interacting with the world, research on personality has created on individual temperament and its influence on the learning process, and research on individual differences, exclusively found in the psychology literature, has helped define limits of human performance. All of these areas of research provide professionals in the field of human research development (HRD) with information about how to structure learning that contributes to maximizing the competence of people in organizations. This information can be quite confusing as the constructs of learning style, cognitive style, personality or personality type, and individual differences are frequently overlapping and provide little clarity about how to apply research results in practice.

The following sections are structured to situate learning style among the constructs of cognitive style, personality or personality type, and individual differences. When it is relevant, connections will be made among the three constructs.

Cognitive Style

Bonham (1988) provided practitioners with a helpful discussion of the difference between cognitive style and learning style. Cognitive styles are described as "fixed patterns for viewing the world. Their purposes are to select information to which the person will attend, to organize and integrate what is attended to, to moderate and control affective aspects of personality, and to adapt to situational constraints imposed by a task" (Bieri as cited in Bonham, 1988, p. 14). Cognitive style, thus, is more about inherent individual differences or abilities. Learning style addresses an individual's preference for learning. Most of the researchers in the area of learning style believe these preferences can be altered, given exposure to or training in alternative approaches.

Bonham (1988) describes three extensive research programs that are classified under the category of cognitive style: the Fells Institute group that investigated conceptual style (examples: the Conceptual Styles Test, measuring analytic and relational styles; Matching Familiar Figures Test, measuring reflection and impulsivity) and cognitive tempo; the Menninger Foundation group that studied cognitive controls (tolerance for ambiguity, constricted vs. flexible control, leveling and sharpening, focusing and scanning); and the Brooklyn group that investigated field-independence and field-dependence. The most well-known of these efforts was Witkin's work that resulted in the Embedded Figures Test (EFT).

Bonham (1988) notes the problem with cognitive style constructs is that the bipolar traits for each theory did not capture the complexity of people's individual differences. Much of the cognitive style research was done in the laboratory, focused mostly on children, and was not very practical to replicate for more widespread use. Learning style, although more practical and complex, has not built up the strong theoretical and well-integrated research base that cognitive style has. Of course, it is often difficult to differentiate the two styles because the terms *learning style* and *cognitive style* are sometimes used synonymously. Cognitive style may be used as a broader term encompassing learning style, or learning style may be seen as the application of cognitive style theory (Bonham). For example, the bipolar concept of field dependence/independence, identified as a cognitive style, is one of the areas measured by Dunn, Dunn, and Price's Learning Style Inventory (1979).

The evolution of the construct of field independence/dependence will be discussed briefly to exemplify the overlap of the constructs of learning and cognitive styles. This discussion may explain why this bipolar concept may have been included in the learning-style instrument of Dunn, Dunn, and Price (1979). Witkin's (1950) exploration started with a question about why some World War II pilots could fly through fog with no problems, and others could not. Using the rod and frame test, he identified that people are different in the way they perceive a rod in relationship to a space. To make this assessment more available, Witkin developed the paper-pencil version of the rod and frame test, the Embedded Figures Test (EFT). The EFT has people locate simple figures within complex patterns. Results indicate that individuals who rely on the visual field (field-dependent) as the primary referent have difficulty locating a simple figure in a complex design, see the whole rather than the parts, and approach things in a global way. Conversely, people who are able to easily locate the simple figure rely on an intrinsic, internal, kinesthetic sense (field-independent), approaching a situation in an analytical way.

Although the initial measurement tools seemed to focus more on individual differences in ability, Witkin (Witkin & Goodenough, 1981) later situated his construct in the broader notion of psychological differentiation. Through 20 years of research, Witkin determined that field-dependent people have a greater openness to external sources of information, which stimulates the development of interpersonal competencies, but does not encourage the development of cognitive restructuring skills. The more autonomous functioning of the field-independent individual fosters the development of cognitive restructuring skills but not the development of interpersonal competencies. Restructuring and interpersonal competencies are seen then as opposite poles of the dimension of field independence/dependence. Witkin suggests that both cognitive restructuring and interpersonal competence are amenable to training. The optimal goal would be mobility that would allow the individual to use the competencies of both poles. Many dissertations and research studies have further examined the construct of field dependence/independence. Goodenough (1985) found that women, as a group, are more field-dependent than are men. Given Witkin's view, women can become more field-independent through environmental influences including training.

The results of assessment of field independence/dependence have implications for education and training. However, there has been little effort to build a framework for the development of instruction.

Individual Differences

Research on individual differences has focused on the abilities of learners, in terms of specific tasks and how to enhance them through instruction. This differs from the learning-style research agenda that features people's preferences for various learning approaches and is more closely aligned with cognitive style research in terms of the measurement of abilities. The individual difference literature notes that people have different inherent traits, abilities, skills, such as spatial abilities, hand-eye coordination, motivation, and intention. Some people are gifted with skills and abilities that set them apart, like a professional golfer's ability to line up and sink putts, a fighter pilot's ability to know his or her position in space during a complex maneuver, and an air traffic controller's ability to track time and speed in his or her head while in three-dimensional airspace. Existing individual attributes can be maximized, less developed attributes strengthened, and new ones developed in an encouraging learning environment.

Fleishman and Mumford (1989) review multiple studies that discuss the relationship between preexisting skills and successful performance in training. In their view, these studies lack "specific information on the kinds of human abilities related to the effectiveness of particular training treatments" (p. 185). The authors further note that principles of instructional design have largely concentrated on common learning environments for groups of learners. Recognizing the significance that individual differences play in the instructional process, the authors note it is a problem to design instruction that accounts for individual differences. Which individual characteristics should be addressed? Readers will remember that this was also noted in the context of matching instruction to the style of learners. Fleishman and Mumford suggest, "One possible solution to this problem is to formulate a taxonomic system capable of describing and summarizing the characteristics of the individuals which are most likely to influence skill acquisition on particular kinds of tasks" (p. 190).

Fleishman (1972) developed a taxonomy of human performance criteria he calls the "ability requirements approach." He describes abilities as general capacities related to the performance of some set of tasks that are enduring attributes of the learner through the impact of genetic influences and the cumulative effects of prior experience. The research behind the development of the approach involved a series of factor-analytic studies where tasks were designed to test hypotheses about the organization of abilities over a wide range of tasks. The tasks were assigned to several hundred subjects, and patterns of correlation were studied. The resulting list of some 50 ability constructs (for example, "wrist-finger speed," "multi-limb coordination," "speed of closure") was reviewed by panels of experts, and then the list was refined. The result of this work was the Manual for the

Ability Requirement Scales (MARS), a tool for the identification and profiling of job-ability requirements (Fleishman & Mumford, 1989).

Fleishman (1972) and Fleishman and Mumford (1989) have contributed to the documentation of specific abilities in which individuals can vary significantly. Their work is valuable in that it breaks down abilities into attributes relevant to task performance and skill acquisition. Knowledge of these abilities can facilitate the selection and assignment of individuals to training based on high or low ability. It can be useful in the design of instructional content and in optimizing learning activities for learners at different stages along the skill acquisition continuum. More research is needed to help identify the means by which existing individual attributes can be maximized, less-developed attributes strengthened, and new ones developed in an encouraging learning environment. Individual differences in abilities are important in determining student performance. Learning style is also likely to influence a person's ability to learn and performance given the nature of a particular learning environment. Individuals and teachers can modify the learning environment by attending to learning-style preferences.

Personality/Psychological Type

Personality is not an area of focus in many of the varied approaches to learning style. Curry's (1987) typology of learning-style measurements includes personality and psychological type. The MBTI, which is oriented to identifying an individual's personality or psychological type, is an example of this category of instrument. However, the construct of personality is much broader. In the past 15 years, there is a modicum of agreement in the psychology literature on the measures of personality. They are referred to in the literature as "the big five" or simply "the five factors." The five factors are

1. Extraversion-Introversion (identical to Jung's and Myers-Briggs constructs; Myers & McCaulley, 1989)
2. Interpersonal relations, how conscientious and considerate one is in dealing with others
3. Conscientiousness, measures of carefulness, planning, and persistence
4. Emotional stability, ego strength vs. emotional disorganization
5. Intellect, measure of inquiring intellect and relative openness to experience (Digman & Inouye, 1986).

All learning-style assessment tools, including the MBTI, are used to inform learners about differences in the way they prefer to approach learning. They and their teachers can use this information in managing the learning process. Personality assessments have often been developed to help professionals to diagnose and categorize persons. HRD professionals probably see personality assessment data (for "normal" personalities) used primarily in preemployment screening to predict whether an individual has the disposition, temperament, and interpersonal characteristics to be successful in different employment settings (Hogan, Hogan, & Roberts, 1996). Learning-style instrumentation was not designed to limit people's choices. Rather, categories and style profiles are intended to provide information to help people be more effective in increasing their levels of competence and career options, in choosing environments that are more comfortable for learning and working.

SUMMARY AND CONCLUSIONS

Remember Marissa? In the introduction, it was suggested this chapter would assist the reader in better understanding the instruments that measure learning style and ways of using learning-style information. Has it? Perhaps you have more answers and as many additional questions. Both are important in this complex and confusing arena to ensure the appropriate use of learning-style instrumentation in practice.

Interest in learning-styles research has waned in recent years. And perhaps it is time for another look. We now know more about the projected diversity of the American workforce in the next century, and much needs to be done to ensure that all people have the best opportunity to learn and succeed. In many ways, we are only beginning to understand the teaching-learning process. Learning-styles research and practice to date give us clues about how to best deal with differences in preference for learning approach.

The literature is not uniform in its enthusiasm for learning-style research and application. Findings have been anecdotal, and as the ATI research suggests, matching learners with prescribed instruction has not yielded consistent results. Given that learners differ in their preference for processing information and approaching a learning task, researchers and developers of learning-style measurements reviewed in this chapter (Learning Styles Inventory, Dunn, Dunn & Price, 1979; Productivity Environmental Preference Survey, Price, Dunn & Dunn, 1982; Learning-Style Inventory, Kolb,1985; Learning Styles Questionnaire, Honey and Mumford, 1989; Myers-Briggs Type Indicator, Briggs & Myers, 1977) suggest that the teacher can create learning environments that provide a variety of learning methodologies and improve learning outcomes. Learners can choose either comfortable approaches or stretch their dominant style through selecting more challenging approaches to learning. Both learner actions are likely to be important to enhance individual learning. Also, in today's environment that calls for self-direction in creating and implementing one's agenda for learning and development, the information about readiness for self-directed learning (Self-Directed Learning Readiness Scale, Guglielmino, 1977; Learning Preference Assessment, Guglielmino & Guglielmino, 1991) could be useful for workers and HRD professionals.

The preceding view assumes that the learners have information about their learning style and that teachers are knowledgeable in constructing diverse approaches to learning in their instructional designs. It also presupposes that teachers understand how to teach the use of learning-style data Of course, one must also assume that people can alter their styles. Although one's psychological type, identified by the MBTI (Briggs & Myers, 1977), is thought to be a stable measure, a person can alter strategies used in learning and making decisions.

Developers of learning-style instruments (Kolb, 1984; Honey and Mumford, 1989; Myers & McCaulley, 1989) also believe that people can receive guidance related to their career choices through being given information about the typical careers of persons of different learning styles. This information is not prescriptive but for self-management of one's career. Also, increased readiness for self-direction (Guglielmino, 1977; Guglielmino & Guglielmino, 1991) might be a supportive factor in being able to self-manage one's career and in successful performance in today's rapidly changing work environment.

Certainly, learning style offers only one piece of the puzzle in terms of the variables that interact to influence learning and performance. It seems clear that data on learning styles can be useful. New research must focus on where and how the data can be practically used and how information on learning styles can be used in tandem with other data to support learners in the successful acquisition of new skills and knowledge. The road to creating such an agenda is fraught with all the complexities and confusion discussed in this chapter. However, as research progresses, psychometrics evolve, and technology becomes more powerful and more accessible, it may be easier to construct holistic learner profiles that may be used to diagnose and prescribe appropriate instruction. It may one day be possible to embed measures of individual difference, learning-style data, and other information in learning workstations that can instantly process all the information through artificial intelligence and prescribe a course of action that best meet an individual's needs. Until that day, HRD professionals are challenged to stay connected with the latest research in the field and embed action research and critical reflection in our practice.

REFERENCES

Allinson, C., & J. Hayes. (1988). "The Learning Styles Questionnaire: An Alternative to Kolb's Inventory?" *Journal of Management Studies*, volume 25, number 3, 2322–2380.

Allinson, C., & J. Hayes. (1990). "Validity of the Learning Styles Questionnaire." *Psychological Reports*, volume 67, 859–866.

Baker, R., J. Simon, & F. Bazeli. (1987). "Selecting Instructional Design for Introductory Accounting Based on the Experiential Learning Model." *Journal of Accounting Education*, volume 5, number 2, 207–226.

Bonham, L. (1991). "Guglielmino's Self-Directed Learning Readiness Scale: What Does It Measure." *Adult Education Quarterly*, volume 41, number 2, 92–99.

Bonham, L. (1998). "Learning Style Use: In Need of Perspective." *Lifelong Learning*, volume 11, number 5, 14–17, 19.

Briggs, K., & I. Myers. (1977). *Myers-Briggs Type Indicator*. Palo Alto, CA: Consulting Psychologists Press.

Brockett, R. (1985). "Methodological and Substantive Issues in the Measurement of Self-Directed Learning Readiness." *Adult Education Quarterly*, volume 36, 1, 15–24.

Brown, H., & R. Burke. (1987). "Accounting Education: A Learning Styles Study of Professional-Technical and Future Adaptation Issues." *Journal of Accounting Education*, volume 5, number 2, 187–206.

Candy, P. (1991). *Self-Direction for Lifelong Learning*. San Francisco: Jossey-Bass.

Canfield, A. (1983). *Canfield Leaning Styles Inventory, Form S-A Manual*. Birmingham, MI: Humanics Media.

Certo, S. & S. Lamb. (1980). "An Investigation of Bias within the Learning-Style Inventory through Factor Analysis. *Journal of Experiential Learning and Simulation*, volume 2, 1–7.

Cullins, R. (1996). "Correspondence in Learning Style between Air Traffic Control Training Providers and Air Traffic Control Training Selectees." Unpublished doctoral dissertation, The George Washington University, Washington, DC.

Curry, L. (1987). *Integrating Concepts of Learning Style: A Review with Attention to Psychometric Standards*. Ottawa, Ontario, Canada: Canadian College of Health Service Executives.

Delahaye, B., & H. Smith. (1995). "The Validity of the Learning Preference Assessment." *Adult Education Quarterly*, volume 45, number 3, 159–173.

Digman, J., & J. Inouye (1986). "Further Specification of the Five Robust Factors of Personality." *Journal of Personality and Social Psychology*, volume 50, number 1, 116–123.

Dixon, N., & D. Adams. (1987). "Adult Reasoning That Leads to Specialization in Learning. Unpublished manuscript.

Dunn, R., K. Dunn, & G. Price. (1979). "Identifying Individual Learning Styles." *Student Learning Styles: Diagnosing and Prescribing Programs* (pp. 39–54), by National Association of Secondary School Principals. Reston, VA: Author.

Durr, R. (1992). "An Examination of Readiness for Self-Directed Learning and Selected Personnel Variables at a Large Midwestern Electronics Development and Manufacturing Corporation." Doctoral dissertation, Florida Atlantic University. Dissertation Abstracts International, 53, 1825.

Durr, R. (1995). "Integration of Self-Directed Learning into the Learning Process at Motorola." *New Dimensions in Self-Directed Learning*, (pp. 335–344), H.B. Long and Associates, editor. Norman, OK: Public Managers Center, University of Oklahoma.

Durr, R., L. Guglielmino, & P. Guglielmino. (1994). "Self-Directed Learning Readiness and Job Performance at Motorola. *New Ideas about Self-Directed Learning*, (pp. 175–186), H.B. Long and Associates, editor. Norman, OK: Oklahoma Research Center for Continuing Professional and Higher Education of the University of Oklahoma.

Excel. (1996). *About Learning*. Barrington, IL: Author.

Excel. (1996). *The 4MAT Research Guide*. Barrington, IL: Author.

Field, L. (1989). "An Investigation into the Structure, Validity, and Reliability of Guglielmino's Self-Directed Learning Readiness Scale." *Adult Education Quarterly*, volume 39, number 3, 125–139.

Field, L. (1991). "Guglielmino's Self-Directed Learning Readiness Scale: Should It Continue to Be Used?" *Adult Education Quarterly*, volume 41, number 2, 100–103.

Finestone, P. (1984). "A Construct Validation of the Self-Directed Learning Readiness Scale with Labour Education Participants." Doctoral dissertation, University of Toronto. Dissertation Abstracts International, 52, 5A.

Fleishman, E. (1972). "On the Relation between Abilities, Learning, and Human Performance." *American Psychologist*, volume 27, 1017–1032.

Fleishman, E.A., & M.D. Mumford. (1989). "Individual Attributes and Training Performance." *Training and Development in Organizations*, (pp. 183–255), I. Goldstein, editor. San Francisco: Jossey-Bass.

Freedman, R., & S. Stumpf. (1978). "What Can One Learn from the Learning Styles Inventory?" *Academy of Management Review*, volume 21, number 2, 275–282.

Golay, K. (1982). *Learning Patterns and Temperament Styles*. Fullerton, CA: Manas-Systems.

Goodenough, D. (1985). "Styles of Cognitive-Personality Functioning." *Personality Assessments in Organizations*, (pp. 217–233), H. Bernardin & D. Bownas, editors. New York: Praeger.

Graeve, E. (1987). "Patterns of Self-Directed Learning of Registered Nurses." Doctoral dissertation, University of Minnesota. Dissertation Abstracts International, 48, 820.

Guglielmino, L. (1977). *Self-Directed Learning Readiness Scale*. Boca Raton, FL: Guglielmino & Associates.

Guglielmino, L. (1978). "Development of the Self-Directed Learning Readiness Scale." Doctoral dissertation, University of Georgia. Dissertation Abstracts International, 38, 6467A.

Guglielmino, L. (1989). "Reactions to Field's Investigation into the SDLRS." *Adult Education Quarterly*, volume 39, number 4, 235–240.

Guglielmino, L., & P. Guglielmino. (1991). *The Learning Preference Assessment*. King of Prussia, PA: Organization Design and Development.

Hall-Johnson, K. (1981). "The Relationship between Readiness for Self-Directed Learning and Participation in Self-Directed Learning." Doctoral dissertation, Iowa State University. Dissertation Abstracts International, 46, 7A.

Hickcox, L. (1995). "Learning Styles: A Survey of Adult Learning Style Inventory Models." *The Importance of Learning Styles*, (pp. 25–47), R. Sims & S. Sims, editors. Westport, CT: Greenwood Press.

Hill, J. (1972). "How Schools Can Apply Systems Analysis." In Phi Beta Kappa Educational Foundation, Bloomington, IN.

Hogan, R, J. Hogan, & B. Roberts. (1986). "Personality Measurement and Employment Decisions." *American Psychologist*, volume 51, 469–477.

Honey, P. & A. Mumford. (1989). *Learning Style Questionnaire—Trainer Guide*. King of Prussia, PA: Organizational Design and Development.

Jones, C. (1990). "A Study of the Relationship of Self-Directed Learning Readiness to Observable Behavioral Characteristics in an Adult Basic Education Program." Doctoral dissertation, University of Georgia. *Dissertation Abstracts International*, 50, 3446.

Keefe, J. (1982). "Assessing Student Learning Styles: An Overview." *Student Learning Styles and Brain Behavior*, (pp. 43–53), National Association of Secondary School Principals, editor. Reston, VA: National Association of Secondary School Principals.

Kirby, P. (1979). *Cognitive Style, Learning Style and Transfer Skill Acquisition.* Columbus, OH: The Ohio State University National Center for Research in Vocational Education.

Knaak, W. (1983). *Learning Styles: Applications in Vocational Education.* Columbus, OH: The National Center for Research in Vocational Education, The Ohio State University.

Kolb, D. (1976a). *Learning-Style Inventory Technical Manual.* Boston: McBer;

Kolb, D. (1976b). "Management and Learning Processes." *California Management Review,* volume 18, number 3, 21–31.

Kolb, D. (1984). *Experiential Learning: Experience as the Source of Learning and Development.* Englewood Cliffs, NJ: Prentice-Hall.

Kolb, D. (1985). *Learning-Style Inventory.* Boston: McBer.

Kolb, D., & D. Smith. (1986). *User's Guide for the Learning-Style Inventory.* Boston: McBer.

Long, H. (1989). "Some Additional Criticisms of Field's Investigation." *Adult Education Quarterly,* volume 39, number 4, 240–243.

McCune, F., L. Guglielmino, & G. Garcia. (1990). "Adult Self-Direction in Learning: A Preliminary Meta-Analytic Investigation of Research Using the Self-Directed Learning Readiness Scale." *Advances in Self-Directed Learning Research,* H. Long and Associates, editor. Norman, OK: Oklahoma Research Center for Continuing Professional and Higher Education.

McCune, S. (1989). "A Statistical Critique of Field's Investigation." *Adult Education Quarterly,* volume 39, number 4, 243–246.

Messick, S. (1976). *Individuality in Learning: Implications of Cognitive Styles and Creativity for Human Development.* San Francisco: Jossey Bass.

Myers, I., & M. McCaulley. (1989). *A Guide to the Development and Use of the Myers-Briggs Type Indicator.* Palo Alto, CA: Consulting Psychologists Press.

Price, G., R. Dunn, & K. Dunn. (1982). *Productivity Environmental Preference Survey Manual.* Lawrence, KS: Price Systems.

Roberts, D. (1986). "A Study of the Use of the Self-Directed Learning Readiness Scale as Related to Selected Organizational Variables." Doctoral dissertation, George Washington University, Washington, DC. Dissertation Abstracts International, 47, 1218A.

Sewall, T. (1986). *The Measurement of Learning Style: A Critique of Four Assessment Tools.* (Report No. CE 043-807) University of Wisconsin-Green Bay. (ERIC Document Reproduction Service No. ED267247).

Simpson, E. (1980). "Adult Learning Theory: A State of the Art." *Adult Development and Approaches to Learning.* Washington, DC: The National Institute of Education.

Sims, R., & S. Sims. (1995). *The Importance of Learning Styles.* Westport, CT: Greenwood Press.

Sims, R., P. Watson, & K. Buckner. (1986). "The Reliability and Classification Stability of the Learning Styles Inventory." *Educational and Psychological Measurement,* volume 46, 753–760.

Tobias, S. (1987). "Learner Characteristics." *Instructional Technology: Foundations,* (pp. 208–231), R. Gagne, editor. Hillsdale, NJ: Lawrence Erlbaum Associates.

Witkin, H. (1950). "Perception of the Upright When the Direction of the Force Acting on the Body Is Changed." *Journal of Experimental Psychology*, volume 40, 93–106.

Witkin, H., & D. Goodenough. (1981). "Cognitive Styles: Essence and Origins. Field Dependence and Field Independence." *Psychological Issues*, volume 14 (Whole No. 51).

Wunderlich, R., & C. Gjerde. (1978). "Another Look at Learning-Style Inventory and Medical Career Choices." *Medical Education*, volume 53, 45–54.

Young, D., & N. Dixon. (1996). *Helping Leaders Take Effective Action: A Program Evaluation.* Greensboro, NC: Center for Creative Leadership.

CHAPTER 3

Organizational Learning

Victoria J. Marsick, Ph.D.
Professor, Adult Education
Department of Organization
and Leadership
Columbia University Teachers College

Karen E. Watkins, Ph.D.
Professor of Adult Education
University of Georgia

In this chapter, the authors examine the research on organizational learning and draw out implications for training and development practitioners. Research on organizational learning effectiveness is not extensive, in part because there are many different ways of understanding and measuring it. Following an introductory overview, the authors explain the different ways in which the idea of organizational learning has been conceptualized and measured in the research. They then discuss selected studies that illustrate several streams of research literature and conclude with implications for practice.

OVERVIEW

What is organizational learning, and how does it differ from the idea of a learning organization? Peter Senge (1990) popularized the learning organization when he advocated that companies adopt five disciplines for competitive advantage. Senge pointed out that everyone must be involved in learning and share their learning to benefit the company. Since then, many scholars and practitioners have struggled to define and implement the learning organization. Most of them agree that its essence is systems level, organizational learning. Of course, organizations are collections of people, and people learn on behalf of the organization. But the learning organization is not just the sum of many individuals who are learning. It speaks to the collective capacity of a company to respond effectively to a rapidly changing, turbulent environment by more effectively fostering, capturing, and sharing learning to reap the benefit of what people know so as to improve performance.

Organizations can learn naturally, without intentional efforts, in order to cope with changes in their environment. But the learning organization involves dynamic, intentional processes to accelerate the creation and utilization of knowledge across the system. This chapter reviews research on the product of the learning organization, that is, on organizational learning, to help human resource developers who want to use these lessons in designing initiatives and measuring results.

In recent years, efforts to understand organizational learning have increased, but we still know comparatively little about this phenomenon from research. Theory is being driven, in effect, by promising experiments and interventions. Companies have adopted practices heralded in the literature as bringing success and profit to well-known Fortune 500 companies (Marquardt & Reynolds, 1994; Watkins & Marsick, 1993, 1996). Sometimes, diagnostic instruments are used to monitor results that could shed light on success. But instruments available to assess dimensions of the learning organization have often been derived from a set of practices that its architects think will benefit the company. They are not based on theory, nor are they designed to tell us much about the relative merits or impact of different interventions (Gephart, Marsick, Van Buren, & Spiro, 1996; Gephart, Marsick & Van Buren, 1997).

Scholars have been interested in organizational learning for a long time, but very little of the scholarly research has been empirically derived. Early writing was aimed primarily at conceptualizing the phenomenon in order to lay a basis for research. Differences in these conceptualizations have led to inconsistency among the variables measured. Thus, even when studies exist, we are left without an integrated database from which we can draw meaningful comparisons. Hence, there is little that we can say about the effectiveness of one approach over another, or the linkages between interventions and performance results.

Even so, the research to date does point to some factors that we should consider in designing interventions and in examining their impact. In this chapter, we start with an overview of the research in order to map the topography of this research. We then lay out the different ways in which organizational learning has been defined, and thus, could be measured. We then examine various research streams in light of these different conceptualizations and examine representative studies in each category. Finally, we conclude with a discussion of implications for practice.

We have based this review on research reports published in refereed journals from 1991 through 1996 that are listed under the key words *organizational learning* and *research* in ABI Inform, Psych Lit, ERIC, and Dissertation Abstracts.[1] We also drew on research reports with which we were

---

1. A search of ERIC from 1995 to 1997 yielded 108 citations; however, many of these citations duplicated ones that we had uncovered through other searches, or they did not report systematic research. A search of Dissertation Abstracts from 1991 through 1996 using the same key words yielded 142 citations, from which we reviewed 22 dissertations plus one additional study known to the authors that addressed organizational learning. Each author had chaired two of these dissertations.

familiar and on earlier literature reviews that were the first to conceptualize its dynamics. Our search uncovered 71 articles, from which we selected 53 for review. We excluded articles that were not based on solid research, although we did not confine ourselves to quantitative or experimental designs. We did not select articles that focused solely on theoretical frameworks (for example, a discussion by Edgar Schein of culture as a missing piece in organizational learning), that reported anecdotally on experience or observations (for example, a discussion of "electronic hippies"), or that seemed insufficiently relevant to human resource development practice (for example, trends in Japanese technological innovation).

OVERVIEW OF RESEARCH ON ORGANIZATIONAL LEARNING

Less research is focused on the *effectiveness* of organizational learning than on its nature and definition. The first task that many researchers face is to clarify their assumptions about what organizational learning is. Then their next task is to build a set of hypotheses and models that enable them to design and conduct empirical research. Many of the early reviews on organizational learning (for example, Argyris & Schön, 1978; Fiol & Lyles, 1985; Hedberg, 1981; Huber, 1991; Shrivastava, 1983) focused on definition. Recent researchers have built on these early reviews to reinterpret the meaning of organizational learning in a rapidly changing environment and to challenge some of the original assumptions on which models were based (for example, Brown & Duguid, 1991; Glynn, Milliken, & Lant, 1991; Isaacs & Senge, 1992; Miner & Mezias, 1996).

The different ways in which researchers have conceptualized organizational learning has greatly influenced what is considered salient, what therefore is measured, the way in which findings shape new insights, and the way in which studies are designed. Glynn, Milliken, and Lant (1991), for example, suggest that these differences are captured by contrasting an adaptive perspective with a knowledge development perspective. An adaptive view casts organizations in the role of almost unconsciously adjusting targets and routines on the basis of their learning from experience. A knowledge development view assumes that the information learning produces can be proactively communicated and institutionalized. These authors suggest that adaptive researchers use abstract modeling and computer simulations in their research, whereas knowledge development researchers focus on applied case studies that are contextually grounded.

Some of this variation is also due to the disciplinary frameworks built over time by individual theorists. Edmondson (1996) illustrates the practical implications of these differences by describing three distinctly different approaches to intervention research by Edgar Schein, Peter Senge, and

---

1. *(continued)* However, we ultimately excluded dissertation research from this analysis because studies were extremely variable in their conceptualization and analysis. In addition, we reviewed existing volumes of *Management Learning*, a relatively new journal devoted to managerial and organizational learning that is not in these databases. We included one article from this journal that fit the research profile we sought.

Chris Argyris, who are all affiliated with M.I.T.'s Organizational Learning Center. Their research differences emerged when confronted with the task of helping the same company in its quest to become a learning organization. Schein took a culture perspective that first sought to understand conflicting cultural assumptions through observation without intervention. Senge wanted to actively experiment with the creation of models in a learning laboratory to illuminate system dynamics. Argyris preferred to work collaboratively with managers to change their reasoning and behavior through the joint mapping of causal links among values, actions, and consequences. Each researcher believes that different phenomena should be measured and influenced. Practitioners following each different research approach will design very different organizational learning interventions.

Research has had to distinguish among levels of learning (individual, interpersonal, group, intergroup, company, industry, community). Research is still not clear as to how learning relates across different levels, as Gephart, Marsick, Van Buren, and Spiro (1996) point out in a review of different models of learning organizations and the diagnostic instruments that theorists have created to assess systems-level learning. Much research has been done on individual learning, but it is not possible to automatically apply models and insights generated about individuals to aggregates; nor is it possible to simply aggregate data collected about individuals and make sound statements about systems-level learning, whether that takes place in groups or larger entities.

Another frequent question about the learning process concerns the differences between incremental and radical learning (or between single-loop and double-loop learning, or adaptive and generative learning) and the relative value of each. Incremental, single-loop, and adaptive learning all refer to knowledge, skills, or attitudes that do not require people to question the basic mental frameworks within which they interpret a situation. Radical, double-loop, and generative learning require people to critically examine the values, assumptions, beliefs, and mental frameworks within which they understand and solve problems. For example, a customer service representative demonstrates incremental learning when he or she is on the phone with a client and uses a computer database to call up product information in response to the customer's request. Radical learning might prompt a customer service representative to notice a puzzling pattern in customer calls that would lead to researching customer preferences in order to suggest improvements in the product itself or how it should be marketed. Many learning organization advocates believe an increase in incremental learning alone is not sufficient and may even be harmful because it perpetuates behavior that is inadequate in a turbulent environment. Miner and Mezias (1996) conclude that research shows that both concepts are meaningful, however, and that both types of learning are useful under some conditions, but harmful under others.

An intriguing line of research suggests that we can identify different types of organizational learning and that even though one or other type might be considered more effective, a company should build on its preferred learning style for quickest results. This advice parallels what we know about individual learning-style preferences. However, until research is done to link speed of learning with longer term success, it is hard to know whether quicker learning is better learning. Miner and Mezias (1996) identify four types of organizational learning: behavioral (trial-and-error), inferential (inductive observation or active experimentation), vicarious (in which organizations learn from observation of one another), and generative (discovery) learning. In a study using in-depth case studies and a survey of 1,359 managers from around the world, Ulrich, Von Glinow, and Jick (1993) identified four comparable categories of organizational learning: competence acquisition (discovery learning), experimentation (inferential learning), continuous improvement (behavioral learning), and boundary spanning (vicarious learning).

According to Miner and Mezias (1996), behavioral theories of learning have begun to focus on learning competencies rather than on information alone, a direction that Miner and Mezias point out is supported by cognitive studies that distinguish between declarative memory (knowing that) and procedural memory (knowing how). To illustrate this shift, they cite practical evidence from the history of VCRs, in which competencies enabled the Japanese to move quickly to market. The inability of U.S. researchers with scientific knowledge to access these competencies prevented similar success. By contrast, little is known about inferential learning even though its importance has been recognized for some time, and claims have been made about such learning in product development studies. Product development studies support the fact of inferential learning (Moorman, 1995; Lynn, Morone, & Paulson, 1996), but Miner and Mezias decry the relative lack of research on organizational experimentation. Vicarious learning may be best represented by benchmarking studies, although as Miner and Mezias note, there is little empirical research of any comparability among such studies. Although Miner and Mezias indicate that research on discovery learning is relatively scant, we note, as do they, that there is a small, but consistent, body of research with this orientation by Argyris and Schön (1996). Research-based simulations and other interventions (Isaacs & Senge, 1992) also describe discovery learning.

DEFINING CHARACTERISTICS OF ORGANIZATIONAL LEARNING

The first step in building a research stream is to agree on what is to be measured, but such agreement is still more a goal than a reality. Learning is measured through its outcomes. Learning is said to have occurred when a learner [or an organization] has changed, for example, by acquiring new knowledge, understanding, skill, or attitudes. We identify several schools of thought in the literature about learning outcomes. The organization has learned when it has

- developed better systems for conscious error detection and correction

- changed its organizational memory by changing some part of how it encodes memory (for example, the management information system, the budget, policies, or procedures)
- changed its mental models
- developed cultures of inquiry and generativity
- extracted knowledge latent in experience, which is then translated into new products or services or skills.

A description of each of these approaches to organizational learning follows:

- **Learning as conscious error detection and correction.** Argyris and Schön (1978) build on John Dewey's understanding of learning as a response to an error. Error is not necessarily a mistake; it is simply that which was not desired. Organizations learn when individuals inquire into error on the organization's behalf, as Argyris and Schön explain:

  > They experience a surprising mismatch between expected and actual results of action that leads them to modify their images of organization or their understandings of organizational phenomena and to restructure their activities so as to bring outcomes and expectations into line, thereby changing organizational theory-in-use. In order to become organizational, the learning that results from organizational inquiry must become embedded in the images of organization held in its members' minds and/or in the epistemological artifacts (the maps, memories, and programs) embedded in the organizational environment. (p. 16)

  What is measured in this conceptualization of organizational learning? Some examples include: changes in mission, vision, and value statements that reflect a transformed underlying consensus on the organization's purposes; structural changes that promote learning; higher levels of inquiry behavior at all ranks; use of mistakes or problems as opportunities for learning rather than blame; and the presence or absence of systems for detecting error rates as well as for addressing causes.

- **Organizational learning as a change in organizational memory.** James March (March & Olsen, 1976; Levitt & March, 1988) pioneered a focus on capturing knowledge gained from experience through organizational memory. Organizations learn by encoding inferences from history into routines that guide behavior. These routines are both formal (forms, rules, procedures, policies, strategies, technologies, or work processes) and informal (culture, beliefs, paradigms). Changes in these routines constitute a measure of the learning of the organization.

  Organizations, like people, learn only if information becomes sufficiently relevant for them to become aware of it. Like people, organizations are limited in their capacity to store and retrieve information, and they are subject to biases that may lead them to store inaccurate information. Experience may or may not lead to learning. A theory of organizational learning must take into account exposure to information, organizational memory, retrieval of information, and learning incentives as well as belief structures and their development in organizations.

March (1991) further differentiated two forms of organizational learning that result from experience-based improvements—exploration and exploitation. Exploitation is investing in continuous, incremental improvements through efficiencies, innovation, and product differentiation, whereas exploration is investing in more long-term, fundamental research and development. This type of experience-based organizational learning involves drawing on the learning that comes from outside the organization, from listening to newcomers, and from basic research. Organizations with a long-term learning capacity balance investments in both exploitation and exploration.

What would be measured in this conceptualization of organizational learning? Some examples include: changes in organizational investments in research and development; whether or not systems are created to buffer and learn from new hires; environmental scanning systems; changes in formal procedures, work processes, or cultural artifacts; and information systems processing capacity.

- **Organizational learning as changing mental models.** According to de Geus (1988), "institutional learning begins with the calibration of existing mental models" (p. 74). De Geus speaks from experience, having been head of planning for Royal Dutch Shell in the 1980s. Mental models (or frameworks by which people understand a situation) prevented managers from believing that oil prices could change. By creating scenarios of good and bad futures, de Geus helped managers learn in advance what they might do should prices fall. Their anticipatory learning helped Shell respond effectively to the severe drop in prices in early 1986, whereas other oil companies were caught off guard.

  Mental models become operationalized in a company's systems and processes. Without conscious examination, these systems can inhibit organizational learning. Shrivastava (1983) highlights this facet of mental models in an early review of research. He identifies two differentiating dimensions for organizational learning systems: the person or persons they serve, and the degree to which they are intentionally designed. Mental models differ if the systems serve a few key individuals, in which case they are highly personalized; or if they serve a larger, and sometimes impersonal, group of decision makers. Likewise, mental models are often incorporated without explicit review when information systems evolve without design. Organizational learning can be enhanced through revamping information systems. However, Shrivastava suggests that the development of learning systems without adequate examination of sociocultural learning norms may explain the frequent *failure* of designed learning systems. To the extent that organizations have embedded norms that suppress learning, designed learning systems are often less effective.

Technology has made it possible for people to work and learn together in new ways, but individuals' and companies' mental models have not always kept pace. A recent nationwide survey of 82 consulting groups by *Consultant News* supports this conclusion (Reimus, 1997). *Consultant News* first conducted fax surveys (52 percent response rate) and followed them with telephone interviews with more than 25 percent of the respondents. These consulting firms are grappling with the same information technology challenges as their clients. Some 60 percent of these firms currently do not maintain an active best practices database. One out of three firms does not use groupware for collaboration. Less that 25 percent do not use the Internet for internal communication, and at least 25 percent believe that technology provides only a slight competitive advantage, at best. The biggest challenge in the use of technology was persuading consultants to collaborate and share knowledge. Other challenges they cited are maintaining the currency and usefulness of information; ensuring security and confidentiality of the database; and providing for consistency and timeliness of data management, storage, and retrieval.

What would be measured in this conceptualization of organizational learning? Some examples include: changes in the overall map of what it means to work together in the organization; changes in capacity to plan strategically or to hypothesize viable futures; changes in the collaborative use of technology for learning and problem solving; and changes in the value and character of formal training systems toward more self-directed, continuous learning.

- **Organizational learning as cultures of inquiry and generativity.** Senge (1990) emphasizes the ability of an organization both to adapt and to create alternative futures. He conceptualizes organizational learning environments as places "where people continually expand their capacity to create the results they truly desire, where new and expansive patterns of thinking are nurtured, where collective aspiration is set free, and where people are continually learning how to learn together" (p. 3). Senge has developed learning laboratories that are characterized by continuous learning and the ability to "run experiments in the margin." He operationalizes organizational learning through five disciplines. Systems thinking is the integrative discipline. The other four disciplines are developing personal mastery with an emphasis on clarifying a personal vision; clarifying mental models that encourage individuals to identify and test their assumptions; building shared visions, and understanding the power of team learning.

  Measures that fit this conceptualization include tests of systemic thinking; employee opinion surveys that assess the degree of congruence between organizationally espoused values and organizational or individual actions, between the vision that top management defines and the one all others see, and between employees' sense of empowerment and management's belief in employee participation; presence and quality of experimentation designed for innovative problem solving; reward systems that support innovation; and assessments of the extent to which all members of the organization are engaged in learning either individually or in teams.

- **Organizational learning as extracting and building knowledge.** Organizational learning has been newly conceptualized as knowledge creation (Nonaka, 1994; Nonaka & Takeuchi, 1995), based on an analysis of the experience of Japanese companies. Knowledge is embodied in a company's goods and services, and as such, is part of its intellectual capital. Nonaka and Takeuchi describe an interactive, spiral, iterative organizational learning process that moves back and forth between implicit (tacit) and explicit knowledge, and that does so through alternating cycles of externalization and internalization. Tacit knowledge is created in socialization through sharing of experiences, mental models, and skills. Knowledge is then drawn out and made explicit so that ideas can be built into archetypes and tested through new product development. New ideas are explicitly shared throughout the organization, or cross-leveled, so that they can be externalized and experimented within other parts of the company. Finally, the newly evolved ideas are again internalized so that they become resocialized. Five organizational conditions support this knowledge creation process: intention, fluctuation/chaos, autonomy, redundancy, and requisite variety. Nonaka and Takeuchi describe an elaborate, integrated knowledge creation system that is built around specialized knowledge roles for all employees at various levels, and that involves a virtual, group-based learning management system.

The four types of organizational learning that were identified earlier in this article might be described as well, using these dimensions of knowledge creation. To be maximally effective, knowledge creation involves all four types of learning. Implicit knowledge creation (behavior learning) is recognized and consciously studied and drawn out. Based on this, experimentation occurs (inferential learning). Results of experiments are shared (vicarious learning) so that others in the organization can adapt what is known to their own settings (discovery learning).

Research from this organizational learning perspective would assess such things as the quality and speed of the research development and diffusion process in the organization; the number of new patents, products, or services per year; the extent to which new ideas are modified and incorporated into other products or services; the roles of individuals and groups in drawing out, testing, and spreading new knowledge; and whether or not the organization has the requisite cultural and structural infrastructure to develop new knowledge.

RESEARCH ON ORGANIZATIONAL LEARNING EFFECTIVENESS

The reports on which this chapter is based, like most research, represent partial windows on effectiveness. As can be seen in the prior discussion, the basis for those studies is differing definitions and assumptions about the nature of organizational learning. Even if the studies are, individually, well designed and analyzed, it is difficult to draw conclusions across studies because of the resulting variability in sampling and in design choices. Given the early trajectory of research in any given vein, studies also report one small part of the picture, and hence make it difficult to link findings across studies.

We found that studies of organizational learning effectiveness frequently fell into the following categories: natural field studies, with or without extensive, complementary data collection strategies; case studies (single or multiple case studies, sometimes combined with modeling); surveys; and simulations. Table 1 provides highlights into some of the more carefully designed studies that we identified in each of these categories. We turn now to a discussion of selected studies to provide a flavor of what researchers have learned about organizational effectiveness.

Field Studies

Alan Meyer (1982) developed a model of organizational learning as error detection and correction, based on a study of 19 hospitals in northern California. He had completed field observations in each hospital when the doctors went on strike. A malpractice insurer dropped 4,000 California doctors and offered to reinsure them as individuals at a 384 percent increase; surgeons and referral physicians supported the strike. Meyer had collected a great deal of information about each hospital's strategy through his personal observations, organizational documents, and interviews. This unanticipated, natural experiment allowed him to collect data on these organizations' responses to the strike.

In Meyer's model, based on business theory, a jolt or surprise triggers a learning cycle. Strategy (the organizations' overall business approach to its environment) and ideology (the beliefs, mission, and values that drive action) determine what captures the organization's attention, and therefore, how its leaders frame the challenge caused by the jolt. The structure and system of relationships in the organization and the slack—the available human, financial, and technological resources available in responding to the shock—influence the organization's response.

Meyer found that the organization either absorbed the impact of the jolt without changing in any fundamental way [resilience], or it retained new practices or information gained during the change experience [retention]. Further, he learned that strategy and slack help organizations absorb the shock of jolts, but they lead to change, which occurs only incrementally and within the same framework (or single-loop learning). Slack gives the organization the cushion it needs to absorb the impact, but the organization's dominant strategy tends to lead organizations to a consistent way of framing problems. Ideology and structure drive retention responses. Hence, for double-loop learning of the organization, changes have to occur at the cultural or vision and values level or at the level of a change in the overall system of relationships.

Meyer found that occupancy, employment, and revenue declined least in those hospitals whose ideologies encouraged surveillance of the environment; fostered strategic reorientations; embraced organizational changes; valued members' capabilities; and encouraged participation. Entrepreneurial strategies and adaptive, participative ideologies therefore enhanced organizational learning, while formalized, complex structures

Table 1: Representative research studies of organizational learning.

Research and Approach	Sample	Methods	What Was Measured	What Was Found
Field study encompassing unplanned natural experiment that shifted focus of study (Meyer, 1982)	• 19 voluntary general hospitals of intermediate size (100-400 beds) in same metropolitan area and not affiliated with medical schools	• Assessments of market strategies by panel of experts • Pictorial diagrams of task environments drawn by CEOs • Questionnaire data measuring structures and processes • Analysis of organizational charts and documents and of archival data from hospital associations and state agencies • Notes from structured interviews with chief executives and other informants • Naturalistic observation before and after strike	• Initial focus on contingency relationships among hospital environments, market strategies, formal structures, and informal processes • Shift to model of adaptive behavior during jolts (doctors' strike)	• "Adaptive behavior involves selective responses to feedback that map environmental attributes into systems capable of learning" (p. 519). • Entrepreneurial strategies and adaptive, participative ideologies enhanced learning. Formalized, complex structures retarded learning. • Slack contributed less to learning, although organizations that invested in people and technology learned more than those that invested in capital reserves or control systems.

Table 1: Representative research studies of organizational learning (continued).

Research and Approach	Sample	Methods	What Was Measured	What Was Found
Multiple case study (Elmes & Kasouf, 1995)	• Four biotechnology firms (three public and one private) in Massachusetts, ranging from 60 to 200 employees, in various stages of product launch • Cross-section of 44 scientists, managers, and technicians at different levels in hierarchy	• Open-ended interviews (one and a half to three hours each) with 30-question protocol in fall 1993 and spring 1994 • Content analysis • Preliminary focus on common themes using qualitative research software with verbal categories used by participants	• How interviewees thought their organizations learned and what interfered with organizations' ability to learn	• Competing theories of how organizations learn: rational, scientific inquiry, and action versus survival in hostile economic and regulatory climates • Interference factors: setting aggressive deadlines, vertical communication, rapid growth
Case study and model building (Nevis, DiBella, & Gould, 1995)	• Various-sized work groups in four companies: Motorola Corporation, Mutual Investment Corporation (MIC), Electricite de France (EDF), Fiat Auto Company • Workshops in 20+ Fortune 500 companies	• Field observation and unstructured interviews • Case descriptions of learning process shared for member checks • Grounded analysis to build two-part model of critical factors of organizations as learning systems • Testing and revision of model's components	• Seven systems-level learning orientations and 10 facilitating factors	• Nature of learning determined by organization's culture or subcultures • Style varies with learning systems • Best practices facilitate learning regardless of preferred learning style
Diagnostic surveys (Watkins, Selden, & Marsick, 1997; Watkins, Yang, & Marsick, 1997)	• 2% return rate for sample of almost 3,000 family businesses two-hour driving distance from Atlanta	• Item analysis reliability studies • Multiple regression • R square	• Seven action imperatives • 12-item construct of organization performance	• Reliability of coefficient alpha of .818 • More than one-third of variance in overall organizational performance explained by measured learning organization behaviors

Table 1: Representative research studies of organizational learning (continued).

Research and Approach	Sample	Methods	What Was Measured	What Was Found
Survey and field research (Zander & Kogut, 1995)	• 44 innovations identified from study of 100 major Swedish innovations with major share of world market (little variance in "relative advantage") • One key respondent per innovation (or experts for separate sections) identified by technical directors at group level • 80% response rate (remaining 20% similar in size and industry)	• Field research to develop and pretest questionnaire in five case studies and in Swedish technical universities • Measure constructs by forming scales from a priori questions • Form responses into standard normal deviate with 0 mean and variance of 1 (Cronbach alpha for reliability; "within" and "between" average correlations for discriminant validity) • Hazard rate specification for estimating effects of the covariations on time to transfer and time to imitation	• Test thesis that transfer and imitation are related to dimensions of underlying knowledge • Three constructs: manufacturing capabilities, technological competition, and the degree of knowledge diffusion among competitors	• 50% of production sold overseas within a year after introduction; 70% of new products manufactured in at least one plant outside Sweden • Adjusted median time to transfer and to imitate was five years • Codifiability and teachability significantly influence speed of transfer
Computer simulation (Lant & Mezias, 1990)	• 150 organizations created and assigned randomly to three search strategies (fixed, adaptive, imitative); 16 firm types related to ambiguity and high or low levels of performance	• Simulated organizations perform, set aspiration levels, search, and change; firm is bankrupt when resources = 0, and is replaced by random draw from surviving types; population experiences discontinuous shock in period 25; simulation run 100 times each under unambiguous and ambiguous conditions	• Theoretical implications for entrepreneurship in established firms facing discontinuous change using organizational learning perspective	• Different levels of ambiguity have different implications for strategy. • Lessons from experience can result in learning traps when environment changes. • Differences in entrepreneurial strategy and level show differences in performance, growth, and failure-probability outcomes.

retarded learning. Structures that decentralized decision making therefore enhanced organizational learning. Slack contributed less to organizational learning, though Meyer found that organizations that invested in people and technology learned more than those that invested in capital reserves or control systems.

Case Studies

A large number of single or multiple case studies, including many dissertations (for example, Broersma, 1992; Kim, 1993; Muir, 1991; Ziegler, 1995), are being conducted to identify the ways in which companies understand and respond to organizational learning needs. Case studies depict the complexity of variables that might have an impact on organizational effectiveness. However, these case studies are frequently time-bound snapshots rather than longitudinal studies, and hence make a true sense of effectiveness hard to verify, given that effectiveness is likely to vary greatly over time. These case studies have different foci, as well, and thus do not always link strategies and interventions to results.

Two representative case studies include a multiple case study in four technology-intensive biotechnology firms (Elmes & Kasouf, 1995) and a multiple case study leading to the development of a model of the learning organization that is based in Gestalt psychology (Nevis, DiBella, & Gould, 1995). Elmes and Kasouf approach organizational learning as the social construction of a culture. A paradox is that knowledge workers, who are trained in the rational scientific method, found themselves learning through a puzzlelike, nonlinear process of trial and error. Members acquire expertise in whatever way they can find it—literature, conferences, patents, interaction with colleagues and academics, new hires—and they create new knowledge by "mixing and communicating among employees at different levels of the firm and with different scientific and organizational orientations" (Elmes & Kasouf, 1995, p. 410). For those who are directly responsible for product development, aggressive deadlines and lack of time are among the greatest obstacles to organizational learning, along with a structure that interferes with information flows across the organization. The picture that emerges involves two narratives that the authors believe compete with each other:

> a) learning as a process of rational, scientific inquiry and action to identify and develop effective new products and b) learning for the purpose of survival in a hostile economic and regulatory environment." (Elmes & Kasouf, 1995, p. 418)

They link their findings to the differences between a managerial culture and a scientific professional culture, and discuss implications for changes in these biotechnology companies that will emphasize "technology transfer and partnering as firms come to rely on interorganizational alliances" (p. 420).

Nevis, DiBella, and Gould (1995) build their research on a conceptualization of organizational learning as knowledge acquisition, sharing, and utilization. They began with intensive observation in two U.S. and two European companies that were reputed to be strong learning organizations. They did not attempt to study an entire company or to focus on any specific, single work unit. From their interviews, they identified what organizational members claimed they learned and why. Their analysis led to a two-part model of organizations as learning systems: a description of what learning looks like and how the organization goes about learning or its preferred style; and identification of where an organization stands in relationship to best practices that facilitate learning.

Nevis and his colleagues developed an instrument, which a company can use to diagnose its learning system, that has commonalities with some of the survey research that is discussed in the next section. One of the differences between this model and other instruments is the belief of the designers, based on Gestalt psychology and supported by the research findings, that a company might choose to embrace and strengthen its existing orientation to learning instead of trying to make itself over using a normative profile based on an ideal. This case study also recognizes that learning organization interventions must be tailored to the unique strengths and needs of each company. However, it is clear that certain best practices facilitate learning in all organizations, irrespective of the level at which learning happens or its location in the value chain.

Survey Research

A number of studies are currently under way to validate assessment survey instruments that have been based on experience, the literature, and an analysis of practice (Gephart, Marsick, Van Buren, & Spiro, 1996; Gephart, Marsick, & Van Buren, 1997). Examples are companion survey research studies by Watkins, Selden, and Marsick (1997) and Watkins, Yang, and Marsick (1997) to determine the relative fit between an organizations' expressed characteristics and those measured by the Dimensions of the Learning Organization Questionnaire (DLOQ). The theoretical framework undergirding the research together with the DLOQ is a model of the learning organization developed by Watkins and Marsick (1993, 1996) in which critical changes must occur at the individual, group, organizational, and system levels. These changes include creating continuous learning opportunities, promoting dialogue and inquiry, supporting collaboration and team learning, empowering people toward a collective vision, establishing of systems to capture and share learning, connecting the organization to its environment, and providing strategic leadership for learning. Preliminary results indicate Cronbach's alpha coefficients for each dimension of the scale ranged from .716 to .859. Overall, the reliability estimate for the 42-item version of the scale was .940.

A general weakness of these kinds of surveys is the absence of linkages between interventions and impact on performance. Watkins and Marsick have been experimenting with 12 items that they constructed to measure organization performance, which they are beginning to use in conjunction with their DLOQ on data collected from a 2 percent sample of almost 3,000 family businesses within a two-hour drive of Atlanta, Georgia. Watkins, Selden, and Marsick (1997) found a significant correlation between reported financial and knowledge performance and above-average fit with the measured dimensions. Item analysis procedure showed that the 12 measures of organization performance had acceptable reliability estimates and the coefficient alpha was .818. Furthermore, these items showed strong internal consistency as the overall reliability estimate would not be significantly improved by simply discarding inappropriate items. The authors divided the sample between those firms reporting that their current financial performance was above average when compared to last year's [n=36] and those reporting that it was below average [n=28]. Firms reporting above-average financial performance differed significantly on all seven dimensions of the learning organization. Multiple regression analysis yielded an estimated multiple correlation coefficient of .570 and the R-square was .324. This means that over one-third of the variance in overall organizational performance [both knowledge and financial performance combined] was explained by the learning organization behaviors measured in this instrument. It is difficult to speculate on the meaning of these results with such a low response rate. Nevertheless, it is provocative to find that these seven dimensions of the learning organization consistently predicted higher overall responses on both financial and knowledge performance variables.

In looking for studies that link increased organizational knowledge with performance results, the authors found research by Zander and Kogut (1995) that looked at "the effects of the extent to which capabilities can be communicated and understood on the time to their transfer and imitation" (p. 79). As such, they examined the thesis that the transfer and imitation of capabilities are related to the dimensions of underlying knowledge. To test this thesis, they developed a questionnaire through field research that resulted in eight case studies. The questionnaire consisted of two parts. The first part sought facts about such things as the date the innovation was introduced, the number and timing of transfers, and when the first imitation occurred. They used these data to determine a hazard rate specification for estimating the effects of the covariations on the time to transfer and the time to imitation. Hazard rates are "rates by which manufacturing capabilities were transferred to the new sites and by which innovations were imitated" which are "expressed as the probability of transfer or imitation *conditional* on no previous event" (p. 83). The second part of the questionnaire consisted of 43 questions with a seven-point response scale regarding the nature of the firm's manufacture of the innovation. Zander and Kogut developed three constructs for items in the questionnaire: manufacturing capabilities, technological competition, and the degree of knowledge diffusion among competitors.

Zander and Kogut (1995) identified 44 major Swedish innovations that had been developed between 1960 and the time of their study and sent questionnaires to the project engineers that group technical directors had nominated as the ones most familiar with the development and subsequent spread of the innovation. The final sample consisted of 35 innovations. Using correlational models, Zander and Kogut found strong relationships between two characteristics of the innovation and the time to transfer. The more codifiable and teachable an innovation is, the higher the risk of rapid transfer. The characteristics of manufacturing capability do not correlate with the time to imitation, but key employee turnover is significantly associated with faster imitation times. This study suggests that continuous development activities enhance organizational learning, when defined as the development of knowledge. The more an organization invests in knowledge creation and modification, the less the threat of imitation by competitors. Transfer of knowledge and the imitation of innovations are facilitated by making new knowledge explicit and by key employees taking knowledge to competitors.

Simulations

With some exceptions, laboratory and simulation studies include a complex range of variables. Computerized capabilities make it possible for these studies to take into account numerous variables that can be played out over countless scenarios and through various combinations. However, because variables are preset and controlled, such studies cannot easily account for many real-world factors that could have an impact on results should the findings be applied in complex, field settings.

A good example of such research is a computer simulation by Lant and Mezias (1990) that tests the effectiveness of different entrepreneurial strategies in organizations in response to major changes in their environments. The simulation illustrates high and low levels of entrepreneurial activity under three types of strategies: fixed firms that do not search for information from the environment or change as a result; firms that monitor the behavior of industry leaders and change to become more like them; and adaptive firms that continually seek information about organizational characteristics and performance so as to adopt characteristics that get the best results. The study suggests that implications for costs and effectiveness vary depending on the degree of ambiguity that exists in the relationship between organizational characteristics and performance. High costs for entrepreneurial activity, interpreted as environmental scanning, are not justified under unambiguous conditions, although the authors caution that real-life conditions may differ from those set by the simulation. Under conditions of ambiguity, adaptive activity bears high costs, and as such, should often be avoided if possible. Imitative firms should not change too rapidly until industry leaders have emerged whose experience can be first analyzed. Studies such as these, if based on accurate assumptions, enable companies to play out the results of certain choices over time. Results can ward off actions that seem intuitively appropriate, for example in this study, investing in the high cost of constant surveillance, when conditions might not predict desired impact.

LESSONS FOR PRACTICE

What can we learn from the research about the circumstances under which organizational learning is most or least effective, despite the caution we must exercise in generalizing from the research? Like Hedberg, Nystrom, and Starbuck (1976) before us, we find ourselves camping on seesaws of contradictory patterns, recommending a balance of aligned visions and cultures for learning supported by indigenous structural and procedural changes.

There is some evidence to support the suppositions of organizational learning theorists that more open, empowered cultures (Meyer, 1982; Watkins, Selden, & Marsick (1997) support learning at the organizational level and that knowledge creation is enhanced by investment in continuous improvement (Zander & Kogut, 1995).

A clear pattern is that organizations should build on their existing strengths in choosing interventions to promote learning, especially if they are not either beginning a new business (in which case, the company will already be in a natural state of relatively high learning) or radically restructuring the business (in which case, radical changes may create conditions for totally new ways of thinking and working). Even if organizations are in a period of highly discontinuous change (that is, change that is not incremental and is not continuous), they cannot easily change the many dimensions of their culture, mental models, and organizational systems to support totally new approaches to organizational learning. Ulrich, Von Glinow, and Jick (1993) found that companies that learned through experimentation were more competitive and could change more quickly, but a match was essential between learning style and an organization's culture. Nevis, DiBella, and Gould (1995) pointed out that "The nature of learning and the way in which it occurs are determined by the organization's culture or subculture" (p. 75), and that "style variations are based on a series of learning orientations(that members of the organization may not see" (p. 76).

An implication of the research is that learning at the systems level need not involve everyone in the system at all times or in the same way. Organizational learning is catalyzed when there is a general expectation that people should be involved in scanning their environments, independently interpreting the meaning of the information they gather, sharing knowledge more widely, and ensuring that systems and structures support shared learning. In some organizations, expertise resides in everyone, however, and structures must enable everyone to contribute what they know. In other organizations, for better or worse, individuals are vested with the authority to learn on behalf of the organization due to their position in the hierarchy, their relationship to a natural community of practice, or the expertise they hold.

Information technology is a powerful tool for catalyzing the access, use, and retention of information. However, as the study of consulting companies shows (Reimus, 1997), the presence of technology alone does not ensure organizational learning because other factors come into play (such as its design, access and use; the capacity of individuals to understand it; and structures that may or may not get in the way of information flow). An implication is that organizations must place as much emphasis on changes in behaviors and cultures as they do on the design of the technology. In fact, discussions with practitioners reinforce the difficulty that can arise when newly created information systems lock a company into dysfunctional patterns of communication and interaction. So much has been invested that the company finds itself unwilling to discard the system in favor of something new. Creation of new technology for learning and problem solving might proceed with heavy doses of experimentation and equal investments in changing people's use habits.

Clearly, the organization's culture needs to change to support organizational learning because people will not experiment, take risks, share knowledge, and be motivated to contribute to the organization's success unless they believe that they will be supported and rewarded for doing so. Culture change is not easy, and it is not quick. As the study of biotechnology firms illustrates (Elmes & Kasouf, 1995), culture can make it difficult to adopt a new learning style when prevalent professional approaches to knowledge development are at odds with a turbulent environment that demands rapid growth. Organizations often seek strategies that will enhance knowledge acquisition and utilization, which will often result in incremental learning; but to be strategic and targeted toward higher performance, culture needs to reward innovation and out-of-the-box thinking, which often threaten the status quo. From a research standpoint, this is as difficult to measure as it is to develop. John Seely Brown (1993), in speaking about organizational change at Xerox, suggests: "Acknowledge that mistakes will be made. Build in sufficient chances to correct errors. Create opportunities to go off-site and reflect on whether progress is being made at a satisfactory rate and what new problems are coming up" (p. 8).

Organizational learning requires balance between strategies that emphasize smooth alignment of all functions for high performance, and strategies that may disrupt alignment in order to generate creativity and innovation. Conflicts and tension may accompany organizational learning. Managers must learn to work productively with this tension to generate new ideas and solutions (Leonard-Barton, 1996). This paradox calls for the simultaneous encouragement and balancing of conflicting skills, strategies, and structures within the system as a whole, though not necessarily within every individual, team, or set of procedures.

Finally, a review of research suggests that we need to find a theory-based framework within which to locate our studies. (Gephart, Marsick, Van Buren, & Spiro, 1996). Noting the lack of such a framework, Gephart, Holton, Marsick, and Redding (1997) have developed and are testing a research instrument for systems-level learning that has been based on a theory-oriented framework for organizational change and performance (Burke & Litwin, 1992). Based on open systems principles, the Burke-Litwin model "portrays the primary variables that need to be considered in any attempt to predict and explain the total behavior output of an organization, the most important interactions between these variables, and how they affect change" (p. 529). Burke and Litwin have defined the external environment as the input, individual and organizational performance as the output, and 10 organizational variables as throughput. They distinguish between transformational variables that are levers for fundamental, generative change and transactional variables that are needed to implement change, but are incremental in nature. Transformational variables include mission and strategy, leadership, and culture. Transactional variables include management practices, structure, systems, work unit climate, task and individual skills, motivation, and individual needs and values. This new instrument should enable its users to track learning and performance outcomes at the individual and organizational levels that are most linked to systems-level learning. Given that the design of interventions to create learning organizations must remain somewhat unique to each setting, this instrument will, over time, help to identify features of interventions that can be linked more closely with bottom-line results, which is what the learning organization is all about.

REFERENCES

Argyris, C., & Schön, D. (1978). *Organizational Learning: A Theory of Action Perspective.* San Francisco: Jossey-Bass.

Argyris, C., & Schön, D. (1996). *Organizational Learning II: Theory, Method, and Practice.* Reading, MA: Addison-Wesley.

Argyris, C., Putnam, R., & Smith, D.M. (1985). *Action Science.* San Francisco: Jossey-Bass.

Broersma, T.J. (1992). *Organizational learning and aircrew performance.* Dissertation Abstracts International, 53 (05A), 1427. (University Microfilms No. AAI9225534)

Brown, J.S. (1993). "Reenacting the Corporation." *Planning Review,* volume 21, number 5, 5–8.

Brown, J.S., & Duguid, P. (1991). "Organizational Learning and Communities of Practice: Toward a Unified View of Working, Learning, and Innovation." *Organization Science,* volume 2, 40–47.

Burke, W.W., & Litwin, G. (1992). "A Causal Model of Organizational Performance and Change." *Journal of Management,* volume 18, 523–545.

de Geus, A.P. (March/April 1988). "Planning as Learning." *Harvard Business Review,* volume 66, number 2, 70–74.

Edmondson, A.C. (1996). "Three Faces of Eden: The Persistence of Competing Theories and Multiple Diagnoses in Organizational Intervention Research." *Human Relations,* volume 49, number 5, 571–595.

Elmes, M.B., & Kasouf, C.J. (1995). "Knowledge Workers and Organizational Learning: Narratives from Biotechnology." *Management Learning,* volume 26, number 4, 403–422.

Fiol, M.C., & Lyles, M.A. (1985). "Organizational Learning." *Academy of Management Review,* volume 10, number 4, 803–813.

Gephart, M.A., Holton, E.F., Marsick, V.J., & Redding, J.C. (1997). "Assessing Strategic Leverage for the Learning Organization: Group and Organizational Outcomes, Climate, and Support Systems." Unpublished manuscript.

Gephart, M.A., Marsick, V.J., Van Buren, M.E., & Spiro, M.S. (1996). "Learning Organizations Come Alive." *Training & Development*, volume 50, number 12, 35–45.

Gephart, M.A., Marsick, V.J., & Van Buren, M.E. (1997). "Finding Common and Uncommon Ground among Learning Organization Models." *Proceedings of the Fourth Annual AHRD Conference*, (pp. 547–554), R. Torraco, editor. Baton Rouge, LA: Academy of Human Resource Development.

Glynn, M.A., F.J. Milliken, & T.K. Lant. (1991). "Learning about Organizational Learning: A Critical Review and Research Agenda." Manuscript submitted to *The Journal of Management Studies*.

Hedberg, B. (1981). "How Organizations Learn and Unlearn." *Handbook of Organizational Design*, volume 1 (pp. 3–27), P.C. Nystrom & W.H. Starbuck, editors. London: Oxford University Press.

Hedberg, B., P.C. Nystrom, & W.H. Starbuck. (1976). "Camping on Seesaws: Prescriptions for a Self-Designing Organization." *Administrative Science Quarterly*, volume 21, 41–63.

Huber, G.P. (1991). "Organizational Learning: The Contributing Processes and the Literatures." *Organization Science*, volume 2, number 1, 88–115.

Isaacs, W., & P. Senge. (1992). "Overcoming Limits to Learning in Computer-Based Learning Environments." *European Journal of Operational Research*, volume 59, 183–196.

Kim, D. (1993). "A Framework and Methodology for Linking Individual and Organizational Learning: Applications in TQM and Product Development." Dissertation Abstracts International, 54 (06A), 2223. (University Microfilms No. AAI0573289)

Lant, T.K., & S.J. Mezias. (1990). "Managing Discontinuous Change: A Simulation Study of Organizational Learning and Entrepreneurship." *Strategic Management Journal*, volume 11, 147–179.

Leonard-Barton, D. (1996). *Wellsprings of Knowledge*. Cambridge, MA: Harvard University Press.

Levitt, B., & J.G. March. (1988). "Organizational Learning." *Annual Review of Sociology*, volume 14, 319–340.

Lynn, G.S., J.G. Morone, & A.S. Paulson. (1996). "Marketing and Discontinuous Innovation: The Probe and Learn Process." *California Management Review*, volume 38, number 3, 8–37.

March, J.G. (1991) "Exploration and Exploitation in Organizational Learning." *Organization Science*, volume 2, number 1, 71–87.

March, J.G., & J.P. Olsen. (1976). *Ambiguity and Choice in Organizations*. Norway: Universitetsforlaget.

Marquardt, M., & A. Reynolds. (1994). *The Global Learning Organization: Gaining Competitive Advantage through Continuous Learning*. Burr Ridge, IL: Irwin.

Meyer, A. (1982). "Adapting to Environmental Jolts. *Administrative Science Quarterly*, volume 27, number 4, 515–537.

Miner, A.S., & S.J. Mezias. (1996). "Ugly Ducklings No More: Pasts and Futures of Organizational Learning Research." *Organization Science*, volume 7, number 1, 88–99.

Moorman, C. (1995). "Organizational Market Information Processes: Cultural Antecedents and New Product Outcomes." *Journal of Marketing Research*, volume 32, 318–335.

Muir, N.K. (1991). "R and D Consortium Technology Transfer: A Study of Shareholder Technology Strategy and Organizational Learning." Dissertation Abstracts International, 52 (05A), 1815. (University Microfilms No. AAI9131755)

Nevis, E.D., A.J. DiBella, & J.M. Gould. (1995). "Understanding Organizations as Learning Systems." *Sloan Management Review*, 73–85.

Nonaka, I. (1994). "A Dynamic Theory of Organizational Knowledge Creation." *Organization Science*, volume 5, number 1, 14–37.

Nonaka, I., & H. Takeuchi. (1995). *The Knowledge Creating Company.* New York: Oxford.

Reimus, B. (1997). *Knowledge Sharing within Management Consulting Firms: Reports on How U.S.-Based Management Consultancies Deploy Technology, Use Groupware, and Facilitate Collaboration.* Fitzwilliam, NH: Kennedy.

Senge, P. (1990). *The Fifth Discipline: The Art & Practice of the Learning Organization.* New York: Doubleday Currency.

Shrivastava, P. (1983). "A Typology of Organizational Learning Systems." *Journal of Management Studies*, volume 20, number 1, 7–28.

Ulrich, D., M.A. Von Glinow, & T. Jick. (1993). "High-Impact Learning: Building and Diffusing Learning Capability." *Organization Dynamics*, volume 22, number 2, 52–66.

Watkins, K.E., & V.J. Marsick. (1993). *Sculpting the Learning Organization: Lessons in the Art and Science of Systemic Change.* San Francisco: Jossey-Bass.

Watkins, K.E., & V.J. Marsick. (1996). *In Action: Creating the Learning Organization,* volume 1. Alexandria, VA: ASTD.

Watkins, K.E., G. Selden, & V.J. Marsick. (1997). "Dimensions of the Learning Organization in Family-Run Businesses." *Proceedings of the Fourth Annual AHRD Conference,* (pp. 383–389), R. Torraco, editor. Rouge, LA: Academy of Human Resource Development.

Watkins, K.E., B. Yang, & V.J. Marsick. (1997). "Measuring Dimensions of the Learning Organization." *Proceedings of the Fourth Annual AHRD Conference* (pp. 543–546), R. Torraco, editor. Baton Rouge, LA: Academy of Human Resource Development.

Zander, U., & B. Kogut. (1995). "Knowledge and the Speed of the Transfer and Imitation of Organizational Capabilities: An Empirical Test." *Organization Science*, volume 6, number 1, 767–792.

Ziegler, M.F. (1995). "The Learning Organization: Awakening." Dissertation Abstracts International, 56 (07A), 2770. (University Microfilms No. AAI9539886)

CHAPTER 4

Multirater 360 Feedback

Gary N. McLean, Ed.D.

Professor and Coordinator
Human Resource Development
University of Minnesota, St. Paul

Although the use of feedback from multiple raters is on the increase, research supporting its use does not clearly advocate the ways in which it is commonly used. This chapter defines multirater 360 feedback, explores its history, discusses four primary purposes for it, and presents research evidence related to its application, implications for practice, and general conclusions about its usefulness in human resource development.

DEFINITION

Multirater 360 feedback is "the process of receiving perceptions of one's performance from a variety of sources, typically supervisor(s), peers, direct reports, self, and even customers" (McLean, Sytsma, & Kerwin-Ryberg, 1995, p. 1, section 4:4). Another term used is *cross-hierarchical approach* (Hall, Leidecker, & DiMarco, 1996), defined as building "on the subordinate-oriented style by adding ratings from other organizational levels such as peers and superior(s)" (p. 219). To this they add the term *self-inclusive approach* when the individual adds his or her rating to those included in the cross-hierarchical approach.

The term *multirater 360 feedback* is a relatively recent one and usually implies, at minimum, ratings from one or more supervisors as well as from subordinates and peers (Budman & Rice, 1994; Dunnette, 1993; Nowack, 1993; O'Reilly, 1994). Other terms used include "multirater feedback, multiple-source feedback, and full-circle feedback" (Stoner, 1996, p. 228).

Hall, Leidecker, and DiMarco (1996) focused on the term *upward-performance appraisal (UPA)* in their writing, in spite of their use of the terms *cross-hierarchical approach* and *self-inclusive approach*. Stoner (1996) legitimately criticizes the term because

> much of their data did not seem to support a formal performance appraisal process. In most organizations, the term *appraisal* implies that the process will lead to decision points in the areas of compensation, promotion, succession planning, and other similar situations. This is a very different situation with significantly different dynamics than the situation in which a multiple-source feedback process is used solely for developmental purposes. (p. 227)

Noe, Hollenbeck, Gerhart, and Wright (1997) viewed multirater feedback as

> a special case of upward feedback in which managers' behaviors or skills are evaluated not only by subordinates but by peers, customers, their boss, and themselves. (p. 393)

HISTORICAL DEVELOPMENT

Although the term *multirater 360 feedback* and its formal use are relatively recent, it has probably been present in some form since the beginning of communication. "How did I do?" "What do you think of that?" "Do you love me?" are all questions that invite feedback from a variety of sources. Determining how honest or accurate that feedback has been is a different matter. It continues to be one of the primary concerns with the implementation of 360 feedback today.

By 1979, many of the components of what is now called multirater 360 feedback had been developed and were in use. Matejka, Weinrauch, and McCuddy (1979), for example, argued that there were four approaches to performance appraisal: downward evaluation, horizontal (or peer) evaluation, self-evaluation, and upward evaluation. London and Smither (1995) concluded that "multi-source feedback is not a categorically unique method" (p. 804). They claimed that it is "grounded in the philosophy and practice of survey feedback (and performance appraisal" (p. 804).

The extent of its use today is unknown (Hall, Leidecker, & DiMarco, 1996). Nowack (1993) concluded that many organizations use some form of 360 feedback. However, London and Beatty (1993), referencing a Towers Perrin 1992 report, concluded that companies are more likely to give lip service to it than use it. They also argued that "270-degree feedback" is the term that should be used unless customers are included—the implication, of course, being that a complete circle of feedback cannot occur unless all potential parties are involved in providing feedback. London and Smither (1995) concluded that "multi-source feedback appears to be widely used" (p. 806). One of the respondents in London and Smither's survey reported that "the practice is 'nearly universal' among Fortune 500 firms, and another stated that, 'Every Fortune 500 firm is either doing it or thinking about it'" (p. 807). Van Velsor and Leslie (1991) argued that the number of publicly available 360 feedback instruments had increased dramatically since the late 1970s. The number is even higher today with the availability of in-house and customized instruments. However, London and Smither (1995) also concluded that "it is clear that this is an area in which practice is well ahead of theory and empirical research" (p. 807).

As may already be clear from this historical development, 360 feedback may have different meanings depending on the purpose for which it is used. The next section explores the major purposes for which some form of 360 feedback is used.

PURPOSES AND EXPECTED OUTCOMES

Multirater 360 feedback is a process for making "general personnel decisions, such as promotions and terminations" (Hedge & Borman, 1995). It is also used to "identify training and development needs, pinpointing employee skills and competencies that are currently inadequate but for which programs can be developed," and "as a criterion against which selection and development programs are validated" (Hedge & Borman, 1995, p. 453). Bernardin and Beatty (1987) also suggested that at least one component of 360 feedback, upward appraisal, contributes to worker satisfaction because workers believe that their opinions are valued and that they are being listened to. Extending this argument, a fourth purpose of 360 feedback is to improve organizational culture or climate.

Personnel Decisions

A wide range of tasks are important in organizations, and some of them may be informed by the use of multiple ratings, including selection, performance appraisal, compensation, promotions, team assignments, transfers, downsizing, and succession planning. Historically, an employee's supervisor or, at best, a small group of managers has made these decisions. The argument for 360 feedback is that people other than the supervisor or managers may have different, and perhaps more accurate, perspectives of the employee. Reliance on the limited perspective of one or a few people for such important decisions may not lead to the best decisions for the organization (and, in some cases, for the individual involved).

Development

Multiple ratings used for development often result in an action or development plan for the person being rated (Nelson-Horchler, 1988). A third-party consultant (perhaps someone from human resources), a supervisor, a cross-hierarchical group of raters, or a workshop facilitator may provide assistance, always with the ratee involved.

The process for conducting 360 feedback, according to Noe et al. (1997), focuses on development as the purpose of using the process:

Managers are presented the results, which show how self-evaluations differ from the other raters. Typically, managers are asked to review their results, seek clarification from the raters, and engage in action planning designed to set specific development goals, based on the strengths and weaknesses identified. (p. 393)

The main reason for using 360 feedback for development purposes is that different raters provide different ratings because "they are privy to different sets of ratee behaviors, provide complementary assessments of *different* aspects of ratee performance (Lance, Teachout, & Donnelly, 1992), one of the main premises upon which 360 feedback logic is built (Tornow, 1993)" (p. 24).

Validation of Selection and Development Programs

Kirkpatrick (1959a, 1959b, 1960a, 1960b) established four levels for the evaluation of training and development activities: reaction, learning, on-the-job behavior, and organizational impact. Although often criticized (Holton, 1996), his approach is well entrenched in the human resource development literature. Level three, on-the-job behavior, has traditionally been measured through supervisory rating scales, similar to those used in performance appraisals, though perhaps more focused. Such measures are subject to the same criticisms as those directed at performance appraisal (see, for example, Scholtes, 1990). For many, it seems clear that there are perceived advantages to using the multiple inputs that occur in a 360 feedback process as compared with the singular input from a supervisor in the more traditional evaluation systems.

Improvement of Organizational Culture

Through the selection of items for the 360 feedback instrument and the comprehensiveness of the instrument, those developing it help to create a schema for leadership that helps to set the priorities for leadership within the organization, shape management behavior, and, ultimately, influence organizational culture (for example, London & Smither, 1995). The message sent to those being rated by such a process is that there are behaviors that are important in the organization and that the organization values. Organizations that include feedback from internal and external customers in the process may view their contribution as consistent with the principles of quality (for example, continuous quality improvement) that have had a marked impact on organizational culture.

The rapid growth of application of 360 feedback in organizations mandates that the research in the area, such as exists, be brought to bear on that practice. Otherwise, practice will continue to evolve in a direction that is inappropriate and not supported by the best practices identified by theory, modeling, and empirical research. What, then, does the research suggest about the use of 360 feedback for these various purposes?

RESEARCH EVIDENCE

Although there are many opinions about 360 feedback, there is a paucity of empirical research on its effectiveness, according to a review of the literature and confirmation from Hall, Leidecker, and DiMarco (1996). This section presents a summary of the research, both supporting and challenging its usefulness, on personnel decisions, development, validation of selection and development programs, and improvement of organizational culture. First, though, we include a brief review of some key statistical concepts, which are necessary for understanding the outcomes of research.

Key Statistical Concepts

In the review of research outcomes, some technical language is essential. Such concepts include two psychometric principles—reliability and validity—as well as a statistical measure of relationships—correlations.

For any instrument used for measurement purposes to be useful at all, it must possess both reliability and validity. *Reliability* is a measure of how consistent the results of the instrument are. A perfectly consistent instrument would provide exactly the same measure every time. There are many ways to determine reliability. A common approach is Cronbach's alpha, which provides a measure of internal consistency. A perfectly reliable instrument would yield a coefficient of 1.0. Because of the existence of sampling errors in every measurement, a "perfect" coefficient never occurs. The closer a coefficient is to 1.0, the more consistent the measure is. Thus, an instrument with a coefficient of .8 is more consistent than one with a coefficient of .6. Another way to determine reliability is to conduct a test-retest. That is, a person would fill out the same form after a one- or two-week time lapse. Again, a perfectly reliable instrument would yield a coefficient of 1.0. A third approach to reliability is to determine the amount of agreement among multiple raters. In general, a coefficient of .7 is considered necessary for "adequate" reliability.

There are many different types of *validity*. Simply, validity reports the extent to which an instrument measures what it intends to measure. Statistical measurements of validity include predictive validity, which measures how well a test score predicts future performance, or concurrent validity, which measures how well a test score on one instrument agrees with a test score on a similar instrument. Validity may also be a subjective observation of how well an instrument measures what is intended (as in face validity, where a pool of experts judges the appropriateness of individual items on an instrument).

Correlation coefficients are often used to measure both reliability and validity. A correlation is a number that ranges between -1 and +1; the sign of the coefficient indicates the direction of agreement (a negative number means that as the value on one variable goes up, the value on the other variable goes down). Coefficients are always within this range. A simple way to interpret the coefficient is to square the coefficient. This explains the amount of overlap in variance between two variables. Thus, a reliability of .7 roughly reflects consistency in measurement of 49 percent.

Personnel Decisions

In spite of the many personnel decisions suggested in the "Purposes and Expected Outcomes" section, most of the research about personnel decisions has focused on performance appraisal. The research suggests that performance appraisals are probably the most problematic of all the purposes for which 360 feedback is used. According to Stoner (1996), research

> indicates that rating patterns of respondents in a multirater feedback for a performance appraisal process change and are significantly different from those of raters involved in a multirater feedback for a development process. In general, ...respondents rate people more favorably when the process is tied to performance appraisal than they do when the data are to be used for development only. (pp. 229-230)

One motivator for the increased use of 360 feedback is the increasing criticism directed toward traditional supervisor-focused performance appraisal approaches. Lawler (1995), for example, summarized the situation:

> The problem—and it is well-documented—is that most performance-appraisal systems do not motivate individuals nor guide their development effectively. Instead, they cause conflict between supervisors and subordinates and lead to dysfunctional behaviors. These dysfunctions often are exaggerated when performance appraisals are tied to traditional merit pay systems. They are particularly severe when the system forces supervisors to compare subordinates. (p. 29)

The argument sometimes made for 360 feedback is that the reasons for use of performance appraisals will not disappear, so it is necessary to have a system that does not have the "rater errors, biases, and other inaccuracies" that detract from the validity of performance appraisals (Hedge & Borman, 1995, p. 453).

The following research evidence that focuses on reviews by peers, self, subordinates, and multiple sources provides a further look into the use of 360 feedback for performance appraisal.

PEER REVIEWS. One of the criticisms of relying solely on the supervisor's rating in a performance appraisal is that the supervisor has too few opportunities to observe the ratee's performance and, therefore, is not able to offer a reliable rating. Latham (1986) argued that the inclusion of peers, who are more likely to have daily interactions, increases the reliability of ratings. In contrast, McEvoy and Buller (1987) found that peer ratings are not well accepted by raters or ratees except when they are used for developmental purposes. Hedge and

Borman (1995) suggested further that there is resistance from peers to playing "a major role in the administrative decision process." Further, such "a peer-rating system may hinder coordination and increase intra-group conflict" (p. 456) in a team setting.

SELF-RATINGS. Much of the literature focuses on the appropriateness of self-ratings. Yammarino and Atwater (1993) concluded that "self-ratings...are the most commonly used approach for measuring and understanding individual differences" (p. 231). Based on their review of the literature, however, they further concluded that "self-ratings are inflated, unreliable, invalid, biased, inaccurate, and generally suspect when compared to the ratings of others" (p. 231). Hedge and Borman (1995) echoed Yammarino and Atwater; their review also found self-ratings to be "unreliable, biased, and inaccurate compared to other rating sources" (p. 456). Borman (1991) conducted

> a meta-analysis of relationships between self-assessments on traits or competency dimensions and criteria relevant to those assessments, including objective test scores, academic grades and supervisor ratings, resulted in a mean correlation of .29. (p. 291)

In contrast, Dunnette (1993) concluded that self-descriptions possess accurate components and suggested that it is premature to presume that other people's ratings should always be used to assess the validity of self-ratings. Latham and Wexley (1981) argued for the use of self-ratings from a developmental perspective. They suggested that self-ratings force the employee to focus on what's expected in the job. Also, they allow the supervisor to see how subordinates perceive their level of effectiveness.

Based on this research, self-ratings, for whatever purpose, are not likely to represent "objectivity." Their use in 360 feedback, however, may still be warranted, especially if the goal is to help an individual understand how self-ratings differ from other-ratings.

SUBORDINATE REVIEWS. Finally, Hedge and Borman (1995) concluded that, "despite evidence that use of subordinate appraisal is on the increase, there is almost no empirical research to support upward appraisal for any purpose" (p. 457). They went on to argue that "the biggest potential problem with subordinate appraisals is the fear that supervisors will exact retribution if an honest, but unfavorable, appraisal is received" (p. 458). Antonioni (1995) used a pool of 96 managers to explore the "extent to which managers improved their supervisory behaviors as a result of receiving written upward appraisal reports (feedback) and reviewing them with their immediate supervisors" (p. 157). He found that there were no differences between "managers who receive feedback with or without a performance review" and those "managers who do not receive feedback" (p. 157). In fact, "the scores for mean supervisory behaviors were lower at time 2 than at time 1" (p. 164).

From a review of the literature, Pollack and Pollack (1994) provided several arguments in support of subordinate ratings:

> 1) they typically have frequent contact with the manager, giving them many opportunities to observe the manager's performance, 2) they see different behaviors than supervisors and peers, giving them a unique perspective on the manager's performance, and 3) several subordinates' ratings can be averaged to produce a more reliable assessment of the manager's performance. (p. 12)

However, McEvoy and Beatty's (1989) review of the literature identified few studies that provided psychometric evidence to support upward appraisals. They did identify three studies that had determined correlations between subordinate and supervisor ratings. They were positive but low, ranging between .2 and .3. In their study, they found some predictive validity support for upward appraisals. In a study by Bernardin and Beatty (1987), subordinate appraisals had greater predictive validity than results of an assessment center, though both were low.

In their review of the literature, Hall, Leidecker, and DiMarco (1996) presented a number of arguments found in the literature against upward performance appraisals (and, by extension, against 360 feedback):

- Subordinates lack appropriate information (Bernardin, 1986; McEvoy, 1988).
- Subordinates are biased due to such preconceived mental sets as prejudice toward the ratee or toward participating in the process (Matejka, Weinrauch, & McCuddy, 1979).
- The process could turn into a popularity contest in which managers acquiesce to the wishes of subordinates in order to get a positive rating (Matejka, Weinrauch, & McCuddy, 1979; Nevels, 1989).
- The process is too time consuming and consumes too much administrative time (Edwards, 1990; Edwards & Ewen, 1996).
- There is lack of acceptance by both raters and ratees (Hall, Leidecker, & DiMarco, 1996).
- Employees won't take the time (Markowich, 1990), though Bernardin and Beatty (1987) provide contrary evidence.
- Employees may fear that they risk losing their jobs (Markowich, 1990).
- Managers being rated may fear reprisals from their bosses or may be reluctant to accept criticism from subordinates (Crumine, 1988).
- There may be an insufficient number of raters to provide valid results (Edwards, 1990).
- Supervisors may feel their authority is being undermined (McEvoy, 1990).

Hall, Leidecker, and DiMarco (1996) argued that proper implementation and careful monitoring can overcome these criticisms, though they were also clear that the research does not support the use of upward appraisals for the purpose of evaluation. Rather, they argued that upward appraisals are useful for developmental purposes only.

MULTIPLE RATINGS. Other important issues regarding multiple ratings include leniency tendencies, divergent and discriminant validity, and halo of self, peer, and supervisory ratings. Through a meta-analysis of the literature, Kraiger (1986) concluded, first, that, "while there is a slight leniency effect for self ratings, the effect is not so large that it would cause severe range restriction problems in validation analyses" (p. 10). Second, because none of the studies used external criteria, "any of the three sources would be equally well suited for validation...[though] all three may be good or all three may be bad" (p. 10). Finally, "peer and supervisory ratings may be more prone to halo than self ratings, but again the size of the effect is not so large that it would be a problem in validation studies, particularly when rating dimensions are combined into a single overall criterion" (p. 10). As to validity, "the lack of discriminant validity in all three sources [peer, self, supervisors] revealed by the multitrait-multirater analysis would argue for the formation of composites in most instances" (pp. 10–11).

Regarding convergent validity, according to Kraiger (1986), "Convergent validity appears greatest between peer and supervisory ratings. Self ratings typically show a higher mean than peer or supervisory ratings which in turn are nearly equal" (p. 11). Correlations between groups across five measures were greatest between peers and supervisors, but ran only from .32 to .52. For self-supervisor, the correlations ranged from .16 to .30, and for self-peer from .06 to .30. Clearly, there is little agreement among the groups. Williams and Levy's (1992) research supported some of these findings. The correlation between self- and supervisor ratings was .26, and the self-ratings showed greater leniency than did the supervisors. Hazucha, Szymanski, and Birkeland (1994) found self-boss correlations on 19 managerial dimensions ranging between .16 (personal adaptability) and .50 (financial and quantitative), with most of the correlations in the .2-.3 range. Finally, in another meta-analysis, Harris and Schaubroeck (1988) found peer-supervisor ratings to be correlated at .62, with self-supervisor ratings at .35 and self-peer at .36. Some of these studies, however, focused on development rather than performance appraisal.

Overall, Pollack and Pollack (1994) concluded from the literature that "older, more tenured, and higher educated employees, which managers typically are, generally are more resistant" to 360 feedback (p. 3). The difficulty that this creates in using it to evaluate management development activities is evident. However, they also pointed out that

> the organizations surveyed and research literature... [indicated]... that subordinates and peers provide a unique perspective on job performance that the supervisor of that employee may not have. The research literature also showed that subordinate and peer ratings are reliable and valid predictors of job performance. (p. 3)

Using a sample of 2,350 managers, Mount, Judge, Scullen, Sytsma, and Hezlett (1997) concluded that multiple raters at four levels (boss, peer, subordinate, and self) produced "idiosyncratic" results. They concluded further that these findings challenge the common practice of providing feedback based on average ratings by level: "Such a practice may be no more meaningful than summarizing the results based on groups of randomly chosen raters" (p. 18). Their recommendation was to provide feedback across all raters rather than by level.

Development

Few experimental studies are available to determine whether managers or supervisors that receive multiple-source feedback can actually improve their performance more than those receiving single-source feedback or no feedback, which is, after all, the goal of supervisory or management development.

Hegarty (1974) randomly assigned 56 first-line janitorial managers in a university setting to an experimental group and a control group. In the experimental group, the managers received a summary report of feedback from five of their subordinates and then met with a consultant to discuss the results. In the control group, there was neither a report nor a meeting. After three months, those in the experimental group improved their supervisory behaviors significantly more than those in the control group.

Nemeroff and Cosentino (1979) investigated the use of subordinate feedback to improve managers' performance-appraisal interviewing skills when combined with setting improvement goals. Managers who received feedback and set goals with the assistance of a human resource development (HRD) trainer improved significantly over those who received feedback only and those who received no feedback.

Kluger and DeNisi (1996) conducted a meta-analysis, concluding that feedback does not always improve performance. They found that, using standard deviations to compare those who received feedback with those who did not, the average difference, favoring those receiving feedback, was .41. About one-third, however, showed negative effects. Given this mixed review, London and Smither (1995) concluded that "feedback alone does not lead to skill development and performance improvement" (p. 823). Rather research on goal setting and control theory, as well as the role of training and development, is needed to explain when multiple-source feedback positively affects performance.

Perhaps the most important conclusion from the literature, related to this study, is Pollack and Pollack's (1994) recommendation to

> use the information [from 360-degree feedback] for developmental, not evaluation, purposes. Research and practice both overwhelmingly indicated that the data collection and feedback processes are most effective and efficient when performance ratings are collected for developmental rather than evaluation (for example, to determine pay or promotions) purposes. (p. 4)

Many authors echo this conclusion, including London and Wohlers (1991), Matejka, Weinrauch, and McCuddy (1979), McEvoy and Beatty (1989), and Nelson-Horchler (1988). Among 128 public-sector managers, McEvoy (1990) found wider acceptance of subordinate ratings for developmental purposes.

Smither et al. (1995) applied only upward appraisal in which subordinates rated 238 first- through fifth-level managers six months apart. Managers whose initial level of performance was moderate or low improved over the six-month period, and this improvement could not be attributed solely to regression to the means. Both "managers and their subordinates became more likely over time to indicate that the managers had an opportunity to demonstrate behaviors measured by the upward feedback instrument" (p. 1). The changes, however, were modest, and, when managers received low or moderate ratings and also rated themselves low, there was no change. Smither et al. concluded that "people seek to minimize the discrepancy between their self-evaluation and feedback from others" (p. 25). Although inconsistent, there also appears to be a pattern of association with length of time the rater has known the ratee. Another interesting finding was that managers who did not complete a self-rating improved more than did managers who completed self-ratings.

Most of the studies used quantitative methodologies. Callender (1996) used qualitative methodologies (in-depth interviews using a constant comparative method to develop process descriptions) to examine the experience of five managers who received 360 feedback. From an analysis of more than 10,000 lines of text, Callender concluded that

> those who started a developmental dialog with direct reports or peers experienced the deepest and most resilient change. Source credibility in feedback givers was essential for acceptance of the feedback, and, when missing, led to both deflection of the feedback and a worsening relationship. Organizational turmoil minimized the effect of the feedback....some who engaged in developmental dialog broadened their perspective..., suggesting that 360-degree feedback can go beyond skill-building and be effective as a means to establish a developmental dialog. (p. iii)

Validation of Selection and Development Programs

There are many problems associated with the use of 360 feedback for this purpose. One of the main problems concerns the interpretation of the ratings from various groups that provide different feedback. Which rating should predominate when they differ? Should the supervisor's rating predominate, as has been the case historically? Or should more attention be paid to the ratings of those with whom the ratee has the greatest contact? Or should the self-rating predominate, especially for developmental purposes, because the greatest likelihood is that the ratee will accept it? Before a group accepts 360 feedback as the instrument for making evaluative decisions, it must receive answers to these questions.

The biases that have been explored extend to those who are charged with evaluating the effectiveness of development programs. Hazucha, Hezlett, and Schneider (1993) investigated

> changes in the skill levels of managers which occurred two years following the managers' participation in 360-degree feedback. The major objective was to investigate how skill development, development efforts, and environmental support for development are related. The *Management Skills Profile (MSP)* was used to measure skills and to give feedback. Of the original 198 managers who received feedback, 48 accepted the opportunity to complete the instrument again two years later. (p. 325)

Participants' skills increased during the two years (though the cause of the improvement is unclear), and self-other agreement was greater at time 2 than at time 1. Those with greater skill at time 1 were more likely to have advanced. While providing evaluative information, the change in scores at time 2 are not clearly as a result of either having received feedback at time 1, having received the training provided at time 1, nor the developmental activities that occurred between time 1 and time 2.

McLean, Sytsma, and Kerwin-Ryberg (1995) studied managers who had gone through a weeklong leadership training program. Prior to the workshop, they completed the Management Skills Profile (MSP), a 122-item inventory designed to assess skills across 19 managerial dimensions. The MSP was completed by the manager being assessed as well as by his or her immediate superiors, subordinates, and peers, but only the manager received the results, not the manager's supervisor. Holt and Hazucha (1991) reported on a number of studies supporting the reliability and validity of the instrument. However, interrater correlations for pairs of supervisor raters ranged from .30 to .52; for subordinates, .28 to .48; and for peers, from .21 to .37. Average interrater reliability ranged from .28 to. 47. Of those who participated, 72 agreed to retake the MSP.

One of the important findings, for the purposes of this chapter, was the correlation matrices that were run to determine whether skills remained relatively the same over time or whether they had changed and the correlations matrices to measure the relationship among the various raters. These two sets of tests were designed to explain the difficulty in using 360 feedback to evaluate the effectiveness of management development activities. Correlations were determined on each dimension of the MSP for each rater group comparing time 1 with time 2 ratings. For both self and subordinate, the correlations are essentially zero, with the range in the former from -.06 to .26 and in the latter from .07 to -.24. The supervisor ratings ranged from 0 to -.26. The peer ratings were consistently positive and are the highest, ranging from .11 to .41.

The correlations between the two times are consistently low. Although the peer correlations reflect the largest number of significant correlations,

Table 1. Highest correlation within each ratings group comparison at time 1 and time 2.

Group	Self	Peer	Subordinate
Peer	.24/.08		
Subordinate		.40/.29	-.23/.12
Supervisor	.36/-.15	.28/.21	.22/.20

the highest is .41 for planning, which is still a low correlation. It would appear from these figures that there is no consistent pattern of continuing development of managers that can be predicated on the time 1 ratings by any of the rating groups. The peer ratings hold the best possibility. None of the other ratings is consistent across the time spans involved in this study.

Correlations by MSP dimension were also run among the four rating groups at both rating times. This analysis yielded 114 correlations for each time, for a total of 228 correlations. Given the number of correlations calculated and the low correlation required for statistical significance, the more critical question for analysis has to do with practical rather than statistical significance. A review of all correlations calculated revealed that the highest correlation obtained was .40, a level considered to be low. The highest correlations in each of the ratings group comparisons appear in table 1.

The correlations show clearly that there is very little relationship among the various groups in terms of how they completed the MSP. The perspective of each group is very different, and each group appears to view performance in each of the 19 dimensions in a different way from that of the other groups.

The low to moderate correlations among the rating groups underscore the difficulty of deciding for evaluative purposes whose perspective is important. This same question must be raised for other applications of 360 feedback as well. For developmental purposes, it is helpful to be able to view one's own performance from the perspective of several different groups. But when a decision needs to be made, such as evaluating a developmental activity or making an administrative decision, such as pay or promotion, varied and contradictory evidence creates confusion rather than options.

Without providing details, such as those outlined above, Stoner (1996) argued that it was important for an organization to test, using a multiple-rater feedback instrument at time 2, to determine whether development had occurred since time 1. He concluded that such a process can yield "interesting and compelling results" (p. 232).

Improvement of Organizational Culture

Both in practice and research, 360 feedback appears to be applied less to the improvement of organizational culture or climate than to the other purposes described. Bernardin (1986) found that subordinate appraisal of supervisors or managers fosters greater attention to subordinates' needs, which positively correlates with job satisfaction. Amsbary and Staples (1991) found a negative correlation between workers' opportunities to express dissatisfaction with working conditions and employee turnover.

Antonioni's (1995) research does not support these conclusions, however. Managers who received subordinate feedback with an oral performance review were not judged to be more satisfactory as supervisors than were those who received feedback without verbal performance review, those who received a verbal performance review without subordinate feedback, and those who received neither. Thus, multiple-rater feedback in Antonioni's study did not result in greater employee satisfaction.

Much more research is needed relative to this purpose, especially given the complexity of managing organizational change.

IMPLICATIONS FOR PRACTICE

The research evidence suggests both advantages and disadvantages to the use of 360 feedback. In general, Noe et al. (1997) described the benefits of 360 feedback as including

> collecting multiple perspectives of managers' performance, allowing employees to compare their own personal evaluation with the views of others, and formalizing communications between employees and their internal and external customers. (pp. 393-394)

The limitations potentially include

> the time demands placed on the raters to complete the evaluation, managers seeking to identify and punish raters who provide negative information, the need to have a facilitator to help interpret results, and companies' failure to provide ways that managers can act on the feedback they receive (for example, development planning, meeting with raters, taking courses). (p. 395)

The important question for this section, given the limitations of its use, is to identify how the advantages of its use can be maximized. Suggestions from various authors are provided below, followed by a summary list.

Based on their review of the literature, Hall, Leidecker, and DiMarco (1996) identified "twelve recommendations for effective use of the UPA [upward performance appraisal] process" (p. 211):

> 1. Guarantee anonymity to participants.... 2. Use UPAs for development, not for evaluation.... 3. The timing of the survey in relation to other organizational events is critical.... 4. Clarify expectations regarding procedures with participants.... 5. Provide support for the ratee.... 6. Training of all participants is crucial to success.... 7. Have a commitment from top management.... 8. Get people involved and

keep them informed.... 9. Participation by the raters should be voluntary.... 10. Focus only on observable aspects of ratee's job.... 11. Provide both average and range information in results provided to ratee.... 12. Control for bias. (pp. 211–216)

Stoner's (1996) advice is also sound:

> Clearly defining and articulating the purpose of the multiple-source feedback process are essential to understanding how implementation should occur and whom to involve in the process. This point cannot be overemphasized. (p. 230)

Stoner (1996) also added suggestions for implementation to those of Hall, Leidecker, and DiMarco (1996):

- Assess organizational readiness.
- Use competency models.
- Construct a solid questionnaire.
- Manage the administrative process.
- Use training.
- Use normative data when appropriate.
- Don't stop with the feedback; support development with the use of "workshops, coaching, various learning opportunities, software, and other means" (p. 232).

Regardless of the purpose of a 360 feedback instrument, it must not be a hastily constructed instrument, but must meet psychometric requirements, including reliability and validity, although neither Hall, Leidecker, and DiMarco (1996) nor Stoner (1996) emphasized these needs.

Based on the research reviewed and regardless of the use of a 360 feedback instrument, personnel should follow these suggestions:

1. Be clear about the purpose for which 360 feedback is being used and communicate it to everyone involved in the process.
2. Raters' and ratees' involvement in 360 feedback, for whatever purpose, must be voluntary.
3. The organization must provide consistent, continuous, and nonwavering support to ratees throughout the process, including a guarantee that competent support personnel, including clinical psychologists, will be available, as needed.
4. Raters, ratees, and third parties must be well trained in their roles.
5. Instruments must be psychometrically sound, reflecting sound validity and high reliability. Except in very unusual organizations, this characteristic probably requires the use of instruments that expert psychometricians have developed commercially. Hastily constructed, in-house instruments are likely to cause more damage than good.
6. Be aware of other factors occurring in the organization at the time of the administration of the questionnaires. Systems thinking is critical in understanding the factors that affect both the feedback provided and the ways in which the feedback is received.

7. Do not rely on the 360 feedback instrument alone to accomplish its purpose. Again, a systemic perspective is necessary. Both one-on-one and group dialogue are useful adjuncts to the instrument. Another useful supplement is documentation (for example, statistical process control, artifacts).

Personnel Decisions

I admit to being unconvinced that performance appraisals, whether traditional or based on 360 feedback, can perform any useful function for an individual or for an organization. Numerous authors have pointed to the many deficiencies that reside in a performance appraisal concept. Most practitioners recognize these deficiencies, but rather than discarding the concept, they continue to work at trying to improve an inherently flawed process that is not susceptible to improvement.... Much of the rush to the use of 360 feedback seems to be from organizations that have recognized the deficiencies of their traditional performance review and appraisal process and are desperately looking for a way to improve it—a way that is destined for failure.

As many writers have recognized (see McLean, Damme, & Swanson, 1990), individual performance is heavily influenced by the systems in which one performs, whereas typical performance appraisals make the assumption that the individual heavily influences his or her own performance. Although feedback is important, perhaps even necessary, feedback that people request for themselves is much more powerful than that which is imposed on them, and contiguity of feedback is critical (that is, that which is received at the time the performance occurs is more powerful than receiving feedback on something that might have occurred months earlier).

Although it is not appropriate here to lay out alternatives to traditional performance appraisals, suffice it to say that 360 feedback is not likely to be the answer to the many deficiencies that exist with performance appraisals.

Development

All of the available evidence suggests that the greatest power residing in 360 feedback is in development. But as many authors indicated, it is not sufficient simply to give the manager the information. That person receiving feedback needs support as he or she struggles with what to do with the feedback. An external coach or mentor can be a useful part of the development process. A facilitated discussion with those involved in doing the rating can be helpful. In fact, Stoner (1996) concluded that

> it is not the most complete or prettiest plan that leads to development but rather the act of planning for development and of soliciting the support of others that actually brings about behavioral change and growth. (p. 232)

This process will lead to an action plan or development plan for the ratee. However, the process must not stop here. It is important to determine whether or not development then occurs.

Because of the research suggesting that 360 feedback is ineffective for personnel decision making and the differences among raters in decision-making settings, it is important to separate the development uses of 360 feedback from its use in personnel decisions. That means that 360 feedback should not be administered in a context that might lead both raters and ratees to assume that it is being used for personnel decision-making purposes. Thus, if a traditional performance review system is in place (questionable as such systems are), the 360 feedback instrument should not be administered with temporal contiguity. Second, unless there is a high level of trust in the organization, the results of the feedback should belong to the ratee only and no one in the ratee's line of supervision, including the ratee's supervisor, should see them. Thus, any discussion focused on the results or any assistance in developing action or development plans should be with a neutral third party, preferably with an external consultant. Even human resource (HR) or human resource development (HRD) personnel could be problematic because employees associate them with performance appraisals.

Eventually, however, HRD needs to know the results of the feedback, perhaps in an aggregated form, so that appropriate developmental tasks can be developed and supported. Although this may include traditional training, it also might include the provision of coaching or mentoring, providing resources for workshops or seminars, assignment to more challenging tasks, team assignments, transfers, access to a library of media (books, videotapes, software), and other appropriate developmental activities.

Some implementation guidelines are critical for success in using 360 feedback for development. Maurer and Tarulli (1996) found that employees doing the rating and being rated must believe that the right dimensions are being assessed. Second, raters must believe that ratees can change as a result of receiving feedback. Finally, there must be a belief that the raters have had sufficient time to observe the behaviors being rated.

Kaplan (1993) added these additional suggestions to the implementation of 360 feedback to improve or "boost" its power: Ask co-workers to complete open-ended questions, obtain nonwork feedback (for example, from friends or family), and attempt to get a historical perspective based on early influences on the managers (family of origins, childhood friends, and so on). Kaplan recognized, however, that "the more the power of 360-degree feedback, the greater the potential benefits and risk, and the greater the responsibility that the program staff...assume" (p. 312). To counter these risks, he recommended the following precautions: Recognize that this approach is not for everyone (assess readiness and make the program voluntary), communicate why the program is being proposed for a specific person, support the person throughout the entire process, and use only competent staff (including clinical psychologists).

Validation of Selection and Development Programs

We now reach an interesting twist in the cycle of questions that the research in 360 feedback raises. If its most appropriate application is in development, as the research indicates, if it is ineffective as a source for personnel decisions, and if it provides mixed results in validating selection and development programs, how, then, do we determine whether appropriate development occurred, especially if we want to tie it to an action or development plan? In fact, we can probably do nothing more than was done originally in the development process, that is, give the results to the ratee and ask whether they suggest that development occurred. The cycle then begins over again, appropriate to the organization's development plan and the support that is provided.

This process, obviously, will leave frustration in its path. Human resource development will not have the "objective" data that it is seeking to determine the effectiveness of its programming. Management that sponsored the development activities and may have been intimately involved will not have external validation that its time, effort, and resources have been used wisely. The target of the development, the manager, may also feel frustration with not having his or her observations confirmed or challenged. The external consultant (or consulting firm) may not obtain the strong evidence necessary to market the process with the next client.

Yet, the iterative nature of this task may be its greatest strength. It maintains the ambiguity that exists for adult development and avoids dichotomous or dualistic thinking, acceptance of which, in itself, helps produce development. It puts the onus of development squarely where it belongs—on the individual who is seeking development. It forces the organization away from individual blaming behavior and encourages more systemic thinking. It helps consultants and consulting firms to avoid the off-the-shelf, one-size-fits-all solutions for clients and forces them, too, to think about clients more systemically. So, rather than bemoaning these results, one can well celebrate the "growing edge" thinking that such conclusions can encourage.

Improvement of Organizational Culture
Of all of the purposes for 360 feedback, this may be the most important. Yet the paucity of research in this area gives us little direction about what our practice should reflect. The "practice" that is most needed here is additional research. How does the use of multiraters for any of the three purposes affect employee morale? And the most important question may be, how does the use of multirater feedback for developmental purposes affect the mission of the organization? Does improved managerial development improve profitability, quality, customer service, employee satisfaction, and so on? Until research can provide answers to these questions, the use of 360 feedback *for any purpose* remains wishful and based mostly on conjecture.

From a systems perspective, though, it is evident that the use of any multirater feedback will have an impact on the organization's culture or climate. What this lack of research does, however, is leave us in the dark about what impact it will have and unable to project with confidence what the effects will be.

CONCLUSIONS

Although the desire to move to higher levels of evaluation in Kirkpatrick's model is important and valid, the use of 360 feedback, in its current state of development, is not likely to provide the solution that will allow for improved Level 3, on-the-job behavior, evaluation. The use of 360 feedback seems well established when used for developmental purposes when supplemented with other necessary components. The attempt to use it for evaluative or administrative purpose is a response to the frustration of those who continue to work at improving performance appraisal systems instead of recognizing the inherent deficiencies in the system itself. A better approach is to change the system to one that is theoretically sound and truly answers the important questions. The challenge to human resource development, then, is to determine explicitly the outcomes that are expected from management development activities and design an evaluation system that responds specifically to these outcomes. Multirater 360 feedback is not the management development evaluative tool to do that. Without careful application and evaluation, 360 feedback has the potential to be one of many other fads that have come and gone in the business world, and it will not find its appropriate place as an essential HRD tool.

REFERENCES

Amsbary, J.H., & J.P. Staples. (1991). "Improving Administrator/Nurse Communications: A Case Study of Management by Wandering Around. *Journal of Business Communication,* volume 28, number 2, 101–112.

Antonioni, D. (1995). "Problems Associated with Implementation of an Effective Upward Appraisal Feedback Process: An Experimental Field Study." *Human Resource Development Quarterly,* volume 6, number 2, 157–171.

Bernardin, H.J. (1986). "Subordinate Appraisal: A Valuable Source of Information about Managers." *Human Resource Management,* volume 25, number 3, 421–439.

Bernardin, H.J., & R.W. Beatty. (1987). "Can Subordinate Appraisals Enhance Managerial Productivity?" *Sloan Management Review,* volume 28, 421–439.

Borman, W.C. (1991). "Job Behavior, Performance, and Effectiveness." *Handbook of Industrial and Organizational Psychology,* volume 2 (2d edition) (pp. 271–326), M.D. Dunnette & L.M. Hough, editors. Palo Alto, CA: Consulting Psychologists Press.

Budman, M., & B. Rice. (1994). "The Rating Game." *Across the Board,* volume 31, number 2, 35–38.

Callender, S.M. (1996). "Response to 360-Degree Feedback as a Management Development Intervention: Deflection, Change, and Transformation." Doctoral dissertation, Virginia Polytechnic Institute and State University, Blacksburg, VA.

Crumine, L. (Summer 1988). "Subordinate Appraisals: How Credit Union Employees Rate Managers." *Executive Journal,* 18–20.

Dunnette, M.D. (1993). "My Hammer or Your Hammer?" *Human Resource Management,* volume 32, 373–384.

Edwards, M.R. (1990). "Implementation Strategies for Multiple Rater Systems." *Personnel Journal,* volume 69, number 9, 130–138.

Edwards, M.R., & A.J. Ewen. (1996). *Providing 360-Degree Feedback: An Approach to Enhancing Individual and Organizational Performance.* Scottsdale, AZ: American Compensation Association.

Hall, J.L., J.K. Leidecker, & C. DiMarco. (1996). "What We Know about Upward Appraisals of Management: Facilitating the Future Use of UPAs." *Human Resource Development Quarterly,* volume 7, number 3, 209–226.

Harris, M.M., & J. Schaubroeck. (1988). "A Meta-Analysis of Self-Supervisor, Self-Peer, and Peer-Supervisor Ratings." *Personnel Psychology,* volume 41, 43–61.

Hazucha, J.F., S.A. Hezlett, & R.J. Schneider. (1993). "The Impact of 360-Degree Feedback on Management Skills Development." *Human Resource Management,* volume 32, number 2–3, 325–351.

Hazucha, J.F., C. Szymanski, & S. Birkeland. (1994). *Will My Boss See My Ratings? Effect of Confidentiality on Self-Boss Rating Congruence.* Minneapolis: Personnel Decisions.

Hedge, J.W., & W.C. Borman. (1995). "Changing Conceptions and Practices in Performance Appraisal." *The Changing Nature of Work,"* (pp. 451–481), edited by A. Howard. San Francisco: Jossey-Bass.

Hegarty, H.H. (1974). "Using Subordinates' Ratings to Elicit Behavioral Changes in Supervisors." *Journal of Applied Psychology,* volume 59, number 6, 764–766.

Holt, K.E., & J.F. Hazucha. (1991). *Management Skills Profile Technical Summary.* Minneapolis: Personnel Decisions.

Holton, E.F. III. (1996). The flawed four-level evaluation model. *Human Resource Development Quarterly,* 7(1), 5–21.

Kaplan, R.E. (1993). "360-Degree Feedback PLUS: Boosting the Power of Co-worker Ratings for Executives." *Human Resource Management,* volume 32, numbers 2–3, 299–314.

Kirkpatrick, D. (1959a). "Techniques for Evaluating Training Programs." *Journal of the American Society of Training Directors,* volume 13, number 11, 3–9.

Kirkpatrick, D. (1959b). "Techniques for Evaluating Training Programs." *Journal of the American Society of Training Directors,* volume 13, number 12, 21–26.

Kirkpatrick, D. (1960a). "Techniques for Evaluating Training Programs." *Journal of the American Society of Training Directors,* volume 14, number 1, 13–18.

Kirkpatrick, D. (1960b). "Techniques for Evaluating Training Programs." *Journal of the American Society of Training Directors,* volume 14, number 2, 28–32.

Kluger, A.N., & A. DeNisi. (1996). "The Effects of Feedback Interventions on Performance: A Historical Review, a Meta-Analysis and a Preliminary Feedback Intervention Theory." *Psychological Bulletin,* volume 119, number 2, 254–284.

Kraiger, K. (April 10, 1986). "An Analysis of Relationships among Self, Peer, and Supervisory Ratings of Performance." A paper presented at the First Annual Conference of the Society of Industrial/Organizational Psychologists, Chicago, IL.

Lance, C.E., M.S. Teachout, & T.M. Donnelly. (1992). "Specification of the Criterion Construct Space: An Application of Hierarchical Confirmatory Factor Analysis." *Journal of Applied Psychology,* volume 77, 437–452.

Lance, C.E., & W. Bennett Jr. (April 11, 1997). "Rater Source Differences in Cognitive Representation of Performance Information." A paper presented at the Annual Conference of the Society for Industrial and Organizational Psychology, St. Louis, MO.

Latham, G.L. (1986). "Job Performance and Appraisal." *International Review of Industrial and Organizational Psychology*, volume 1, edited by C.L. Cooper & I. Robertson. Chichester, England: John Wiley.

Latham, G.L., & K.N. Wexley. (1981). *Increasing Productivity through Performance Appraisal*. Reading, MA: Addison-Wesley.

Lawler, E.E., III. (1995). "Performance Management: The Next Generation." *Quality Digest*, volume 15, number 2, 29–31.

London, M., & R.W. Beatty. (1993). "360-Degree Feedback as a Competitive Advantage." *Human Resource Management*, volume 32, numbers 2–3, 352–372.

London, M., & J.W. Smither. (1995). "Can Multi-Source Feedback Change Perceptions of Goal Accomplishment, Self-Evaluations, and Performance-Related Outcomes? Theory-Based Applications and Directions for Research." *Personnel Psychology*, volume 48, 803–839.

London, M., & A.J. Wohlers. (1991). "Agreement between Subordinate and Self-Ratings in Upward Feedback." *Personnel Psychology*, volume 44, number 2, 375–390.

Markowich, M.M. (1990). "Is It Risky to Give the Boss a Good Idea?" *Management Review*, volume 79, 28–29.

Matejka, J.K., J.D. Weinrauch, & M.K. McCuddy. (1979). "Upward Evaluation of Management: A Viable Alternative." *Arkansas Business and Economic Review*, volume 12, number 1, 17–21.

Maurer, T.J., & B.A. Tarulli. (1996). "Acceptance of Peer/Upward Performance Appraisal Systems: Role of Work Context Factors and Beliefs about Managers' Development Capability." *Human Resource Management*, volume 35, number 2, 217–241.

McEvoy, G. M. (1988). "Evaluating the Boss." *Personnel Administrator*, volume 33, number 9, 115–120.

McEvoy, G.M. (1990). "Public Sector Managers' Reactions to Appraisals by Subordinates." *Public Personnel Management*, 19(2), 201–212.

McEvoy, G.M., & R.W. Beatty. (1989). "Assessment Centers and Subordinate Appraisals of Management: A Seven-Year Examination of Predictive Validity." *Personnel Psychology*, volume 42, number 1, 37–52.

McEvoy, G.M., & P.F. Buller. (1987). "User Acceptance of Peer Appraisals in an Industrial Setting." *Personnel Psychology*, volume 40, 785–797.

McLean, G.N., S.R. Damme, & R.A. Swanson, editors. (1990). *Performance Appraisal: Perspectives on a Quality Management Approach*. Alexandria, VA: American Society for Training & Development.

McLean, G.N., M. Sytsma, & K. Kerwin-Ryberg. (March 1995). "Using 360-Degree Feedback to Evaluate Management Development: New Data, New Insights." *Academy of Human Resource Development 1995 Conference Proceedings (Section 4-4)*, edited by E.F. Holton III. Austin, TX: Academy of Human Resource Development.

Mount, M.K., T.A. Judge, S.E. Scullen, M.R. Sytsma, & S.A. Hezlett. (April 10–13, 1997). "Trait, Rater and Level Effects in 360-Degree Performance Ratings." Paper presented at the Annual Conference of the Society for Industrial and Organizational Psychology," St. Louis, MO.

Nelson-Horchler, J. (Sept. 19, 1988). "Performance Appraisals." *Industry Week*, p. 64.

Nemeroff, W.F., & J. Cosentino. (1979). "Utilizing Feedback and Goal Setting to Increase Performance Appraisal Interviewer Skills of Managers." *Academy of Management Journal*, volume 22, number 3, 566–576.

Nevels, P. (1989). "Why Employees Are Being Asked to Rate Their Supervisors." *Supervisory Management*, volume 34, 5–11.

Noe, R.A., J. Hollenbeck, B. Gerhart, & P. Wright. (1997). *Human Resource Management: Gaining a Competitive Advantage* (2d edition). Homewood, IL: Richard D. Irwin.

Nowack, K.M. (1993). "360-Degree Feedback: The Whole Story." *Training & Development*, volume 47, number 1, 69–72.

O'Reilly, B. (October 17, 1994). "360-Degree Feedback Can Change Your Life." *Fortune*, 93–100.

Pollack, L.J., & D.M. Pollack. (June 26–30, 1994). "Using 360-Degree Feedback in Performance Appraisal." Paper presented at the International Personnel Management Association Assessment Council Conference, Charleston, SC.

Scholtes, P.R. (1990). "An Elaboration on Deming's Teachings on Performance Appraisal." *Performance Appraisal: Perspectives on a Quality Management Approach* (pp. 24–52), edited by G.N. McLean, S.R. Damme, & R.A. Swanson. Alexandria, VA: American Society for Training & Development.

Smither, J.W., M. London, N.L. Vasilopoulos, R.R. Reilly, R.E. Millsap, & N. Salvenini. (1995). "An Examination of the Effects of an Upward Feedback Program Over Time." *Personnel Psychology*, volume 48, 1–34.

Stoner, J.D. (1996). "Invited Reaction: Reaction to Hall, Leidecker, and DiMarco." *Human Resource Development Quarterly*, volume 7, number 3, 227–232.

Tornow, W.W. (1993). "Editor's Note: Introduction to Special Issue on 360-Degree Feedback." *Human Resource Management*, volume 32, 211–219.

Van Velsor, E., & J.B. Leslie. (1991). *Feedback to Managers 1991*. Reports #149R & #150R. Greensboro, NC: Center for Creative Leadership.

Williams, J.R., & P.E. Levy. (1992). "The Effects of Perceived System Knowledge on the Agreement between Self-Ratings and Supervisor Ratings." *Personnel Psychology*, volume 42, 835–847.

Yammarino, F.J., & L.E. Atwater. (1993). "Understanding Self-Perception Accuracy: Implications for Human Resource Management." *Human Resource Management*, volume 32, numbers 2–3, 231–247.

CHAPTER 5

Evaluating Training

Joan Hilbert
M.A. Candidate
University of New Mexico

Hallie Preskill, Ph.D.
Associate Professor
College of Education
University of New Mexico

Darlene Russ-Eft, Ph.D.
Director
Research Services
Zenger Miller

This chapter looks at the last four decades of training evaluation research. After reviewing the scholarly literature, the authors conclude that the research on human resource development (HRD) evaluation has focused on a limited number of questions using only a few tools and methods. Because of its insular and parochial approach, evaluation has failed to show HRD's contribution or value to organizations. The authors argue that as trainers move into the role of learning and performance consultants and as organizations seek to do things faster and better, HRD professionals should consider additional and alternative ways of integrating evaluative inquiry into their work. When well conceived and implemented, evaluation should be considered a key strategic initiative that highlights the critical information needs of designers, trainers, and managers, and provides the means to ensuring quality training interventions.

HISTORY OF TRAINING EVALUATION

There is little doubt that today's organizations are experiencing unprecedented changes in how they define themselves and accomplish their work. Nowhere are these changes more evident than in organizations' training and development departments. Human resource development (HRD) professionals are now being called on to do the following: move from training to performance improvement, keep up with the pace of reengineering, manage and train current and new employees, maximize training technologies, facilitate learning to achieve their organization's goals, and know their organization's business inside and out (Bassi,

Benson, & Cheney, 1996). All of this is occurring in the midst of downsizing, outsourcing, budget cutting, and frequent turnover in the leadership of many organizations.

HRD professionals are also increasingly being asked to show how their efforts add value to the organization. In many companies, evaluation of training is thought to be the most appropriate method of demonstrating this value. However, findings from the American Society for Training & Development's (ASTD) benchmarking survey found that 94 percent of the respondents collected participant reaction information, 34 percent measured learning, 13 percent evaluated transfer of learning, and only 3 percent were evaluating financial impacts from training (Bassi et al., 1996, p. 37). Given that training provided in the public and private sectors is now equaling $55.3 billion (Benson, 1996, p. 58), HRD professionals have an ethical obligation, if not a pragmatic one, to invest in developing effective evaluation systems for their organization's learning efforts.

Models and Taxonomies of Training Evaluation

During the past four decades, numerous models of training evaluation have been proposed. Donald Kirkpatrick created the one that is most familiar to trainers and that they use most widely. He originally called his conceptualization a "four-step approach" to evaluation. Since then, it has been variously called a model, a system, a framework, a taxonomy, a methodology, a typography, and a vocabulary. The four steps themselves have also been called stages, criteria, types, categories of measures, and most commonly, levels of evaluation. Kirkpatrick himself now calls it the four-level model of evaluation (Kirkpatrick, 1994).

As the first attempt to formalize the notion of training evaluation, Kirkpatrick's model offered a solid starting point. Interestingly, most models found in the literature either directly or indirectly build on Kirkpatrick's model. The following section presents the most common and relevant models of evaluation found in the HRD literature over the last 40 years, starting with Kirkpatrick's four-level model. Figure 1 summarizes the levels or stages of each model discussed.

KIRKPATRICK'S FOUR-LEVEL EVALUATION MODEL. Kirkpatrick (1959a, 1959b, 1960a, 1960b) noticed that training evaluation could be conducted with four possible training outcomes in mind: reactions, learning, behavior, and results. At Level 1, evaluating reactions means finding out if training participants enjoyed the training, if the training environment was suitable and comfortable, and if the trainers were capable and credible. In short, at this level trainers are trying to ascertain what the trainees think and feel about the training.

At Level 2, evaluating learning means determining the extent to which trainees have improved or increased their knowledge or skills as a result of the training. The evaluation questions at this level are, What can trainees do now that they couldn't do before? What do they know now that they didn't know before?

Figure 1. General models of training program evaluation.

Kirkpatrick's Four Level (1959a, 1959b, 1960a, 1960b) • Reactions • Learning • Behavior • Results	**Hamblin's Five Level (1974)** • Reactions • Learning • Job behavior • Organization • Ultimate value (cost benefit)	**Training Effectiveness Evaluation System (Swanson & Sleezer, 1987)** • Satisfaction • Learning • Job/organization performance • Financial performance
Brinkerhoff Six-Stage Model (1987, 1989) • Goal setting • HRD program design • Program implementation • Immediate outcomes • Intermediate or usage outcomes • Impacts and worth	**Input, Process, Output Model (Bushnell, 1990)** • Inputs (trainee qualifications, materials, facilities) • Process (ISD steps) • Outputs (short-term results) • Outcomes (long-term results)	**Richey (1992)** • Trainee characteristics • Knowledge • Attitude • Behavior
Kaufman, Keller, Watkins' Five Level (1994) • Enabling • Reaction • Acquisition • Application • Organizational outputs • Societal outcomes	**Training Efficiency and Effectiveness Model (Lincoln & Dunet, 1995)** • Analysis • Development • Delivery • Results	**Holton's HRD Evaluation Research and Measurement Model (1996)** • Learning • Individual performance • Organizational results

At Level 3, evaluating behavior means determining if the trainees are using or transferring their newly learned knowledge and behaviors back on the job.

At Level 4, evaluating results means determining if the training has affected business results or has contributed to the achievement of organizational goals. Questions asked at this level might be, Was the training worthwhile? How has the organization benefited? Has productivity increased? Have customer complaints been reduced? Have scrap and rework decreased?

Kirkpatrick did not explicitly state that his model was hierarchical in nature. However, it has predominated the training evaluation literature as the de facto standard and has been popularly accepted as a hierarchy. That is, trainers have assumed that positive reactions (Level 1) are a prerequisite for learning (Level 2) to occur; behavior (Level 3) depends on learning (Level 2); and behavioral changes (Level 3) drive organizational results (Level 4).

Another implicit assumption in Kirkpatrick's four-level model is that each succeeding step or level is somehow "better" than the previous one. Better might be in terms of information gleaned or value to the organization. As we will discuss later in this chapter, there is little research to support these assumptions.

The ubiquity of Kirkpatrick's model stems from its simplicity, its understandability, and the "reasonableness" of its implicit assumptions. Just how pervasive is this model? While researching material for this article, we found 57 journal articles in the HRD and psychology literature describing or mentioning evaluation models. Of those, 44 (or 77 percent) included Kirkpatrick's model (either alone or in comparison with another model). A mere 13 articles discussed a model other than Kirkpatrick's. The 57 articles describe 21 different models published between 1959 and 1996:

1959	1970s	1980s	1990s
1	2	3	15

Although this list is not exhaustive, it does illustrate the tenacity of Kirkpatrick's model and the lack of challenge until recent years. Even as late as 1993, there were assertions that "Kirkpatrick's recommendations continue to represent the state-of-the art training evaluation" (Kraiger, Ford, & Salas, 1993).

For all the attention it has received over the years, Kirkpatrick's model has been subject to a modest level of scrutiny and has not been widely implemented in its entirety (Alliger & Janak, 1989). Most commonly, training interventions are evaluated at the reaction and learning levels (Bassi et al., 1996; Bramley & Kitson, 1994; Plant & Ryan, 1992). The reliance on reaction and learning measures may be due to the perceived difficulty and cost in measuring performance or behavior and organizational benefits. With many organizations' increased emphasis on the bottom line comes concomitant pressure on trainers to "prove" the value of training. In the eyes of management, this often means providing enough evidence to show an acceptable return-on-investment or other concrete benefits to the organization.

Kirkpatrick's model has provided a solid foundation for the development of other models, as evidenced by a host of evaluation models with a similar look and feel. The remainder of this section describes the salient features of some of these models. Several authors advocate expanding Level 4 to include financial results that are related to organizational results. Typically, financial results are expressed as a return-on-investment. Other authors suggest adding a fifth level for evaluating financial results. Still another (Rowe, 1995) splits Level 2, learning, into knowledge and skills, and renames "results" to "business needs." These changes result in a five-level model of obvious parentage.

HAMBLIN'S FIVE-LEVEL MODEL. Hamblin (1974), also widely referenced, devised a five-level model similar to Kirkpatrick's. In addition to measuring reactions, learning, job behavior, and organizational impact (noneconomic outcomes of training), he adds a Level 5 that measures "ultimate value variables" or "human good" (economic outcomes).

Hamblin was more explicit about his model being hierarchical than was Kirkpatrick, asserting that reactions lead to learning, learning leads to behavior changes, and so on. Accordingly, evaluation at a given level is not meaningful unless the evaluation at the previous level has been performed.

TRAINING EFFECTIVENESS EVALUATION (TEE) SYSTEM. The Training Effectiveness Evaluation System (Swanson & Sleezer, 1987) highlights three evaluation processes. First Swanson and Sleezer advocate developing an effectiveness evaluation plan, then tools for measuring training effectiveness, and finally an evaluation report. Like Kirkpatrick's model, the TEE system focuses on measuring participants' and supervisors' satisfaction, trainees' knowledge and skills, and organizational, process, job, and financial performance.

The model specifies that a minimum of four tools are required to evaluate training: two satisfaction measures, at least one learning measure, and at least one performance measure. Scores from each tool are calculated and used to compile the Effectiveness Evaluation Report, which compares before and after snapshots of a specific performance goal.

BRINKERHOFF'S SIX-STAGE MODEL. Brinkerhoff's evaluation model provides a cyclical approach, subjecting every phase of the HRD process to evaluation (Brinkerhoff, 1988, 1989). Although similar to Kirkpatrick's model, Brinkerhoff's six-stage model adds a Stage 1, called goal setting or needs analysis. This is when the training need is clarified and verified before any efforts begin to design a program. Brinkerhoff also adds a Stage 2 that focuses on evaluating the training program's design. His model then picks up with evaluating the training program's operation or implementation, which is similar to Kirkpatrick's reactions (Level 1).

The six-stage model is intended to be used to aid in decision making throughout the HRD process. It can be used formatively to improve programs and results by recycling evaluative information from one stage to the next.

INPUT, PROCESS, OUTPUT MODEL. Combining and enhancing features of both Kirkpatrick's four-level model and Brinkerhoff's six-stage model, IBM has developed its own model for evaluating training. Called input, process, output (IPO), Bushnell (1990) described this model as IBM's corporate education strategy for the year 2000. In the early stages of evaluation it takes into account some of the factors (inputs) that may affect training's effectiveness. Among these factors are trainee qualifications, trainer qualifications, program design, materials, facilities, and equipment. The inputs, themselves subject to evaluation, feed into the process stage where the mechanics of planning, designing, developing, and delivering the training are accomplished.

After the delivery of the training, the end results are evaluated. These results are subdivided into outputs and outcomes. Outputs, which are defined to be short-term benefits, consist of trainee reactions, knowledge and skill gains, and job performance improvement. Outcomes, or long-term results, are associated with the bottom line. Outcome measures include profits, customer satisfaction, and productivity, and they are derived from short-term outputs. Evaluative information from outputs and outcomes are recycled into both the process and input stages, thereby improving the training program cyclically.

Because the goal of training is to effect an organizational-level change, the payoff comes when trainees use their new skills, knowledge, and attitudes on the job in a fashion consistent with organizational goals. Ultimately then, it should be possible to express the training impact in terms of dollars and cents, rather than in training seats filled or number of favorable reactions generated.

SYSTEMIC MODEL OF FACTORS PREDICTING EMPLOYEE TRAINING OUTCOMES. Richey (1992) model, a Systemic Model of Factors Predicting Employee Training Outcomes, includes factors affecting training outcomes: knowledge, attitudes, and behavior. It acknowledges that instructional design and delivery do have an impact on training outcomes, but it deemphasizes this process in favor of trainee characteristics and perceptions of the organization.

According to the systemic model, trainees' backgrounds (age, education, training experience, work environment, motivation, and ability to learn) and their perceptions of the organizational climate (working conditions, management style) affect their attitudes. In turn, their attitudes directly influence knowledge, attitudes, and behavior.

KAUFMAN, KELLER, WATKINS FIVE-LEVEL MODEL. In recent years there has been a new twist to Kirkpatrick's four-level model. Kaufman and Keller (1994) and Kaufman, Keller, and Watkins (1995) have expanded Kirkpatrick's model by increasing the scope of the first four levels (enabling and reaction, acquisition, application, and organizational outputs). By adding a fifth level (societal outcomes), they take into account the societal impact of training or of any HRD intervention. The "good neighbor" aspect of the model draws attention to an area in which businesses have not always realized or admitted their impact—the environment outside their organizations. The effects of their programs on their clients and on society at large should be a major concern of any organization, according to this model.

Specifically, evaluation at the societal outcomes level seeks to answer whether the clients of the organization have been satisfied and whether the contributions to society have been worthwhile. These "megalevel" (Kaufman et al., 1995, p. 375) results are seen to be vital in determining how an organization benefits the society to which it is inextricably linked. For example, the authors suggest that manufacturing organizations be held accountable for side-effects of production such as pollution. This model strives to present a holistic view of the nature and purposes of evaluation.

TRAINING EFFICIENCY AND EFFECTIVENESS MODEL (TEEM). Similar to Brinkerhoff's six-stage evaluation model is the training efficiency and effectiveness model (Lincoln & Dunet, 1995), which labels the evaluation stages as analysis, development, delivery, and results. TEEM emphasizes that evaluation should occur throughout the training development process by using evaluative information to shape the decisions made at each stage. The model also strongly advocates the role of stakeholders in the evaluation process and recommends that trainers identify all those with a stake in the program so that all points of view and information needs can be considered in the evaluation's design and implementation.

HOLTON'S HRD EVALUATION RESEARCH AND MEASUREMENT MODEL. So far we have seen several frameworks that claim to be models, but may more correctly be called taxonomies, or classification systems. The authors call them models so we have adopted the same nomenclature for consistency. We have found more than 20 such models and have described some of them in the preceding pages. Holton (1996) has offered a model with the full panoply of objects, relationships, influencing factors, hypotheses, predictions, and limits of generalization—in short, a model that is testable.

Holton's model identifies three outcomes of training (learning, individual performance, and organizational results) that are affected by primary and secondary influences. The similarity to Kirkpatrick's Levels 2, 3, and 4 is readily apparent, but where are Level 1 reactions? Holton maintains that reactions should not be considered a primary outcome of training. He points to several studies suggesting that favorable reactions and learning are unrelated or are weakly related at best. Instead, reaction is shown in his model to influence the learning outcome, so its affect is not completely disregarded.

A summary of Holton's view of the influences on learning, individual performance, and organizational results follows:

Outcome	Influences
Learning	A. Trainee reactions
	B. Cognitive ability
	C. Motivation to learn
	1. Readiness for training
	2. Attitudes toward job and organization
	3. Personality characteristics
	4. Motivation to transfer learning
Individual Performance	A. Motivation to transfer
	1. Job attitudes
	2. Expectations about training
	3. Expected utility (How useful will it be?)
	4. Learning outcomes
	5. Transfer conditions (constraints from the workplace that inhibit training transfer)

Organizational Results

B. Transfer design (how and when to apply the learning)

C. Transfer conditions (constraints from the workplace)

A. Expected utility/return-on-investment
(Does the forecast show a payoff?)

B. Link to organizational goals

C. External events/factors (economic climate, resource availability, and so on)

Essentially Holton's HRD evaluation research and measurement model shows the expected outcomes from training and the influences that promote or inhibit them. It is an intriguing addition to the roster of training evaluation models in that it identifies several variables known to affect training's effectiveness.

MODELS OF TRAINING TRANSFER

Each of the general evaluation models described earlier includes a stage or level or process that focuses on training transfer—to what extent and in what ways are trainees applying their learning? In recent years, training transfer has rightly grown to be an important issue in training evaluation. The extent to which trainees' skills, knowledge, and attitudes are transferred to the workplace highlights the effectiveness of the training. Because of its importance, we include four models of training transfer to help conceptualize the components that may affect successful transfer. Table 1 summarizes each of these models.

Table 1. Training transfer models.

Training Transfer Process (Baldwin & Ford, 1988)	Navy Civilian Personnel Command Model (Erickson, 1990)	Stages of Transfer Model (Foxon, 1994)	Transfer Design Model (Garavaglia, 1996)
• Training input —trainee characteristics —learning principles —delivery —management support —opportunity to transfer —new skills • Training output —learning • Conditions of transfer —ability to generalize and maintain new behaviors	• Learning • Transfer	• Intention to transfer • Initiation • Partial transfer • Conscious maintenance • Unconscious maintenance	• Baseline performance • Systemic design features • Instructional design factors • Training event • Maintenance system • Transfer performance measure

A Model of the Transfer Process

Baldwin and Ford's (1988) model of the transfer process conceptualizes the transfer process in three parts: training input, training output, and conditions of transfer. Each of these categories is further reduced to its essential components.

Training input includes (1) trainee characteristics such as ability, personality factors, and motivation; (2) training design, which includes principles of learning and sequencing and delivery of training; and (3) the work environment, consisting of managerial support and opportunity to use new behaviors. Training output includes the actual learning that occurred during training and the retention of that learning at the end of the training intervention. Conditions of transfer include the ability to generalize learned behaviors to the job and to maintain them over time.

Navy Civilian Personnel Command (NCPC) Model

Trainers at NCPC are similarly concerned about the knowledge and competencies gained during training, but they test for them in a different fashion (Erickson, 1990). Instead of completing detailed questionnaires, trainees in staffing and placement undergo intensive interviews three to six months after training. The interviews are designed to test their knowledge by presenting real-life situations with which trainees will be or have been confronted. By explaining how to handle the situation to a subject matter expert (SME), trainees divulge their grasp of the course material and the degree to which they have been able to apply the material on the job. The SME uses a check sheet to note which actions the trainee would take to resolve the problem under question. Analyzing the results of many trainees, trainers are able to determine what portions of the training are not working or appear irrelevant.

Stages of Transfer Model

Foxon's (1994) stages of transfer model illustrates transfer not as an outcome, as it is often described, but as a process. From intention to transfer to unconscious maintenance, supporting or inhibiting factors affect each of the model's following five stages:

- Stage 1: Intention to transfer begins when a trainee decides to apply newly acquired knowledge and skills. The training environment, work environment, and organizational environment affect motivation to transfer. At this stage, the risk of transfer failure, or not attaining acceptable transfer, is high.

- Stage 2: Initiation occurs when the trainee makes a first attempt to apply new knowledge and skills at the job. Factors that affect transfer at this stage include the organizational climate, trainee characteristics, training design, and training delivery. The risk of transfer failure is medium to high.

- Stage 3: Partial transfer is when the trainee applies only some of the knowledge and skills learned or applies them inconsistently. Factors affecting training transfer are the opportunity and motivation to apply the learning, skill mastery, and confidence to apply skills and knowledge. Risk of transfer failure is further reduced at this stage.

- Stage 4: Conscious maintenance occurs when the trainee chooses to apply what he or she learned in training. Motivation and skills influence transfer, and the risk of transfer failure is medium to low.
- Stage 5: Unconscious maintenance occurs when trainees apply their new knowledge and skills unconsciously and have integrated them completely into their work routines. At this stage training transfer is considered successful.

Transfer Design Model

Garavaglia (1996) combines various aspects of each of the preceding three models in his Transfer Design Model. As with Foxon's (1994), this model is organized into stages. The first stage establishes a baseline performance measure from which the trainee is expected to improve.

Stage 2, systemic design factors, and Stage 3, instructional design factors, operate simultaneously and feed back into each other. Systemic design factors include trainee characteristics and work environment, trainee background, trainee emotions, self-efficacy, expected outcomes, and other psychological variables. An important feature of the transfer design model is the identification of instructional design factors that improve the chances transfer will occur.

Stage 4, the training event, "is where the rubber meets the road, and we begin to get a sense of the effect the training will have on the original performance problem" (Garavaglia, 1996, p. 8). If the trainer adequately addressed transfer issues before this stage, he or she should be able to determine if the training is appropriate.

At Stage 5, the maintenance system comes into effect as the trainee returns to the work environment. This stage is especially concerned with the level of support managers and supervisors provide to trainees.

Finally, Stage 6 is implemented to determine the transfer performance measure. This measure, when compared with the initial performance measure (Stage 1), indicates the extent to which the original performance problem has been corrected. If there has been insufficient transfer, the model suggests that the problem may lie in the training program's design or in the maintenance system.

RESEARCH USING TRAINING PROGRAM EVALUATION MODELS

Our next discussion focuses on research that has been conducted using various training evaluation models. Many of the researchers measuring the effects of training have looked at one or more of the outcomes that Kirkpatrick identified—reactions, learning, behavior, results. These possible training outcomes provide a simple and understandable structure for organizing and reporting the results. Because of its usefulness, we have adopted a similar organization for the following discussion on measuring training's effectiveness.

Evaluating Trainee Reactions

The first level of training evaluation according to several evaluation models is to assess trainees' reactions. Kirkpatrick pointed out in 1959 that positive reactions to training did not imply that any learning had occurred. Since then, perhaps because of the minimal cost and ease of conducting reaction evaluations, many trainers have apparently forgotten Kirkpatrick's caveat. They routinely use positive reactions as evidence of training's success.

It seems reasonable to assume that enjoyment is a precursor to learning, and that if trainees enjoy training, they are likely to learn. To put this assumption in perspective, consider diversity training, which often brings out feelings of discomfort as trainees are compelled to examine their deeply held values and beliefs. For this reason, diversity training likely will not garner a high score on the enjoyment scale. However, the learning and insights gained from such training may prove invaluable. Training that offers challenges and forces trainees to confront or experience uncomfortable or difficult situations need not be enjoyable to be effective. Numerous research efforts have attempted to determine the extent to which there is a relationship between trainee reactions and training outcomes (see table 2).

In 1990 Dixon published her findings on the relationship between trainee reactions and posttraining learning scores. From her study that involved 1,200 participants from a large manufacturing concern, she concluded that participants' reactions were not related to how much or what they learned. The results did show, however, that the instructors' ratings were related to the participants' level of enjoyment. Because the study was undertaken at a single organization, its results may not be widely generalizable. They do, however, suggest that trainers consider other means of determining training effectiveness besides the usual reaction form.

In 1982, Clement described the results of a study of a modified version of Hamblin's five-level hierarchical evaluation model. Using a pretest/posttest control group experimental design, 50 new supervisors participated in a general supervisory training course. At the end of the course, the participants completed course reaction forms and a knowledge test. The results showed a positive relationship between reactions and learning: The more favorable the reactions, the greater the learning. This finding contradicts Dixon's. But like Dixon's study its generalizability may be questionable if the results are extrapolated to other types of organizations or other types of training or trainees.

In a reaction study, Faerman and Ban (1993) tested the link between reactions and changes in work behaviors. The authors contend that past failures to find a strong link between reactions and behavior are due to "statistical artifacts" introduced by measuring individual change. In other words, the relationship is there, but the statistics researchers used were not sensitive enough to find it. Furthermore, they argue that a gain score (the difference between pretest score and posttest score) commonly used to determine improvement or lack of it is not necessarily the correct mea-

Table 2. Evaluating trainee reactions.

Author(s)/Date	Focus of Research	Design and Methods	Findings
Dixon (1990)	Relationship between trainee reactions and posttraining learning scores	1,200 employees of large manufacturing company; pretest/posttest of content and performance demonstration in three courses by employee type	Participants' reactions were not related to how much they learned. Ratings of instructors were related to the participants' level of enjoyment.
Clement (1982)	Relationship between trainee reactions and knowledge test scores	Pretest/posttest control group; 50 new supervisors; knowledge test	Positive relationship between reactions and learning: the more favorable the reactions, the greater the learning
Faerman & Ban (1993)	Relationship between trainee reactions and changes in work behaviors	Three-day managerial leadership training program for first-level supervisors; pretest/posttest at three months and posttest at six months; supervisor behavior and reactions	Moderate relationship between participants' reactions and subsequent job behavior
Noe & Schmitt (1986)	Degree of influence of trainee attitudes on training effectiveness	60 educators (randomly selected); pretest/posttest of learning, behavior, and performance	No link between trainee reactions and learning
Warr & Bunce (1995)	Relationship between trainee characteristics and reactions to training	Open learning environment with 106 junior managers in a four-month training program; pretest/posttest on performance; reactions and learning assessed during training and reported later	Neither enjoyment nor usefulness is related to learning. Pretraining motivation was related to both enjoyment and usefulness, but not to perceived difficulty.

sure to use. "[A gain score] is generally not considered appropriate by those psychometricians who have been engaged in the methodological debate over how to measure change" (Faerman & Ban, 1993, p. 302). The reliability of gain scores is also a serious concern when measuring change and must be accounted for by using appropriate statistical methods.

Faerman and Ban employed an upgraded statistical model to evaluate a three-day managerial leadership training program for first-level supervisors. At the end of the study, they reported a moderate relationship between participants' reactions and their subsequent behavioral changes.

Even when appropriate statistical methods are used during an evaluation, Faerman and Ban do not recommend using reactions to predict behavior changes. They advocate measuring behavior changes as rigorously as possible and speculate that favorable reactions may increase the likelihood of transferring learned behaviors to the job. Additionally, carefully designed reaction forms may provide a forum for participants to describe their ability or intent to transfer their learning and any inhibiting organizational constraints they envision.

Noe and Schmitt (1986) conducted a study to determine the influence of trainee attitudes on training effectiveness. Sixty randomly selected educators completed pretest and posttest instruments measuring learning, behavior, and performance. Using Kirkpatrick's four-level evaluation model, Noe and Schmitt measured trainee reactions and learning and found no link between the two. However, they discovered a direct effect on trainees' satisfaction with the training program. Specifically, they noted that trainees tended to have positive reactions to the program when they felt the precourse assessment of their training needs and current work skills was credible, relevant, and accurate.

In another study based on Kirkpatrick's four levels, Warr and Bunce (1995) conducted an evaluation of an open learning environment. Using 106 junior managers in a four-month management program, they studied the relationship between trainee characteristics and reactions. This study is somewhat different from others because it investigated three kinds of reactions—enjoyment, usefulness, and perceived difficulty. Enjoyment of training is self-explanatory. Usefulness indicates the potential applicability of the training content back at the job. Perceived difficulty comprises the cognitive and emotional work required of the trainee during training.

Before training, participants completed questionnaires about their individual characteristics. Line managers rated participants' on-the-job performance before training, directly after training, and three months later. Tutors supplied learning scores attained during training. From the compiled data, Warr and Bunce concluded that neither enjoyment nor usefulness is related to learning. Although they hypothesized that perceived difficulty would be negatively related to learning scores, and did in fact find such a result, the relationship was not significant. This result counters the expectation that trainees who find the material difficult will also have difficulty learning. In addition, pretraining motivation was related to both enjoyment and usefulness, but not to perceived difficulty. Trainees who felt anxiety about the program reported significantly higher levels of perceived difficulty and lower levels of enjoyment than those who did not feel anxiety. Warr and Bunce maintain that the results from this study argue for the construct validity of this three-pronged approach to measuring reactions. However, even they agree that more research is needed to determine if this framework provides a useful framework for evaluating trainee reactions in other settings.

Although the results of these studies are mixed, it seems certain that it is risky to use only trainee reactions to assess learning or behavior changes. Many researchers suggest evaluating other training outcomes in addition to reactions for a more holistic view of training's impact.

Evaluating Trainees' Learning

After reactions, learning measurements are most often used to assess the impact of training ("Industry Report," 1996; Plant & Ryan, 1992) (see table 3).

In testing Hamblin's hierarchical model, Clement (1982) found mixed results relating learning to behavior improvements. Participants with the greatest learning improvements did not necessarily improve their work behaviors correspondingly. He found that learning was related to some behavior changes but not to others.

In their study of trainees' attitudes on training effectiveness, Noe and Schmitt (1986) attempted to identify the factors influencing learning in a training environment. To improve their administrative and interpersonal skills, 60 educators, approximately half of each sex, underwent a two-day training program. The authors hypothesized that trainee's motivation to learn had a direct influence on learning. In turn, motivation to learn was influenced by trainees' attitudes toward their jobs and careers, expectations about the effort required during training and the rewards to be gained after, reactions to the skills and needs assessment, and the favorability of the environment, including organizational climate and support.

The results of the study showed slight improvements in the knowledge of interpersonal skills and behaviors. Finding little support for the original hypothesis, the authors found pretraining motivation to be weakly related to learning. Job involvement, the psychological attachment to the job, was a stronger predictor of learning than any other measured attitude.

In 1991, Baldwin, Magjuka, and Loher published the results of their research showing how the choice of training is related to trainee motivation and learning. The authors note that "choice" in this context refers to the selection of training content and not to the decision to attend or not attend training. When trainees have been given a choice of possible training courses, it is possible that some will not be granted their choice. Therefore, the authors are careful to distinguish between choice and choice-accepted, a differentiation which they say has generally not been made in the literature.

The main hypothesis of this study is that trainees who received their choice of training would be more motivated to learn and would have higher learning scores. To test this hypothesis, 242 subjects, divided about equally

Table 3. Evaluating trainees' learning.

Author(s)/Date	Focus of Research	Design and Methods	Findings
Clement (1982)	Relationship between learning and behavior improvement	50 new supervisors; pretest/posttest control group; measured knowledge, behavior, and performance	No relationship between increase in learning and work behavior.
Noe & Schmitt (1986)	Relationship between learning and motivation to learn	60 educators in a two-day administrative and interpersonal skills training program; pretest/posttest of learning, behavior, and performance	Pretraining motivation was weakly related to learning; job involvement and psychological attachment to the job were stronger predictors of learning than attitude.
Baldwin, Magjuka, & Loher (1991)	Relationship between choice of training to trainee motivation and learning	242 divided into three groups that were trained on skill-based performance appraisal and feedback; groups were divided into choice-not-received group, choice-received group, and no-choice group; pretest/posttest control group design	The choice-received group had higher levels of motivation to learn, but there were no significant differences in terms of learning outcomes between trainees who received their training choice and those who were not given a choice.
Gist, Stevens, & Bavetta (1991)	To determine the impact of self-efficacy on the acquisition and retention of negotiation skills	79 self-selected predominantly white male M.B.A. students; four-hour salary negotiation training program; self-efficacy report, checklist of goal-setting activities, questionnaire on self-set goals; trainees randomly assigned to a two-hour workshop (pretest/posttest control group design)	Self-efficacy is positively related to the acquisition and retention of salary negotiation skills; trainees with high self-efficacy negotiated the largest salaries.

Table 3. Evaluating trainees' learning (continued).

Author(s)/Date	Focus of Research	Design and Methods	Findings
Warr & Bunce (1995)	Relationship between trainee characteristics and training outcomes	106 mostly male junior managers; four-month open learning program for first-line managers	The following characteristics positively related to learning outcomes: • attitude about training • motivation learning the topic • learning self-efficacy • management experience • analytic learning strategy The following characteristics were negatively related to learning: • learning task anxiety • (greater) age.
Ree & Earles (1991)	The extent to which specific abilities combined with general cognitive ability predict learning outcomes	78,041 air force enlistees, mostly white, 17–23 years old, high school graduates; battery of tests for cognitive ability; training on one of 82 military job training topics—learning measured by technical knowledge and procedure tests	Test battery predicted general cognitive ability; general cognitive ability was the best predictor, and measures of specific ability were not needed to predict training success.
Dixon (1990)	Relationship between trainees' perceptions of how much they have learned and actual learning scores	1,200 employees of large manufacturing company; pretest/posttest of content and performance demonstration in three courses by employee type	No relationship between perception of how much learned and learning scores.

by sex, were divided into three groups. Each group participated in an identical two-hour, skill-based performance appraisal and feedback training module. The first group received a carefully compiled list of training module titles. Based on the results of a pilot survey, three of these titles were intended to be more attractive to the trainees than the performance appraisal module. Therefore, the performance appraisal module was the one that trainees were least likely to select as the preferred option (choice-not-received group). By manipulating the list of titles, researchers were able to induce the second group to request the performance appraisal module as its preferred choice (choice-received group). The third group did not get a choice of training modules (no-choice group).

Prior to training, trainees' cognitive abilities and pretraining motivation were measured. The three groups experienced identical training and were given several outcome tests to measure motivation and learning. The study's results showed that the choice-received group had higher levels of motivation to learn than did the other two groups. Trainees who did not receive their chosen training had the lowest motivation to learn and subsequent learning outcomes. Baldwin et al. concluded that motivation to learn can be enhanced by offering trainees a choice, but only if the requested training is ultimately received. The more highly motivated choice-received group was expected to attain higher learning scores than the other two groups; however, there were no significant differences in terms of learning outcomes between trainees who received their training choice and those who were not given a choice.

Given these results, trainers and managers should consider what the authors call the perils of participation—the possibility that offering a choice of training will result in decreased motivation and learning outcomes. They suggest that this possibility could be lessened by providing no choice at all. This no-choice scenario is also problematic, in that trainees' learning is predicted by their (lower) motivation to learn.

Other published research has sought to determine what other trainee characteristics influence learning outcomes. Gist, Stevens, and Bavetta (1991) conducted a study with 79 self-selected M.B.A. students, primarily male Caucasians, who received a four-hour training course in salary negotiation. The researchers' goal was to determine the impact of self-efficacy on the acquisition and retention of negotiation skills. After completing training, trainees completed a self-efficacy report and engaged in a role-playing exercise with trained scorers to simulate a salary negotiation scenario. The scorers had strict guidelines from which to assess and score trainees. Trainees were then randomly assigned to a two-hour workshop to be conducted a week later. In the workshop, they were taught either goal-setting or self-management techniques to enhance their skill maintenance. Six weeks after the workshop, subjects engaged in a second salary negotiation exercise with a different scorer. Before the second negotiation trainees completed three instruments: the same self-efficacy report; a checklist of goal-setting or self-management activities, whichever was applicable; and a questionnaire regarding any self-set goals.

At the conclusion of the study, the authors found self-efficacy to be positively related to both the acquisition and retention of salary negotiation skills. An additional finding suggests that self-management training administered after the initial training may enhance skills performance for trainees with low self-efficacy. Trainees with high self-efficacy who attended the goal-setting workshop negotiated the largest salaries. The authors note that this goal-achievement focus served trainees well. The self-management workshop apparently caused trainees to focus on their weak skills rather than on the task of maximizing their salaries. The authors caution about generalizing these results to other interpersonal skills or over longer periods of time. Additionally, the sample population of self-selected predominantly white, male, university students significantly limits the generalizability of these results.

In exploring the relationship between trainee characteristics and training outcomes, Warr and Bunce (1995) found that trainees' general attitude about training, their motivation for the specific course of training, learning self-efficacy, management experience, and analytic learning strategy are positively associated with learning outcomes. Characteristics shown to be negatively associated with learning outcomes are learning task anxiety and (greater) age.

Trainees who achieved higher learning scores had more positive attitudes toward training in general, had analytical learning styles, and were relatively young. The authors are unclear why age was negatively related to learning, expecting that the open learning environment, in which trainees proceed at their own pace, would support older trainees.

Ree and Earles (1991) conducted a study to determine the extent to which specific abilities combined with general cognitive ability to predict learning outcomes. The subjects were 78,041 air force enlistees, who were primarily white (80 percent), male (83 percent), 17 to 23 years old (86 percent), high school graduates (99 percent). They were given a battery of tests consisting of 10 subtests, each of which contributed to the estimation of general cognitive ability. Nine of the 10 subtests provided measures of specific ability.

Subjects received training in one of 82 military job training courses. Their learning was typically measured by technical knowledge and procedures tests, and was reported as a numerical grade. Results showed the predictive power of the test battery was due to general cognitive ability. Specific ability was shown to have statistical significance in predicting learning. However, "[general cognitive ability] was the best predictor, and measures of specific ability were not needed to predict training success" (Ree & Earles, 1991, p. 330). The generalizability of this research is questionable because the subjects were predominantly young, white, male, high school graduates in the air force. Further research is needed to determine whether a diverse group of trainees in a corporate setting would also show general cognitive ability predicting learning outcomes.

Dixon's (1990) research shows that trainees' perceptions of how much they have learned are not related to their actual learning scores. This result contradicts the intuitive notion that individuals know whether or not they've learned. Dixon offers two possible explanations for this result: First, trainees truly were not aware of the extent of their learning achievements, perhaps due to a lack of introspection about their knowledge, and second, posttraining reaction forms showed a high level of enjoyment for the training. Because trainees enjoyed it, they may have reported high learning as a reward for the trainer. In either case, using trainee assessments of their learning appears to be a questionable policy.

Obviously many questions remain about how to truly evaluate learning from training. Much of the research reported here may be limited in its generalizability given the lack of the subjects' diversity with regard to gender, race, and ethnicity; the small populations studied; the different variables studied; and the variety of environments in which the research took place.

Evaluating Training Transfer

Training transfer is defined as applying the knowledge, skills, and attitudes acquired during training to the work setting. According to Tziner, Haccoun, and Kadish (1991),

> The fundamental purpose of training is to help people develop skills which, when applied at work, will enhance their average job performance. Hence the ultimate purpose of training evaluation must be to assess the level of on-the-job transfer. (p. 167)

Training for training's sake is not a viable business practice, and today's economic realities mandate highly focused training to remedy organizational deficiencies or to gain business advantage. The paucity of research dedicated to transfer of training belies the importance of transfer issues. The following discussion describes several well-known training transfer studies and provides empirical evidence on the factors affecting transfer of training. Table 4 summarizes the results of these studies.

Wexley and Baldwin's (1986) study of 256 university students was designed to indicate which of three posttraining strategies best enhanced retention and application of time-management skills. All subjects attended a three-hour time management workshop conducted by a professional trainer who was unaware of the research project. After training, subjects were randomly assigned to one of four groups: assigned goal setting, participative goal setting, behavior self-management using a relapse-prevention model, or control.

Two days later, the 60 subjects in the assigned goal-setting group attended a one and one-half hour transfer session. They received a list of behavioral goals and a behavior checklist to be completed three times per week. During a group discussion, subjects described their commitment and specific plans and activities in which to use the specified behaviors. At the end of four weeks participants received feedback on their performance, including the number of times they exhibited each of the behavioral goals. In a group setting, subjects openly discussed their accomplishments.

Table 4. Evaluating training transfer.

Author(s)/Date	Focus of Research	Design and Methods	Findings
Wexley & Baldwin (1986)	Which of three posttraining strategies best enhanced retention and application of time-management skills	256 university students who attended a three-hour time-management workshop; subjects were randomly assigned to one of four groups: (1) assigned goal setting, (2) participative goal setting, (3) behavior self-management, (4) control; measures included learning and behavioral self-reports.	Assigned and participative goal-setting conditions were positively related to behavior performance; learning was not related to experimental conditions.
Gist, Bavetta, & Stevens (1990)	Whether goal-setting or self-management training would better facilitate transfer of training	68 M.B.A. students with a mean age of 29; all participants completed a seven-hour negotiation skills course independently reported behavior measures of performance; learning was measured by written responses to nine scenarios; subjects were randomly placed into one of the two groups.	Trainees in the self-management group negotiated greater compensation on the transfer task than did trainees in the goal-setting group; some form of posttraining transfer strategy may facilitate training transfer.

Table 4. Evaluating training transfer (continued).

Author(s)/Date	Focus of Research	Design and Methods	Findings
Tziner, Haccoun, & Kadish (1991)	To determine whether personal and situational factors affect training transfer	81 Israeli military instructors; divided about equally by sex, with a mean age of 20; subjects randomly assigned to a relapse prevention module after the training program; other subjects assigned to a control group; nine instruments administered to measure locus-of-control, work environment support, reactions to training, motivation to transfer, content mastery, trainee self-report of skills used, trainee self-report of transfer strategies used, supervisor assessment of trainee skills used, and supervisor assessment of transfer strategies used.	Trainees who attended the relapse prevention module learned more, attempted to use transfer skills more often, and used their new skills on the job more often than members of the control group.
Rouillier & Goldstein (1993)	Relationship between organizational climate and training transfer	102 assistant managers at a large fast-food franchise; nine-week training program on administration, customer service, and food handling; surveys administered to assess organizational climate; measures of trainees' learning, transfer behavior, and job performance taken; trainers assessed learning during and after training.	Learning and transfer were positively related; trainees who learned more also performed well on behavior measures; transfer behavior was found to be positively related to job performance; learning was not related to job performance; the amount of learning combined with transfer climate affects the degree to which training is transferred.

Table 4. Evaluating training transfer (continued).

Author(s)/Date	Focus of Research	Design and Methods	Findings
Brinkerhoff & Montesino (1995)	Relationship of management support to training transfer	91 randomly selected employees from a Fortune 500 company; subjects participated in one of five different skill development courses; course members assigned to either the experimental or comparison group; survey questionnaire administered to assess amount of transfer, factors affecting transfer, and meetings held with supervisors.	Management support and training transfer are related; trainees who reported more skills transfer also perceived greater supervisor support and reported fewer transfer inhibiting factors.

Similarly, the 65 subjects in the participative goal-setting group met for a one and one-half hour transfer workshop. In collaboration with the trainer, subjects recorded specific behavioral goals and specified the days on which they would record their performance on each goal. Group discussion allowed participants to express their commitment and intentions to meet the behavioral goals. Four weeks later the group met for an hour. Individuals received feedback on their performance toward each goal based on their self-ratings.

The relapse-prevention group of 63 subjects spent two and a half hours in its transfer workshop. To facilitate further application of their time-management skills, trainees discussed various self-control strategies. These included an awareness of the relapse process, identification of potential situations in which time management skills might be abandoned, and a written list of coping responses for each problem situation. Subjects were encouraged to try out their relapse-prevention strategies and to add new ones as they were needed over the next weeks.

The 68 control group members did not receive any form of transfer training. Eight weeks after the initial time-management training, all subjects completed learning and behavioral self-reports. The major finding showed both assigned and participative goal-setting conditions to be positively related to behavior performance. Additionally, subjects in the goal-setting groups displayed significantly greater behavioral changes than subjects in either the relapse-prevention or control groups. Learning was not related to any of the experimental conditions.

The researchers suggest that the explicit, public statement of intentions, record keeping, monitoring, and subsequent public discussion of accomplishments promoted transfer of training for the two goal-setting groups. Relapse-prevention subjects were not required to show a similar level of behavioral commitment. They received more latitude in selecting a coping strategy that may have reduced their commitment to a particular behavior.

Expanding on Wexley and Baldwin's (1986) research, Gist, Bavetta, and Stevens (1990) sought to determine whether goal-setting or self-management training would better facilitate the transfer of training. Several notable differences between the two studies warrant mentioning. Wexley and Baldwin (1986) relied primarily on self-report behavioral measures. Two months after the workshop, trainees reported the frequency of behaviors exhibited during that period. Furthermore, the posttraining self-management (relapse-prevention) workshop did not include a goal-setting component. In contrast, Gist et al. (1990) used independently reported behavioral measures of performance rather than self-reports. The self-management workshop they offered included a goal-setting component, which is not unusual for this type of training (Andrasik & Heimberg, 1980).

Participating in the study were 68 M.B.A. students at a large state university. Of these, 45 were male, 23 were female, and the mean age was 28.6 years. All participants completed a seven-hour negotiation skills course, based on salary negotiation and consisting of classroom instruction, negotiation preparation and review, and a negotiation simulation with a trained confederate. Learning assessment consisted of written responses to nine scenarios in which trainees identified and justified the negotiation strategies they would use in each scenario.

Subjects were randomly placed into either the goal-setting or self-management group for a two-hour transfer training workshop designed to facilitate generalization of salary negotiation skills to other negotiation situations. The content of the goal-setting workshop included a definition of goals and discussion of how to set goals, characteristics of goals, reasons why people set goals, examples of goals, and so on. Subjects were encouraged to use self-set goals to facilitate transfer of training. Members of the self-management group were instructed to focus on desired outcomes and ways to achieve them. Goal setting was discussed as one self-management technique. Other techniques included identifying obstacles and plans for overcoming them, monitoring plans, and reinforcing accomplishments.

After the transfer training workshop, subjects engaged in a second negotiation simulation (the transfer task). This second scenario was substantially different from the first, allowing researchers to explore the degree to which trainees could generalize salary negotiation skills to another context. Again, trained colleagues assessed trainees on their negotiation skills.

The researchers found trainees in the self-management group negotiated greater compensation on the transfer task than did trainees in the goal-setting group, illustrating a higher level of training transfer. Self-management trainees also used more negotiation strategies, suggesting greater skill generalization. Although the results regarding the superiority of the two transfer conditions (goal setting versus self-management) are mixed, it seems clear that some form of posttraining transfer strategy may facilitate training transfer. The differences in results may be due in part to the inclusion of goal setting as a part of a self-management strategy in one study (Gist et al., 1990) and the exclusion of goal setting from the self-management (relapse-prevention) strategy in the other (Wexley & Baldwin, 1986).

Tziner et al. (1991) undertook research to determine whether personal and situational factors affect training transfer. The subjects were 81 Israeli military instructors, approximately half of each sex and with a mean age of 20.3 years. Researchers randomly assigned 45 subjects to participate in a relapse-prevention module that was conducted after the regular training program. The 36 subjects who did not receive relapse-prevention training were assigned to the control group. The purpose of the research was to determine the extent to which exposure to the relapse-prevention module affected training transfer, to determine the impact of trainee locus-of-control and perceptions of work environment on the degree of learning and training transfer.

All 81 subjects received the same two-week training program. The experimental group then received a two-hour relapse-prevention module consisting of a general discussion of training transfer, identification and discussion of situations in which trainees might find it difficult to use trained skills, and further discussions suggesting possible solutions to those problematic situations.

Nine instruments were administered to measure locus-of-control, work environment support, reactions to training, motivation to transfer, content mastery (learning), trainee self-report of skills used, trainee self-report of transfer strategies used, supervisor assessment of trainee skills used, and supervisor assessment of transfer strategies used. Six of the nine instruments were derived from English-language instruments that Noe (1986) and Wexley and Baldwin (1986) developed. These instruments were translated to Hebrew before being administered.

Significant results showed trainees who attended the relapse-prevention module learned more, attempted to use transfer skills more often (self-reported), and actually used their new skills on the job more often (supervisor-reported) than members of the control group. These results were strengthened for trainees with an internal locus-of-control and who believed their work environment would support transfer of training. No direct relationship was found linking transfer to locus-of-control and perception of work environment support.

Based on this research, relapse-prevention training appears to be helpful in "combating long-term skills use decay" (Tziner et al., 1991, p.175). The likelihood of transfer may increase if appropriate transfer strategies are introduced during or just after training. Caution must be taken, however, in generalizing the results of this research to other groups. Subjects were young, Israeli military officers, a population quite different from what American trainers would expect to find in their classrooms. Another issue is the validity of instruments administered to subjects and their supervisors. Six of the instruments required translation from English to Hebrew. This implies that the instruments were normed on an English-speaking population and may not be valid for other populations.

Another factor thought to affect transfer of training is the organizational climate to which a trainee returns after the training intervention. Rouillier and Goldstein (1993) addressed this issue in the study of a managerial program for 102 assistant managers at a large fast-food franchise. The nine-week training program consisted of a variety of administrative, customer service, and food handling topics. Existing managers were surveyed to determine the organizational climate at the stores before newly trained assistant managers were brought in.

Measures were taken to assess trainees' learning, transfer behavior, and job performance. Trainers assessed learning during and after the training course. During the first several weeks on the job, managers and experienced staff assessed transfer behavior using a 92-item survey of key behaviors. The head manager assessed job performance eight to 12 weeks after assistant managers began work. Standardized, company-developed evaluation forms were used in job performance assessment.

The study's results showed that learning and transfer behavior were positively related, so that assistant managers who performed well on learning measures also performed well on behavior measures. In turn, transfer behavior was positively related to job performance, indicating that trainees' learning had transferred to the work setting. Interestingly, learning was not directly related to job performance. Other results showed that organizational climate affects job performance, and the amount of learning combined with transfer climate affects the degree to which training transferred.

In this study Rouillier and Goldstein (1993) found support for their main hypotheses: Greater learning means better on-the-job performance, and a positive organizational climate is important if transfer is to occur. In addition to a healthy transfer climate, management support of trainees is expected to influence the transfer of training. Brinkerhoff and Montesino (1995) sought support for this position.

They conducted research using 91 randomly selected employees from a Fortune 200 company. Subjects participated in one of five different skill-development courses. Members of each course were assigned to either the experimental group or to the comparison group. Supervisors of trainees in the experimental group were instructed to provide management support before and after training. Supervisors of the comparison group were not instructed to provide support.

Pretraining management support entailed supervisors meeting with trainees for approximately 15 minutes to discuss the purpose and content of the training, expectations for trainee application of the content, and supervisor encouragement to use the course content. Posttraining management support consisted of another brief meeting between supervisor and trainee to discuss the skills learned, what barriers the trainee might encounter, opportunities to use the skills, supervisor coaching, and the supervisor's expectations of improved job performance.

Trainees completed a survey one and a half months after training. The survey included items such as the degree of transfer, factors affecting transfer, and the meetings held with supervisors. Results showed that management support and training transfer were related. Furthermore, trainees reporting more skills transfer also perceived more supervisor support and reported fewer transfer inhibiting factors. These results show that even a modest supervisor intervention before and after training can have a significant impact on whether trainees use their newly developed skills. The small effort that supervisors expended seemed to yield a large payoff in terms of increased training transfer.

Evaluating Training Results

One of the hottest evaluation topics of the 1990s is the evaluation of business results, financial results, and return-on-investment (ROI). Popular and research literature from 1990 through 1996 is laden with such articles (we found 30 articles published within this time). Most offer anecdotal evidence or conjecture about the necessity of evaluating training's return-on-investment or financial results and methods trainers might use to implement such an evaluation. The current research on this topic is not so voluminous, however. Following is a look at studies conducted in the past decade. Each gives insights into different aspects of evaluating financial or business results. Table 5 provides a summary of these studies.

Table 5: Evaluating training results (organizational impact).

Author(s)/Date	Focus of Research	Design and Methods	Findings
McLinden, Davis, & Sheriff (1993)	To determine ROI of tax consultant training	Collected reaction, learning, and job performance data; assigned dollar amounts to various training benefits; payback = revenues attributed to training = cost of training	Substantive positive impact on the financial productivity of the tax consultancy; trainees generated more revenue for their organization than did untrained employees.
Russ-Eft, Krishnamurthi, & Ravishankar (1990)	To determine ROI of interpersonal skills training program	Pretest/posttest control group design; fixed and variable costs computed; skill changes from training were converted to monetary benefits using the fixed and variable costs	Training improved interpersonal skills and the program showed a favorable ROI.
Jacobs, Jones, & Neil (1992)	To determine whether unstructured or structured on-the-job training produced greater financial benefits	Case study at Midwest assembly plant; studied three critical tasks; performance value and costs calculated for each task	Structured OJT resulted in significantly lower mastery times for all three tasks; structured OJT found to provide almost twice the financial benefits as unstructured OJT for all three tasks.
Bernthal & Byham (1994)	To determine the ROI of an interactive skills training program for supervisors	Predominantly white male maintenance supervisors, ages 20–60; pretest/posttest control group design to measure turnover, absenteeism, overtime; five training modules assessed	Training group showed reduced turnover, less absenteeism; results saved organization between $200 and $20,000.

Because training and development are costly endeavors, they "should be evaluated in the same way as other large investments, in terms of costs and benefits" (Mosier, 1990, p. 45). To assist managers in selecting appropriate evaluation approaches, Mosier reviewed numerous common capital budgeting techniques. Among these are payback time, average rate of return, present value or worth, internal rate of return, and cost-benefit ratio. She notes that many managers and trainers still evaluate by the "gut feel" method and insists that a rational financial model is essential for evaluating training's effectiveness. She concludes by speculating that there are four reasons why financial analyses are rarely conducted or reported:

- It is difficult to quantify or establish a monetary value for many aspects of training.
- No usable cost-benefit tool is readily available.
- The time lag between training and results is problematic.
- HRD managers and trainers are not familiar with financial analysis models.

To justify continuation of their training programs, Mosier suggests that managers or trainers collect and analyze quantitative data.

McLinden, Davis, and Sheriff (1993) conducted an evaluation study to determine the ROI of tax consultant training. One of its goals was to illustrate the practicalities of determining the financial impact of training. To assess financial impact, the authors used Kirkpatrick's four-level model and Brinkerhoff's six-stage model to guide the evaluation. Accordingly, they collected reaction, learning, and job performance data.

Two steps in the analysis drove the financial impact of the training. The authors had to determine reasonable dollar amounts to attribute to various training benefits, and they wanted to determine if complete payback could be achieved. Payback would occur when revenues attributed to training equaled the cost of training. They computed the cost of training as the cost of trainees' time plus the costs associated with development and delivery of training.

The results of this study showed a "substantive positive impact" on the financial productivity of the tax consultancy (McLinden et al., 1993, p. 376). Trainees generated more revenues for their organization than did untrained employees. Additionally, complete payback was achieved in only two months.

Russ-Eft, Krishnamurthi, and Ravishankar (1994) computed the return-on-investment (ROI) of a typical interpersonal skills training program. They conducted the research at a large international information services company. An externally developed training program was provided to professional and support people from three locations. The study used a pretest-posttest, control group evaluation design.

Russ-Eft, Krishnamurthi, and Ravishankar (1994) computed the fixed and variable costs for training. Fixed costs included trainers' salaries during the design of the training session and certification costs. Variable costs included costs associated with the time spent away from the job for each trainee, preparation and training delivery time for each trainer, and training materials. Skill changes resulting from training were converted to monetary benefits using the fixed and variable costs and other relevant information. The authors used the following calculations:

- Annual salaries plus fringe benefits were averaged over all members of the training group.
- Before and after training trainees estimated the percentage of time spent in each of five key skills areas.
- The average annualized salary figure (step 1) was multiplied by the percentage time a trainee spent in each skill area (step 2), resulting in a dollar amount for each skill area.
- Pretraining and posttraining returns to the organization for each skill were calculated using supervisors' skill ratings and the cost figure (step 3).
- The difference between the pre- and posttraining returns (step 4) indicated the benefit to the organization attributed to a single trainee.
- Total benefits of the program were computed as the sum of the benefits (step 5) accrued over all trainees.

The results of this study showed training improved interpersonal skills. Additionally, the interpersonal skills program showed a favorable ROI, demonstrating "bottom-line results can be useful in obtaining management's support for skills training and development" (Russ-Eft et al., 1994, p. 210).

In a case study forecasting financial benefits of two training options, Jacobs, Jones, and Neil (1992) based their study on the widely referenced Swanson and Gradous (1988) financial forecast model. In essence the model states the benefit for each of the optional training interventions should be computed as

$$\text{Benefit} = \text{Performance Value} - \text{Cost}$$

Benefit is the return for work produced; performance value is the financial worth of the work; and cost is the sum of training expenses, including expenses due to salaries, materials, equipment, and other costs incurred by selecting that training option. The most desirable option, then, would be the one yielding the largest benefit.

The case study at a Midwest assembly plant was undertaken to determine which training option, unstructured or structured on-the-job (OJT) training, produced the better financial benefit. Unstructured OJT consists of experienced workers imparting information and skills training to less experienced workers on an ad hoc basis, that is, in an unplanned fashion. Structured OJT is planned, purposeful training in which experienced workers deliver specific training in specific situations to inexperienced workers.

Comparing the financial benefits of unstructured and structured OJT required the calculation of performance value and cost for each option. Researchers identified three tasks as critical for the study because of high work area turnover rates and task difficulty associated with them. Work area turnover rate for each task was computed using existing personnel and plant records. Task difficulty for each task was estimated for both training options, resulting in six time estimates for task mastery.

Not surprisingly, structured OJT resulted in significantly lower mastery times for all three tasks. In accordance with the Swanson and Gradous (1988) financial forecast model, performance value and cost had to be calculated for each task. Performance value was calculated using mastery times (task difficulty), work area turnover rate, plant production rates, and performance value per employee. Start-up expenses associated with structured OJT (for analysis, development of materials, external consultant, and evaluation) caused this option to cost more than unstructured OJT, which incurred no cost. Using these performance and cost data, benefit was forecasted for each task for both training options.

Results showed that structured OJT would provide approximately twice the financial benefits as unstructured OJT over all three tasks. In addition, the authors found that turnover rate had greater impact on financial benefit than task difficulty in this case. Although it is not a typical training scenario, the case study results confirm what many trainers already know or suspect: Formalizing training to some extent is likely to increase mastery of knowledge and skills in shorter time frames than unstructured on-the-job training. In addition, this study shows the Swanson and Gradous financial forecast model can be used in settings other than the traditional training environment.

Bernthal and Byham (1994) conducted a study to assess the ROI of an interactive skills training program for supervisors. The organization under study was concerned about employee turnover and overall organizational improvement, especially the effect supervisors' core skills and behaviors had on them. Supervisor behaviors targeted for training had to fulfill two criteria: (1) They had to be important for the job, and (2) they had to be behaviors at which supervisors were not already proficient.

The training program consisted of five modules of an independently produced interpersonal skills program, which trainers selected. The trainees were male maintenance supervisors who were predominantly white, in their mid-20s to early 60s. A pretest-posttest control group design was implemented to measure turnover, absenteeism, and overtime. Each training session, in which all five modules were covered, took three days. All training sessions were completed within two months. Before training, the control group and training group had equivalent turnover rates. After training, however, the training group showed a significant reduction (46 percent) in turnover from their pretest turnover rate. The control group showed no such reduction. Therefore, training appears to have decreased turnover.

Absenteeism in the training group fell by 17 percent; however, this was not a statistically significant result. Overtime also displayed a nonsignificant drop of 7 percent. Although two of the three decreases were not significant, trainers interpreted these results as showing an overall positive impact at the organizational level. Turnover, which can be costly in terms of hiring and training new people, was nearly halved. This reduction alone would save the company from $200 to $20,000 per year, depending on who provided the estimate. No other effort was expended to estimate dollar benefits for the results of training.

In spite of the interest in ROI and cost-benefit outcomes, research on this topic is hard to find, and those studies that do exist do not provide much guidance for trainers in designing and conducting their own ROI evaluations. Generally, the studies reported do not discuss alternative methods of calculating ROI or justify the method ultimately selected. Mosier (1990) discussed, in quite technical terms, several financial models and techniques for calculating costs and benefits. How they would translate to a real world ROI evaluation would be of great interest.

It is not clear whether the ROI calculations used in the studies are appropriate and relevant and whether the results are truly meaningful. More research needs to be done to identify appropriate financial models for certain evaluation applications. Mosier (1990) notes that using the same data and different techniques can result in vastly different ROI results. Trainers and their managers have a definite interest in determining which models and techniques will give them the answers they seek.

LESSONS LEARNED

Training Evaluation Models

Although Kirkpatrick's (1959a, 1959b, 1960a, 1960b) model has provided many trainers a place to start in evaluating training, criticism about the limited nature of the model is increasing. The model's lack of diagnostic capability and its inability to account for factors that affect the outcomes at each level are just two of the model's inherent weaknesses. The same can be true for most of the models reviewed in this chapter. Nearly all of them in some way incorporate the outcomes of Kirkpatrick's four levels (reactions, learning, behavior, and results) and use similar, if not identical, terminology. Where the labels differ, the models' underlying ideas have common traits. However, most of these "models" are not true models, but are taxonomies that merely describe anticipated training outcomes. They fail to offer any direction on what critical variables need to be studied or how to conduct a rigorous, credible, useful evaluation in dynamic, evolving, and political environments. Further limiting their usefulness is the fact that very few of the models have undergone rigorous forms of research to determine the extent to which the models describe training's effects or how various organizational variables affect training outcomes. For example, individual trainees have different personalities, skills, motivations, attitudes, and expectations. The organizations in which they work have their own cultures, management structures, organizational goals, and so on. It is likely that these factors and many more have an effect on the conduct and outcome of any training program. Yet, the models that have been proposed provide limited guidance on how these variables interact with one another and affect the impact of training on individuals, teams and organizations.

Training Evaluation Research

Research on training evaluation models and methods over the last 40 years leaves us still with many unanswered questions about the effectiveness of training interventions. The one area in which there has been research, however, is on the transfer of training. The findings reported in this chapter provide some important lessons for trainees, trainers, and managers. For trainers and other organization members who want to enhance training transfer, several simple, practical, and relatively easy-to-implement techniques have been found to be effective for facilitating transfer. For example, we know that management support, consisting of brief discussions between trainee and supervisor before and after training, yields significant transfer results. A posttraining self-management workshop with a goal-setting component also appears to have significant effects on transfer. Ensuring a satisfactory organizational climate for transfer may be more difficult to ensure, but appears to be a critical element in the transfer equation.

What we have learned from what works and what doesn't in the training evaluation research is that there are many variables that ultimately affect how trainees learn and transfer their learning in the workplace. Unless we carefully consider and study these variables, we will be unable to describe and explain any effects that training may have on individual, team, and organizational performance. We have composed the following list of variables, most of which have been identified in the training and evaluation literatures, that are thought to influence training's effects and evaluation's effectiveness. Although this list is not exhaustive, we hope it helps training evaluators determine the focus of their training evaluation efforts:

Selected variables that affect training's effects and evaluation effectiveness.

Organization
- risk-taking capacity
- orientation to change
- commitment to training and learning
- resources for training and learning
- extent to which it has systems and structures that support transfer of training and learning
- degree of alignment between goals and actions
- experiences with previous change efforts
- financial situation
- orientation toward evaluation
- organization culture
- organization climate

Trainees
- motivation to learn
- work history
- ability to learn
- readiness for training

- motivation to transfer learning
- attitude about and commitment to the job
- expected utility of training content
- personality factors
- enjoyment of the training experience
- opportunity to apply learning
- choice to be in training
- self-efficacy
- learning task anxiety
- (greater) age
- goal setting before training
- locus-of-control
- involvement in the program's design
- prior experience with training
- perceptions of the organization

Trainers
- facilitation skills
- content knowledge
- training delivery skills
- level of interest/enthusiasm
- written and verbal communication skills
- credibility
- demographics
- understanding of adult learning theories and principles
- level of organization and preparedness
- listening skills

Managers
- ability and willingness to coach on new skills
- ability and willingness to model new skills
- expectations of improved job performance
- pretraining meeting with trainees
- provision of time for trainees to use new knowledge and skills
- provision of resources to use new knowledge and skills
- provision of incentives to use new knowledge and skills
- communication of the value of training and learning

Training Program Design
- training program is based on a needs assessment
- training population is clearly identified and has training needs
- goal and objectives are related to the needs identified (focused on organizational, team, or individual performance improvement)
- a variety of learning/teaching strategies are used to appeal to all learning styles and abilities
- design is based on adult learning theories and principles

Training Program Implementation
- materials facilitate learning
- facilities are adequate for delivering the program effectively
- necessary equipment is available for delivery

- trainer's training skills and level of expertise with content matter
- trainees' group dynamics

Evaluator Characteristics
- credibility
- experience with the program
- previous experience in conducting evaluation
- knowledge of evaluation theory and methods
- position within the organization relative to the program being evaluated
- commitment to evaluation and use of findings
- understanding of the organization's culture and politics
- commitment to ethical behavior—integrity
- group facilitation skills
- verbal and written communication skills
- understanding of program content
- data analysis skills

Evaluation Design
- stakeholder involvement
- agreed-upon key questions
- appropriateness of the evaluation design and data collection methods
- communication and reporting of results
- adherence to professional evaluation standards

Evaluation Implementation
- quality of data collection instruments (ensures data validity)
- political environment
- evaluator's and participant's time
- evaluation resources (for example, incentives, refreshments, facilities)
- support of management to participate in the evaluation
- change in evaluation's stakeholders
- adherence to professional evaluation standards
- quality of data analysis procedures
- focus on evaluation questions
- confidentiality and anonymity of data and sources

When HRD researchers and practitioners study these variables in the context of evaluation, they may more effectively measure the benefits expected from the training program. These benefits may include:
- increased profits
- improved customer satisfaction
- increased productivity
- improved employee morale
- improved loyalty and commitment of employees
- improved individual, team, and organizational performance
- reduced employee and customer/client turnover
- greater sales
- improved efficiency

Using a Logic Model to Advance Training Program Evaluation

Drawing upon the literature on large-scale social, educational, and health programs, we can suggest an approach to evaluating training that incorporates several of these variables. The creation of a logic map of the training can help identify objectives, elements, processes, and approaches (for example, Russ-Eft, 1986; Schmidt, Scanlon, & Bell, 1979; Wholey, 1975, 1976, 1979). The logic map helps determine the extent to which the program has clearly defined and measurable objectives, a logic or rationale for reaching the training goals, and a sequence of activities that represents that logic or rationale. It shows logical linkages among activities, immediate outputs, and a range of outcomes.

A key distinction to this approach is that the development of such a logic model is an iterative and collaborative process. Typically the evaluator involves a stakeholder group in the development of the logic model. The approach can take the form of generating a series of "if-then" statements of the type: "If Event X occurs, then Event Y will occur"; or "If trainees participate in training, they will increase their use of the skill being trained." A more structured approach involves the use of specific questions to aid in the model's development. (See Jordan, 1996, for more details.) These questions include the following:

- How does this program operate; and what resources are needed? (Key measurements here include resources, activities, milestones, and counts of things produced.)
- Who is reached by these resources in terms of users and clients? (Key measurements here include the number and percent of customers (for example, trainees, managers), partners (for example, trainers, managers), and stakeholders.)
- What results are expected from the program, and why are these results necessary? These results include both direct or immediate outcomes, as well as long-term outcomes. (Key measurements here include independent technical assessment of quality, perceived value of the training, and economic benefits.)
- What external factors may be influencing each stage of the training and evaluation process?

Data collection to confirm the model can involve surveys, document review, individual and focus group interviews with customers, partners, and stakeholders, as well as observation. Furthermore, as data are collected, it may be necessary to revise the model to reflect the actual program.

Figure 2 presents a simple logic model for a training process in an organization. In this case, the evaluator has identified outcomes for both the organization and the trainee. The evaluator and stakeholders may want to refine this model to include external variables that may affect the training activities as well as the outcomes.

The use of this logic model approach to evaluating training provides some distinct advantages. First, key stakeholders become involved with training from the program's initial design through the evaluation process. These stakeholders should come to realize that specific training outcomes

Figure 2. Logic model for a training process.

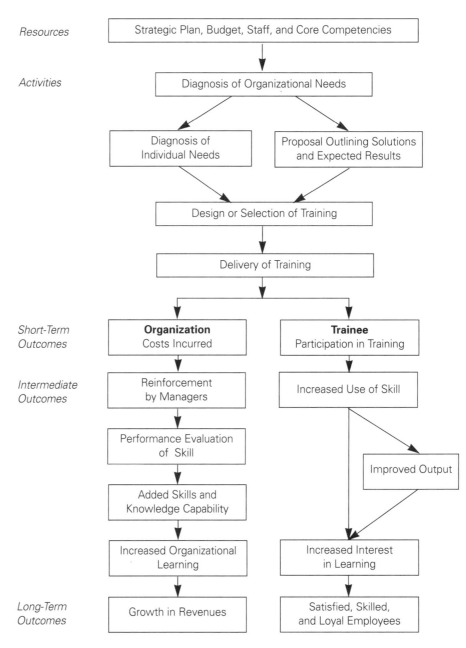

can result only if certain resources are allocated and certain activities occur. Second, because the evaluator and stakeholders are examining the training process from beginning to end, needed modifications and improvements can be undertaken to enhance the impact of training. Finally, because external factors and other intervening variables are identified up-front, action can be taken if such factors threaten the training outcomes and evaluation.

Training Evaluation Practice

What stands out as one reads the training evaluation research is that most of the evaluation models are not grounded in a philosophy or theory of evaluation (Dionne, 1996; Kraiger, Ford, & Salas, 1993; Preskill, 1997). The articles we reviewed tend to position evaluation as a periodic event that is the sum of a set of technical skills and activities focused on a narrow set of expected outcomes. Of particular concern is how little training professionals and researchers have tapped other disciplines such as education and the government or military in their development of evaluation theories, models, and methods. Over the past 30 years, an enormous amount of research has been conducted in the evaluation field manifested by several evaluation journals (for example, *Evaluation, Evaluation & Program Planning, Evaluation Practice, New Directions in Program Evaluation, Evaluation Review*).[1] Research on evaluation models, methods, philosophies, standards, ethics, utilization, and cultural issues have continued to develop outside of the HRD field.

For the past four decades, training evaluation has focused on a limited number of questions, using only a few tools and methods. This pattern has led to a constricted view of what training evaluation can offer organizations. Evaluation of training programs has been parochial in its approach and, as a result, has failed to show HRD's contribution or value to organizations. We have failed to understand the learning potential from evaluation endeavors and the concept of intended use (of evaluation findings) by intended users (stakeholders). As trainers move into the role of learning and performance consultants, as organizations seek to do things faster and better, HRD professionals should consider additional and alternative ways of integrating evaluative inquiry into their work. This shift requires establishing a culture of information in the organization, "where information collection, development and utilization becomes a matter-of-fact, ongoing activity for all those working in the organization" (Bhola, 1995, p. 81). We should also look to other disciplines to expand our notion of evaluation theory and practice. As Scriven (1996) reminds us,

> Evaluation is not only a discipline on which all others depend, it is one on which all deliberate activity depends. It follows that significant improvements in the core concept and techniques of evaluation, of which we have seen many in recent years, and of which many more could be made within the next few years, have the potential for huge improvement in the quality of life and work, as well as in the level of achievement in all disciplines. (p. 404)

CONCLUSIONS

We wish to leave the reader with a sense of untapped opportunities that exist if they choose to establish effective evaluation processes and systems in their organizations. Our experiences have shown us that when trainers be-

---

1. For a detailed history of the evolution of program evaluation, see House (1993).

come evaluators of their programs, using insightful and well-informed practices, their efforts do not go unnoticed. Organization members become aware of training's commitment to continuous improvement and the relationship between training and the organization's goals. Without ongoing training evaluation systems, trainers have no basis on which to judge the merits and contributions of what they do in organizations. When we are told that it "costs too much to evaluate," we ask, "Can we afford not to evaluate?"

We believe that trainers should consider the following:

1. Recognize that HRD professionals are responsible for supporting the transfer of learning when trainees go back to the job; that evaluation efforts must go beyond measuring reactions.
2. Improve the quality of reactions surveys and understand their limited usefulness when it comes to assessing the impact of training. We should stop collecting useless survey data that pile up on our desks and focus more on collecting relevant and useful information.
3. Use more collaborative approaches in conducting training program evaluations. The more stakeholders are involved in the evaluation's design and implementation, the greater the likelihood they will use evaluation results to make formative and summative program decisions.
4. Facilitate organization members' understanding of evaluation purposes, methods, standards, and uses.
5. Become more skilled in evaluation theory and methods. Take workshops and graduate-level courses on training program evaluation.
6. Help organizations develop a spirit of evaluative inquiry that is interwoven into all work processes.
7. Focus on the questions and key variables each evaluation should seek to address. Avoid the one-size-fits-all mindset—that one method (for example, a survey that uses the same questions time after time) will meet all decision makers' information needs.
8. Emphasize the concept of intended use by intended users. This means focusing on the kinds of information needed to make the necessary decisions about a particular program.

Top-level management in organizations has not given training program evaluation the respect it deserves. We believe this is largely because trainers lack sufficient evaluation skills, and management does not truly understand the role evaluation can play in helping to solve complex learning and performance problems. Well-conceived and implemented evaluation is a key strategic initiative that highlights the critical information needs of designers, trainers, and managers, and provides the means to ensuring quality training interventions.

REFERENCES

Alliger, G.M., & E.A. Janak. (1989). "Kirkpatrick's Levels of Training Criteria: Thirty Years Later." *Personnel Psychology,* volume 42, 331–340.

Andrasik, F., & J.S. Heimberg. (1980). "Self-Management Procedures." *Behavioral Medicine: Changing Health Life Styles,* P.O. Davidson & S.M. Davidson, editors. New York: Brunner/Mazel.

Baldwin, T.T., & J.K. Ford. (1988). "Transfer of Training: A Review and Directions for Research." *Personnel Psychology,* volume 41, number 1, 63–105.

Baldwin, T.T., R.J. Magjuka, & B.T. Loher. (1991). "The Perils of Participation: Effects of Choice of Training on Trainee Motivation and Learning." *Personnel Psychology,* volume 44, 51–65.

Bassi, L.J., G. Benson, & S. Cheney. (1996). "The Top Ten Trends." *Training & Development,* volume 50, number 11, 28–42.

Benson, G. (1996). "How Much Do Employers Spend on Training?" *Training & Development,* volume 50, number 10, 56–58.

Bernthal, P.R., & W.C. Byham. (1994). "Interactive Skills Training for Supervisors: Penske Truck Leasing Company." *In Action: Measuring Return on Investment, Volume 1* (pp. 23–32), J. Phillips, editor. Alexandria, VA: American Society for Training & Development.

Bhola, H.S. (1995). "Informed Decisions within a Culture of Information: Updating a Model of Information Development and Evaluation." *Adult Education for Development,* volume 44, 75–85.

Bramley, P., & B. Kitson. (1994). "Evaluating Training Against Business Criteria." *Journal of European Industrial Training,* volume 18, number 1, 10–14.

Brinkerhoff, R.O. (1988). "An Integrated Evaluation Model for HRD." *Training & Development,* volume 42, number 2, 66–68.

Brinkerhoff, R.O. (1989). *Achieving Results from Training.* San Francisco: Jossey-Bass.

Brinkerhoff, R.O., & M.U. Montesino. (1995). "Partnerships for Training Transfer: Lessons from a Corporate Study." *Human Resource Development Quarterly,* volume 6, number 3, 263–274.

Bushnell, D.S. (1990). "Input, Process, Output: A Model for Evaluating Training." *Training & Development,* volume 42, number 3, 41–43.

Clement, R.W. (1978). "An Empirical Test of the Hierarchy Theory of Evaluation." Doctoral dissertation, Michigan State University.

Clement, R.W. (1982). "Testing the Hierarchy Theory of Training Evaluation: An Expanded Role for Trainee Reactions." *Public Personnel Management Journal,* volume 11, 176–184.

Dionne, P. (1996). "The Evaluation of Training Activities: A Complex Issue Involving Different Stakes." *Human Resource Development Quarterly,* volume 7, number 3, 279–286.

Dixon, N.M. (1990). "The Relationship Between Trainee Responses on Participant Reaction Forms and Posttest Scores." *Human Resource Development Quarterly,* volume 1, number 2, 129–137.

Erickson, P.R. (1990). "Evaluating Training Results." *Training & Development Journal,* volume 44, number 1, 57–59.

Faerman, S.R., & C. Ban. (1993). "Trainee Satisfaction and Training Impact: Issues in Training Evaluation." *Public Productivity and Management Review,* volume 16, number 3, 299–314.

Foxon, M.J. (1994). "A Process Approach to Transfer of Training. Part 2: Using Action Planning to Facilitate the Transfer of Training." *Australian Journal of Educational Technology,* volume 10, number 1, 1–18.

Garavaglia, P.L. (1996). "Applying a Transfer Model to Training." *Performance and Instruction,* volume 35, number 4, 4–8.

Gist, M.E., A.G. Bavetta, & C.K. Stevens. (1990). "Transfer Training Method: Its Influence on Skill Generalization, Skill Repetition, and Performance Level." *Personnel Psychology,* volume 43, 501–523.

Gist, M.E., C.K. Stevens, & A.G. Bavetta. (1991). "Effects of Self-Efficacy and Post Training Intervention on the Acquisition and Maintenance of Complex Interpersonal Skills." *Personnel Psychology,* volume 44, 837–861.

Hamblin, A.C. (1974). *Evaluation and Control of Training.* London: McGraw-Hill.

Holton, E.F., III. (1996). "The Flawed Four-Level Evaluation Model." *Human Resource Development Quarterly,* volume 7, number 1, 5–21.

House, E.R. (1993) *Professional Evaluation.* Thousand Oaks, CA: Sage.

"Industry Report." (October 1996). *Training Magazine,* volume 33, number 10, 37–79.

Jacobs, R.L., M.J. Jones, & S. Neil. (1992). "A Case Study in Forecasting the Financial Benefits of Unstructured and Structured on-the-Job Training." *Human Resource Development Quarterly,* volume 3, number 2, 133–139.

Jordan, G. (November 1996). "Using the Logic Chart and Performance Spectrum in Corporate Performance Management: A DOE Case Study." Paper presented at the Annual Meeting of the American Evaluation Association, Atlanta.

Kaufman, R., & J.M. Keller. (1994). "Levels of Evaluation: Beyond Kirkpatrick." *Human Resource Development Quarterly,* volume 5, number 4, 371–380.

Kaufman, R., J. Keller, & R. Watkins. (1995). "What Works and What Doesn't: Evaluation Beyond Kirkpatrick." *Performance and Instruction,* volume 35, number 2, 8–12.

Kirkpatrick, D.L. (November 1959a). "Techniques for Evaluating Programs." *Journal of the American Society of Training Directors (Training & Development),* volume 13, number 11, 3–9.

Kirkpatrick, D.L. (December 1959b). "Techniques for Evaluating Programs, Part 2: Learning." *Journal of the American Society of Training Directors (Training & Development),* volume 13, number 12, 21–26.

Kirkpatrick, D.L. (January 1960a). "Techniques for Evaluating Programs, Part 3: Behavior." *Journal of the American Society of Training Directors (Training & Development),* volume 14, number 1, 13–18.

Kirkpatrick, D.L. (January 1960b). "Techniques for Evaluating Programs, Part 4: Results." *Journal of the American Society of Training Directors (Training & Development),* volume 14, number 1, 28–32.

Kirkpatrick, D.L. (1994). *Evaluating Training Programs: The Four Levels.* San Francisco: Berrett-Koehler.

Kraiger, K., J.K. Ford, & E. Salas. (1993). "Application of Cognitive, Skill-Based, and Affective Theories of Learning Outcomes to New Methods of Training Evaluation." *Journal of Applied Psychology,* volume 78, number 2, 311–328.

Lincoln, R.E., & D.O. Dunet. (1995). "Training Efficiency and Effectiveness Model (TEEM)." *Performance and Instruction,* volume 34, number 3, 40–47.

McLinden, D.J., M.J. Davis, & D.E. Sheriff. (1993). "Impact on Financial Productivity: A Study of Training Effects on Consulting Services." *Human Resource Development Quarterly,* volume 4, number 4, 367–375.

Mosier, N.R. (1990). "Financial Analysis: The Methods and Their Application to Employee Training." *Human Resource Development Quarterly,* volume 1, number 1, 45–63.

Noe, R.A. (1986). "Trainees' Attributes and Attitudes: Neglected Influences on Training Effectiveness." *Academy of Management Review,* volume 11, number 4, 736–749.

Noe, R.A., & N. Schmitt. (1986). "The Influence of Trainee Attitudes on Training Effectiveness: Test of a Model." *Personnel Psychology,* volume 39, 497–523.

Plant, R.A., & R.J. Ryan. (1992). "Training Evaluation: A Procedure for Validating an Organization's Investment in Training." *Journal of European Industrial Training,* volume 16, number 10, 22–38.

Preskill, H. (March 1997). "HRD Evaluation as the Catalyst for Organizational Learning." Paper presented at the Annual Conference of the Academy of Human Resource Development, Atlanta.

Ree, M.J., & J.A. Earles. (1991). "Predicting Training Success: Not Much More Than g." *Personnel Psychology,* volume 44, 321–332.

Richey, R.C. (1992). *Designing Instruction for the Adult Learner.* London: Kogan Page.

Rouillier, J.Z., & I.L. Goldstein. (1993). "The Relationship Between Organizational Transfer Climate and Positive Transfer of Training." *Human Resource Development Quarterly,* volume 4, number 4, 377–390.

Rowe, C. (1995). "Incorporating Competence into the Long-Term Evaluation of Training and Development." *Industrial & Commercial Training,* volume 27, number 2, 3–9.

Russ-Eft, D. (1986). "Evaluability Assessment of the Adult Education Program (AEP)." *Evaluation and Program Planning,* volume 9, 39–47.

Russ-Eft, D., S. Krishnamurthi, & L. Ravishankar. (1994). "Getting Results with Interpersonal Training." *In Action: Measuring Return on Investment, Volume 1,* (pp. 199–212), J. Phillips, editor. Alexandria, VA: American Society for Training & Development.

Schmidt, R.E., J.W. Scanlon, & J.B. Bell. (November 1979). *Evaluability Assessment: Making Public Programs Work Better.* Human Services Monograph Series, No. 14.

Scriven, M. (1996). "The Theory Behind Practical Evaluation." *Evaluation,* volume 2, number 4, 393–404.

Swanson, R.A., & D.B. Gradous. (1988). *Forecasting Financial Benefits of Human Resource Development.* San Francisco: Jossey-Bass.

Swanson, R.A., & C.M. Sleezer. (1987). "Training Effectiveness Evaluation." *Journal of European Industrial Training,* volume 11, number 4, 7–16.

Tziner, A., R.R. Haccoun, & A. Kadish. (1991). "Personal and Situational Characteristics Influencing the Effectiveness of Transfer of Training Improvement Strategies." *Journal of Occupational Psychology,* volume 64, 167–177.

Warr, P., & D. Bunce. (1995). "Trainee Characteristics and the Outcomes of Open Learning." *Personnel Psychology,* volume 48, 347–375.

Wexley, K.N., & T.T. Baldwin. (1986). "Posttraining Strategies for Facilitating Positive Transfer: An Empirical Exploration." *Academy of Management Journal,* volume 29, number 3, 503–520.

Wholey, J.S. (1975). "Evaluation: When Is It Really Needed?" *Evaluation Magazine,* volume 2, number 2.

Wholey, J.S. (1976). *A Methodology for Planning and Conducting Project Impact Evaluation in UNESCO Fields.* Washington, DC: The Urban Institute.

Wholey, J.S. (1979). *Evaluation: Promise and Performance.* Washington, DC: The Urban Institute.

CHAPTER 6

Return-on-Investment

Ann P. Bartel, Ph.D.

Professor of Business
Columbia University Graduate School of Business

More than half of American businesses do not evaluate the results of their training programs but focus instead on reactions, learning, and behavior changes. Even among those companies that do consider business results, only a fraction actually monetize productivity gains and calculate a return-on-investment (ROI). Many companies use faulty methodologies that result in estimated ROIs that are too high to be believed. Practitioners that are considering conducting an ROI analysis for their firm's training investments can learn from these mistakes. The author provides eight guidelines for a sound ROI analysis.

1. BACKGROUND

In November 1959, Donald Kirkpatrick introduced his four-level model of training evaluation.[1] Since that time, this model has been the guide for evaluating training in virtually all American businesses. The four levels in the model are (1) reaction, how participants feel about the contents and delivery of the training program; (2) learning, the knowledge acquired or skills improved; (3) behavior, the extent to which participants change their on-the-job behavior because of the training; and (4) results, the final results that occur due to training, such as increased sales or higher productivity.

Funding for this research was provided by the U.S. Department of Labor under Contract Number F-4956-5-00-80-30.

1.The original Kirkpatrick articles as well as his contemporary reassessment of the model are reprinted in Kirkpatrick (1996).

Phillips (1996a) suggests that calculating the return-on-investment in training can be thought of as the fifth level in the Kirkpatrick model. In this level, the results documented in Level 4 are monetized and compared to the costs of the training program.

Phillips (1994) identified four trends that are creating pressure on firms to use ROI analysis to evaluate training programs. First is the increase in training budgets and the increase in the number of employees who receive formal training. Between 1994 and 1995, budgets increased 3 percent and the number of trainees increased 5 percent. With more resources devoted to training, there is an increased need for accountability. Second, in many companies, human resource development is being used to create competitive advantage, and there is a need to more precisely document the impact of training and development. Third, training is a key element of total quality management (TQM) efforts, which, by definition, emphasize the measurement of quality and productivity. Fourth, there is a general trend toward increased accountability of all business functions.

There are many reasons why conducting an ROI analysis is beneficial to the organization. First, it provides an objective quantitative standard against which to judge the training department. Second, it facilitates a comparison of the relative success of the various training programs that the company offers. Third, it enables the company to compare investment in training with alternative investment opportunities (for example, physical capital). Fourth, even if the measurement of ROI is imperfect, the attempts to measure it will focus attention on the issue of profitability of training, encouraging designers of the training program to incorporate this level of evaluation.

As documented in the following section, part 2, many firms avoid conducting an ROI analysis for training investments, in spite of its many benefits, largely because of difficulties in gathering the relevant data and isolating the influence of training on performance improvement from other factors. Part 3, "Data and Methodological Issues," discusses the methodological issues in conducting an ROI analysis and highlights the pitfalls of different approaches. In Part 4, "Findings from Case Studies," seven case studies of companies that calculated ROIs for their training programs are reviewed and evaluated. Part 5, "Evidence from Econometric Studies," provides a brief overview of the results from studies that have used econometric techniques to calculate the return on training investments. Finally, part 6, provides conclusions and advice for practitioners.

2. EVALUATION PRACTICES OF U.S. BUSINESSES

Surveys of evaluation methods American businesses have used generally show that little evaluation occurs beyond Level 3. A 1986 survey of Fortune 500 companies found that only 15 percent of the respondents measured change in performance on the job, and only 8 percent measured change in company operating results that were traceable to training (see

Phillips, 1991a, p. 7). In 1988, an American Society for Training & Development (ASTD) poll of organizations that led in training evaluation found that only 20 percent evaluated in terms of training's economic effect on the organization (see Carnevale & Schulz, 1990). A December 1989 survey of human resource executives conducted by *Human Resource Executive* found that only 13 percent of the respondents evaluated changes in organizational performance (see Scovel, 1990, for a description of the survey and its results). Data from ASTD's Benchmarking Forum indicates that the number of companies performing some type of Level 4 evaluation grew from 27 percent of Benchmarking Forum companies in 1994 to 40 percent in 1995, but it is not clear how many of these firms convert the results from training into monetary terms in order to calculate an ROI on the training investment (see Bassi & Cheney, 1996).

Why do many firms fail to calculate the ROI on their training investments? In a 1989 study, 35 training managers were interviewed to determine why cost-benefit analysis of training is rarely used (see Lombardo, 1989). Managers were recruited from small, medium, and large companies in central Ohio and were interviewed from 45 minutes to two hours. Most of them did not use cost-benefit analysis for the training programs in their firms, and their reasons for nonuse were as follows:

- the difficulty of quantifying training benefits
- the subjectivity and questionable nature of the assumptions underlying cost-benefit analysis
- the inability to separate the influence of training on performance improvement from other factors
- the cost in time and dollars of doing the analysis
- the difficulty of quantifying skills, especially soft skills such as team building
- top management's perceived lack of interest in the ROI on training
- the lack of an established data network in their company from which to obtain the data necessary for an ROI calculation

Many of these training managers voiced the opinion that training is an art, and, therefore, not easily or meaningfully valued in dollars and cents. It is interesting that many of the interviewees admitted that ignorance of the practical details of cost-benefit analysis was a major barrier to using it in their organizations.

3. DATA AND METHODOLOGICAL ISSUES IN EVALUATING THE FINANCIAL RETURNS TO INVESTMENTS IN TRAINING

Assemble the Relevant Data

To calculate the return on a training investment, a firm needs to assemble data on the investment costs and the returns from the investment. There are two components of the cost of delivering the training program: direct and indirect costs. Direct costs include such items as (1) purchased materials, (2) training room and equipment rental, (3) salaries and benefits of staff involved in designing and delivering the training program, and (4) food, travel, and lodging expenses. Recent data show that direct expenses account for close to 50 percent of total program costs (see Bassi, Gallagher, & Schroer, 1996, p. 125). The indirect costs of training, which are invisible, relate to the cost of the trainee's time. When individuals participate in a training program, the company incurs an opportunity cost because time spent in training is time spent away from the job. For each trainee, the cost of this lost time can be calculated by using the trainee's wage rate and fringe benefit rate. Then direct and indirect costs can be summed to give the full costs of training.

Returns from training are much more difficult to calculate precisely because there are a multitude of benefits that can result from a training program. Figure 1, reproduced from Phillips (1991a), lists the various types of data that a company should review in trying to assess training benefits. The list includes such hard data items as number of units of output produced, costs of production, equipment downtime, on-time shipments, work stoppages, error rates, product defects, and number of accidents. To use any of these items in an ROI calculation, it needs to be converted to a dollar value. Output measures are fairly easy to convert. For example, by comparing the average sales before a sales training program with the average sales after the program, one sees the change in sales output. Assuming that the company has data on the average profit per sale, the returns from the training program equal the increase in sales multiplied by the average profit per sale (Phillips, 1991a, p. 212). The second category of hard data, cost savings, need not be converted. The third and fourth categories, time and quality, are somewhat difficult, and sometimes impossible to convert accurately. For example, the dollar value of reduced equipment downtime could be calculated by using information on the value of the additional output that could be produced during the increased uptime, adjusting for any additional costs that might be incurred. It would be even more difficult to monetize the value of an increase in on-time shipments, however. Presumably an increase in on-time shipments will increase customer satisfaction, which should, in turn, increase customer demand for the company's output, resulting in additional profits. It is unlikely that most companies would be able to successfully trace these steps and produce a dollar value of on-time shipments. In the quality category, the value of a defective product could be calculated by taking the total cost incurred at the point the mistake is identified and subtracting the salvage value (Phillips, 1991a, p. 222). With this information, the value of the reduction in defective products could be quantified. Improved product quality will lead to an increase in customer satisfaction, but, as demonstrated earlier, it will be difficult to accurately quantify the dollar value of this gain.

Phillips (1991a) also recommends that firms measure training benefits by utilizing soft data items such as absenteeism, tardiness, turnover, job satisfaction, employee loyalty, problem-solving ability, performance appraisal ratings, and initiative. But these items are benefits only to the extent that they lead to increased productivity. If a firm is tracking productivity gains resulting from training, including improvements in the soft data

Figure 1. Hard data items for training returns.

Output	Costs
Units produced	Budget variances
Tons manufactured	Unit costs
Items assembled	Cost by account
Money collected	Variable costs
Items sold	Fixed costs
Forms processed	Overhead cost
Loans approved	Operating costs
Inventory turnover	Number of cost reductions
Patients visited	Project cost savings
Applications processed	Accident costs
Students graduated	Program costs
Tasks completed	Sales expense
Output per worker hour	
Productivity	**Quality**
Work backlog	
Incentive bonus	Scrap
Shipments	Waste
	Rejects
Time	Error rates
	Rework
Equipment downtime	Shortages
Overtime	Product defects
On-time shipments	Deviation from standard
Time to project completion	Product failures
Processing time	Inventory adjustments
Supervisory time	Time-card corrections
Break-in time for new employees	Percent of tasks completed properly
Training time	Number of accidents
Meeting schedules	
Repair time	Source: Phillips (1991a, p. 154) From *Hand-*
Efficiency	*book of Training Evaluation and Measurement*
Work stoppages	*Methods, Second Edition*, by Jack Phillips.
Order response	Copyright © 1991 by Gulf Publishing Compa-
Late reporting	ny. Used with permission. All rights reserved.
Lost-time days	

items as benefits would be double counting. Firms that rely on soft data items instead of the hard data items to measure training benefits should be encouraged to translate observed changes in these soft data items into measurable productivity gains.

Choose an Evaluation Design

To accurately evaluate the return-on-investment in training, it is essential that the firm be able to isolate the impact of training from the impacts of other factors. This requires a careful evaluation design before the training program is actually implemented. Carnevale and Schulz (1990) describe five evaluation designs: (1) pre- and posttest control group design, (2) multiple baseline design, (3) time series design, (4) single group pre- and posttest design, and (5) one-time case study. Table 1 shows these designs with a summary of their attributes in order from most to least rigorous.

Table 1. Description and comparison of evaluation designs.

Type	Description	Strengths	Weaknesses
1. Pre- and posttest control group	Random assignment of employees to training or control group	Controls for other factors	Costly or infeasible to select control group (especially in unionized setting)
2. Multiple baseline	Train different groups in the company at different times; second group is control group for first	No need for rigidly maintained control group	Performance is compared across groups at different times
3. Time series	Performance measured repeatedly before and after training	More practical than control group design	Other events occurring at same time as training may be responsible for productivity changes
4. Single group pre- and posttest	Trainees tested once before and once after training	No control group	No controls for other factors that affect performance
5. One-time case study	Trainees tested only after completion of training	Useful only if participants had no prior exposure to skills	No controls for intervening factors

In the pre- and posttest control group design, the evaluator randomly assigns employees to either a training group or a control group. Data are gathered from both groups through pre- and posttests. Upon completion of the program, if the trained group shows greater posttest performance gains than the control group, the gains are assumed to be due to the training. The validity of this approach depends on the extent to which assignment is truly random. In addition, some companies may be unwilling to withhold training from some employees just because a control group is needed for the study. This design may not be feasible in a union setting where training is considered to be an employee benefit.

The multiple baseline design is useful when a training program is to be introduced to different parts of the organization at different times. Data are collected on each group of participants before and after the training. The second group serves as the control for the first group and the third group for the second group, and so on. The performance of the trainees is compared to the performance of its control group. Although this approach eliminates the need for a rigidly maintained control group, it has the disadvantage of comparing performance across different parts of the organization at different times. These differences may themselves be responsible for the observed performance differentials.

In a time series design, the training group serves as its own control group. Performance is measured repeatedly (for example, monthly) before and after the training program. If the measures show improvement after training, the result is assumed to be due to the training. Although this approach is more practical than the two previous designs, it cannot rule out the possibility that an event occurring simultaneously with the training program (for example, a new advertising campaign) is at least partly responsible for the observed improvements. Another problem is that individuals may change jobs after a few months or even leave the company. When job changes occur, the measurement of training returns relies solely on the employees who remain, thereby ignoring the lost investment in those workers who left. A more sophisticated analysis would account for this lost investment.

The single group pre- and posttest design is widely used because it does not require a control group and is inexpensive. The trainees are tested before the training program and then again some time after the training program. To conclude that the observed performance gains are due to the training, the evaluator must try to account for other factors that may be responsible for the performance change. Phillips (1994) suggests two methods for isolating the effect of a training program when this design is used. One is to have the participants estimate the percentage of their improvement attributable to the training program. He argues that this is appropriate because the participants are very close to the improvement and may know how much of the improvement was due to the training. Unfortunately, the participants may also feel pressure (implicit or explicit) to show support for the training program; alternatively, they may be resentful of the training that would introduce a negative bias. The second method is to have the trainees' supervisors estimate the percentage of improvement attributable to the training program. Phillips argues that the supervisors are likely to be most familiar with the situation and with other factors that may influence performance, but this approach is highly subjective and may not accurately account for the potential impact of factors other than training.

In the one-time case study, the participants are only tested after the training program. This is the least rigorous of the approaches and is only appropriate if the participants have had no prior exposure to the skills being taught.[2]

To summarize, the main issue in choosing an evaluation design is how to isolate the impact of training from other factors that may be responsible for the performance improvement. Although a true experimental design is ideal, it may be infeasible. If an alternative design is used, it is essential that data on other factors be tracked in order to assess their roles in explaining performance.

Discount Future Benefits

When calculating the return-on-investment in training, it is essential that future benefits be properly discounted. Unfortunately, many human resource professionals use the average rate of return method, which does not take account of the time value of money. The average rate of return is

---

2. Carnevale and Schulz (1990) cite the example of IBM's program on beginning Japanese for their international sales representatives. They did not receive a pretest because they had no prior exposure to the language.

calculated as the ratio of average annual returns from the training program divided by the average cost of the program (see, for example, Phillips, 1991a). Advocates of this method urge companies to have a target rate of return in mind and to accept any investment that has an average rate of return above the target. An appropriate target might be the rate of return that the firm expects on capital expenditures that have a similar amount of risk. The main weakness of the average rate of return method is that it ignores the timing of returns. Because returns can be reinvested, investments that offer early returns are more desirable than those that offer later returns, but this method cannot distinguish between such investments. As a result, the average rate of return method should only be used if all the returns occur in the time period immediately following the outlay of expenditures.

A more appropriate method is to calculate the net present value of the investment, which is defined as the discounted value of all costs and benefits associated with the project. If the net present value is greater than zero, the company should undertake the project. The distinct advantage of this approach is that it takes into account the time value of money. One difficulty in implementing it, however, is that the company must know its discount rate, which is measured by its opportunity cost of capital. A publicly traded company should, therefore, use the risk-adjusted rate of return on its securities, whereas a private company could approximate its cost of capital by using the cost of capital of a "similar" public company.

An alternative to calculating the net present value is to compute the internal rate of return (IRR), which is defined as the interest rate that sets the net present value of the stream of costs and benefits equal to zero. The internal rate of return rule is to accept an investment project if the opportunity cost of capital is less than the internal rate of return. Hence, like the net present value approach, the IRR approach requires knowledge of the company's opportunity cost of capital.

4. FINDINGS FROM CASE STUDIES ON ROI[*]

My review of the literature uncovered 20 case studies of companies that measured the business results from their training programs. Table 2 provides a summary of the cases indicating, for each company, the evaluation design, the employee group, type of training, performance measure, and measured return-on-investment. The reader should note that the estimated returns-on-investment are extremely high. Although these returns may reflect the fact that companies do not want weak results publicized, they may also be due to methodological flaws.

Part A presents detailed discussions of four cases that provide good examples of the methodological flaws often found in this literature. These flaws are, as follows:

---

[*]Editors' Note: Many of the cases cited in this chapter come from Phillips (1994). It should be noted that these cases were published originally "to show the application of a wide range of models and techniques, some of which are based on sound theory and logical assumptions, and others of which may not fare as well under the scrutiny of close examination," as Phillips states in the book's preface.

Table 2. Description of case studies.

Company	Employee Group	Type of Training	Performance Measure	ROI	Comments
I. Control Group Design					
1. Garrett Engine Division	Maintenance teams	Team building	Equipment downtime converted to dollars.	125%	Only studied performance for four weeks. Did tasks of control group differ?
2. Information Services	Professional and support staff	Interpersonal skills	Subjective behaviors converted to dollar values.	336%	Subjectivity; behavior changes measured for one month only
3. Insurance Company of America	Newly hired underwriters	Underwriting skills	Test scores six months after training	N.A.	No dollar values; no consideration of factors that differ for control group
4. Penske Truck Leasing Company	Maintenance supervisors	Supervisory skills	Turnover of mechanics and fuel island attendants tracked for nine months before and seven months after training.	N.A.	No dollar values
5. Financial Services Company	District sales managers	Selection	Reduction in turnover of branch manager trainees converted to dollar value.	2,140%	Exaggerated the cost of turnover
6. Southeastern Bank	Managers and tellers	Supervisory skills	Supervisors rate performance six months after training.	370% (5 years)	Post-hoc control group; subjectivity

Table 2. Description of case studies. (continued).

Company	Employee Group	Type of Training	Performance Measure	ROI	Comments
II. Single Group Pre- and Posttest					
7. U.S. Government	New supervisors	Supervisory skills	Managers rate skills one week before and six weeks after training and estimate value of skills.	150%	Subjective valuation of skills; will changes continue after six weeks? Other factors may play a role.
8. Hughes Aircraft Company	Entry-level nonmanagement business jobs	Time management; reducing rework	Supervisors rate performance before and six weeks after training.	3,000%	Extrapolates results for 20 employees to 300 employees; subjective evaluation of performance
9. Wood Panel Plant	Supervisors	Monitoring and rewarding performance	Dollar value of product defects and accidents before and one year after training	680%	No consideration of factors that may have changed during year
10. New York State Employees	First-line supervisors	Supervisory skills	Trainees' supervisors evaluate performance three months and six months after training.	—	Used regressions to see if change in performance will correlate with personal characteristics
11. Midwest Banking Company	Consumer loan officers	Consumer lending	Average monthly loan volume compared for six months before and six months after training; valued at net profit per loan.	1,988%	Selection bias due to best prospects being sent to course; trainees told their performance would be monitored

Table 2. Description of case studies (continued).

Company	Employee Group	Type of Training	Performance Measure	ROI	Comments
II. Single Group Pre- and Posttest (cont.)					
12. Multi-Marques	Supervisors	Time management	Self-report of changes in time use, converted to dollar value using salary data	215%	Subjective self-evaluations; extrapolates results from three months to one year; no evidence that time spent more productively; no consideration of other factors
13. Coca-Cola Bottling Company of San Antonio	Supervisors	Motivation and performance appraisal	Three months after training, trainees report increased sales and reduced waste and absenteeism.	1,447%	Highly subjective; trainees identify dollar value of training. No consideration of other factors
14. Vulcan Materials	First-line supervisors	Supervisory skills	Changes in production worker turnover before and six months after training.	400%	Managers of the supervisors estimated % of improvement due to training.
15. Rochester Methodist Hospital	Managers	Management development	Trainees self-report dollar value of application of training.	—	No costs reported, so no ROI; highly subjective
16. Yellow Freight System	Managers	Performance appraisal	Trainees self-report dollar value of productivity gains due to training.	1,115%	Highly subjective; no consideration of impact of new competitive environment

Table 2. Description of case studies (continued).

Company	Employee Group	Type of Training	Performance Measure	ROI	Comments
III. Time Series					
17. International Oil Company	Dispatchers	Customer service	Tracked pullout costs and customer complaint costs for 11 months before and 11 months after training	501%	Used company database to track costs; no consideration of other factors that may have an impact on performance
18. Magnavox Electronic Systems Company	Entry-level assemblers	Literacy skills	Tracked fees and chargeable hours for 12 months before and 12 months after training	741%	Productivity gain occurred only in first month after training; extrapolated four-month average to a full year; ignored role of other factors.
19. Arthur Andersen & Company	Tax professionals	State and local taxation	Tracked average monthly efficiency for five months before and six months after training; converted to labor cost savings	100% payback in one year	Compared changes in revenue of participating and nonparticipating offices to reject role of other factors; but participants already more experienced
20. CIGNA	Managers	Management development	Manager develops productivity measure that is tracked for three months before and four months after training.	5,900%	Used actual work-unit records to document performance; trainees knew their performance would be measured after four months.

- using supervisors' subjective evaluations of trainees' performance levels (Hughes Aircraft)
- monitoring the impact of training for a relatively short time after the training is completed (Hughes Aircraft)
- ignoring the role of factors other than training that could be responsible for performance changes (Hughes Aircraft)
- extrapolating findings based on a small sample of trainees to a large group of employees (Hughes Aircraft)
- selecting the best employees for the training program (Midwest Banking Company)
- informing the trainees that their performance will be monitored after the training program (Midwest Banking Company)
- utilizing self-reports from the trainees about the productivity gains from training (Yellow Freight System)
- ignoring the impact of operating in a new environment (Yellow Freight System)
- ignoring the fact that the posttraining productivity gain disappeared after one month (Magnavox Electronic Systems)

The discussion of these four cases also makes reference to other cases in table 2 that have similar flaws. Part B discusses three cases (Garrett Engine, New York State Employees, and International Oil Company) that use sounder methodologies and can serve as the basis for a recommended evaluation design. For details on additional cases listed in the table, the reader should consult the appendix.

A. Methodological Problems in Four Representative Cases

HUGHES AIRCRAFT COMPANY (CASE 8). This case, described in Merlo (1988), discusses the evaluation of a training program for non-management personnel who have less than one year of experience at Hughes Aircraft Company and are in entry-level positions in business-management job classifications. Utilizing a single group pre- and posttest design, 20 trainees were selected for the evaluation project, 12 from one course and eight from another. Prior to the start of the training, the trainees' supervisors were asked to complete a questionnaire that required them to assess the trainees' overall performance level. The supervisors were not told that they would receive a posttraining questionnaire. Six weeks after the training program, the supervisors were asked to reevaluate the trainees' performance level. The financial utility of the training program was calculated by computing the difference between the average of the pre-and posttraining scores and then dividing that difference by the standard deviation of the pretraining scores. Each standard deviation in performance was assumed to equal 40 percent of the average annual salary of the trainees. The company then assumed that the observed benefits based on 12 employees for one course and eight employees for the second course could be extrapolated to 300 employees per year. The resulting ROIs were 3,000 percent and 3,227 percent, respectively!

This case is particularly useful to analyze because it demonstrates a number of pitfalls in calculating ROI. First, the supervisors' ratings are likely to be subjective. This subjective approach to measuring performance was also used in case 2, Information Services; case 6, Southeastern Bank; case 7, U.S. Government; and case 10, New York State Employees. Second, the supervisor ratings may also be biased because the supervisors, knowing that the individuals have just completed a training program, may be predisposed to ranking the individuals higher. Case 14, Vulcan Materials, demonstrates this problem in another way. In that case, supervisors of production workers who had attended a training program were asked to decide how much of the observed turnover reduction after training was, in fact, due to the training. A third problem with the Hughes Aircraft case is that there is no follow-up beyond the six weeks after the training program and the improvement in performance may not persist. This problem of a short follow-up also occurred in case 1, Garrett Engine; case 2, Information Services; case 7, U.S. Government; and case 13, Coca-Cola Bottling Company. Fourth, there is no attempt to consider the role of other factors that could be responsible for the increase in performance. This problem also occurred in case 7, U.S. Government; case 9, Wood Panel Plant; case 10, New York State Employees; case 12, Multi-Marques; case 13, Coca-Cola Bottling Company; case 16, Yellow Freight System; and case 18, Magnavox Electronic Systems. Fifth, generalizing the results from eight to 12 employees to 300 employees is inappropriate if trainees in the sample are not representative of the much larger group.

MIDWEST BANKING COMPANY (CASE 11). This case, described in Phillips (1994), is about a bank that evaluated its consumer lending seminar for consumer loan officers, using a single group pre- and posttest design. For this evaluation, the director of the seminar requested that managers send their best prospects to the course. The participants were told that their consumer loan volume would be monitored for six months following the program. An individual's record for the previous six months was averaged and compared with the corresponding figure for the six months after the program. If the loan officer was new to the bank or to the job function, estimates of preprogram productivity were based on information from the previous employer (if available), or were based on the average loan volume of loan officers without the consumer lending seminar training.

Three external factors that could explain changes in loan volume were examined. First, there had been a decrease in interest rates four months after the program was conducted. The marketing department provided an estimate of the sensitivity of consumer loan volume to changes in interest rates, and this adjustment was used in the analysis of the impact of the training program. Second, the researchers considered whether there had been a significant change in loan promotions after the seminar was conducted, but they were able to conclude that the difference in promotional expenditures was negligible. Third, the evaluators used a 10 percent increase in consumer loans as an adjustment to account for the fact that employees new to the job learn on their own.

Using data for six months, an average monthly volume increase for each of the 18 loan officers who had attended the program was calculated. The volume increases were adjusted for the interest rate and learning effects. The resulting volume increase was translated into a total profit figure by using the bank's estimate of its net profit per loan. Combining this with data on training costs resulted in an ROI of 1,988 percent.

Although the authors of this case should be commended for their attempts to adjust for factors other than training that could be responsible for the volume increase, this case demonstrates two noticeable pitfalls. First, the trainees were a targeted group. Researchers selected those individuals whom they considered the best prospects, and it is not clear that other loan officers would produce similar results. Second, the trainees were told that they would be monitored for six months after their training and hence were motivated to show results for that time period. Other cases that suffer from this problem are case 13, the Coca-Cola Bottling Company, and case 20, CIGNA.

YELLOW FREIGHT SYSTEM (CASE 16). This case, described in Phillips (1994), is about a training program that Yellow Freight System, a large trucking company instituted in response to deregulation of the trucking industry. In the new environment, employees were to be rewarded on the basis of their performance, and the company, therefore, established a performance appraisal system. Managers now needed to be trained in how to write performance standards, give feedback, and reward employees. Everyone who conducted performance appraisals participated in the training program. In order to estimate the impact of the training program, a single group pre- and posttest design was used and the trainees were asked the following questions at three and six months after the training:

- What changes in terminal or employee performance have you seen since you began using performance management skills?
- What are these changes worth in dollars to Yellow Freight?
- What percentage of the improvement, if any, is due to their use of the skills taught in the program?

The company collected data from 49 percent of the terminals, and 92 percent of the terminals contacted said that they had some performance improvements due to performance management skills. The total value of the improvements that could be translated into dollars was compared to the cost of the training program, resulting in an ROI of 1,115 percent.

This case demonstrates a number of pitfalls in conducting an ROI analysis. First, it relies solely on trainees' self-reports of productivity gains. The trainees both identify the productivity gains and quantify their value. Other cases that relied on self-reports were case 12, Multi-Marques; case 13, Coca-Cola Bottling Company; and case 15, Rochester Methodist Hospital. A second problem with the Yellow Freight case is that the company made no attempt to consider the impact of operating in a new, competitive environment where the rules of doing business had changed dramatically. These external pressures would be likely to lead to decreased costs and increased productivity, and they could account for some of the observed productivity improvement.

MAGNAVOX ELECTRONIC SYSTEMS COMPANY (CASE 18). This case, described in Phillips (1994), utilizes a time series design. In order to address functional illiteracy in reading and math among their hourly workers, Magnavox Electronic Systems introduced a literacy skills training program for entry-level electrical and mechanical assemblers. These individuals were primarily Hispanic, Asian, and African-American women who, although they held high school diplomas, had average English reading scores around the fourth-grade level and average math scores around the sixth-grade level. Thirty employees agreed to participate in the voluntary 18-week training program.[3] The company had a policy of tracking data on productivity, scrap, and rework on a monthly basis. From this database, it was able to extract the information that pertained to the 30 trainees.

The company found that, prior to the beginning of the training, the average monthly efficiency of the trainees was 18 percent of the ideal efficiency for their positions. In the four months after the program began, their average monthly efficiency rose to 26 percent of the ideal level, or a 44 percent gain. It is important to note that the bulk of the gain in efficiency came in the first month after the training program began, and then fell back almost to the original level. The authors of the case failed to note this point! The productivity for the factory as a whole rose only 5 percent during this time period, and the authors point to this number as evidence that the 44 percent gain was due to the training program.

The gain in productivity is then translated into dollar savings by multiplying the average percentage improvement in productivity (44 percent) times the average hourly wage times the average number of hours worked per month times the number of employees who completed training. This figure represents the monthly labor savings from the program. Of course, this is clearly a gross overestimate because the average increase in productivity is biased by the very large increase in the first month only. The company then added the monthly labor cost savings to the monthly savings from the reductions in scrap and rework that it observed after the training. This figure represented the total monthly benefits from the training program. The company then assumed that these benefits would last for 12 months and multiplied the monthly savings by 12. ROI was calculated by subtracting total program costs from gross benefits to get net benefits, and the resulting figure was divided by costs. This led to an ROI of 741 percent. Because the state provided Magnavox with 34 percent of the program costs, the ROI was recalculated based on Magnavox's expenditures (direct and indirect), leading to an ROI of 1,175 percent.

This case demonstrates the importance of accurately tracking productivity changes after the completion of a training program. The authors ignored the fact that the productivity gain occurred during the first month

---

3. The 18-week program was divided into three six-week terms. Half of the original enrollees completed all three terms.

only. Rather, they took a four-month average and extrapolated this to a full year. I used the actual monthly changes that were reported for the six months after the training, assumed that the change observed in month six would continue for the next six months, and recalculated the average rate of return to be 112 percent, less than one-sixth of the rate of return the authors reported.

B. Examples of Sounder Methodologies

GARRETT ENGINE DIVISION (CASE 1). This case, which Pine and Tingley (1993) discuss, comes from the division of Allied Signal, which manufactures jet engines. The company was concerned about the downtime of its equipment and decided to use a two-day team-building training program for the maintenance teams that repair the equipment. Each team consisted of a manager and hourly employees such as electricians, plumbers, and mechanics. Four similar maintenance teams were identified. Two teams were randomly assigned to the experimental group, and two to the control group.

Prior to the training, all teams were measured in terms of their equipment downtime, job response time, and job completion time. Response time is the time it takes for the team to respond to a call for service. Completion time is the time required to complete the job. The teams were measured on all three dimensions for four weeks after the training. The company found that, prior to the team-building course, the people in the experimental group were slower to respond to job requests than those in the control group. After the program, the experimental group responded more quickly, whereas the control group stayed about the same. Similarly, in the case of job completion time, prior to training, the experimental group performed worse than the control group. After training, the experimental group significantly reduced its completion time, but the control group's time remained about the same. As a result of improvements in response time and completion time, total downtime for the experimental group fell from 18.4 hours to 15.8 hours; the control group's downtime stayed constant at about 16 hours.

The maintenance department had established a burden rate, or the cost of machine downtime, prior to this study. Using this figure, the downtime cost was calculated for the experimental and control groups, before and after the training. Downtime cost was $1,156 per job for the experimental group after training, and it was $1,211 per job for the control group after training. This translates into a $55 savings per job, which is attributable to the training. A less conservative estimate of the cost savings would be to measure the experimental group's performance before and after training; this resulted in $185 savings per job. The company then used the cost-savings estimate to calculate the ROI on the training program. This calculation required making an assumption about the length of time that the effect of the training would last. Using the assumption of four workweeks, the resulting ROI, calculated as total benefits over the four weeks minus the cost of training, all divided by the cost of training, was 125 percent.

In general, Garrett Engine's approach is good. By randomly assigning similar teams to the experimental and control groups, and observing the results over a fairly short time period, the company can be reasonably confident in concluding that the performance gains observed over the four weeks were due to the training. The evaluators noted that, in order to conclude that the training effect would last beyond the four weeks, they would need to monitor performance of both groups for a longer time period. It should be noted, however, that although the control-group design eliminates the selection bias problem, it does not eliminate the need to consider the impact of other factors that could play a role in explaining posttraining performance. For example, did the experimental group have easier maintenance tasks than the control group during the four-week observation period? If so, this could explain the reductions in job completion time. Similarly, information about absenteeism may be relevant. Did the control group experience more absenteeism or absenteeism of key team members (for example, the manager) during this time period?

NEW YORK STATE EMPLOYEES (CASE 10). This case, described in Ban and Faerman (1990), discusses the training program for civil service employees in New York State who are first-line supervisors and utilizes a single group pre- and-posttest design.[4] All first-line supervisors who took courses during the first year of the program (September 1986 through June 1987) were included in the evaluation, for a sample of 814. All participants received a pretraining questionnaire as well as three-month and six-month follow-up questionnaires. The trainees' supervisors also completed all three of these questionnaires. The questionnaires gathered data on the participants' performance level on a range of specific tasks. These were supplemented by in-depth oral interviews with 94 individuals approximately four to six months after training. The performance scores showed increases after three months, which remained stable at the six-month mark. The supervisors' assessments supported the results based on the self-assessments. The in-depth interviews provided evidence of specific examples of improved performance. Unfortunately, there was no attempt to quantify the value of the improved performance, and no ROI was reported.

This case has many good qualities. First, the authors of the case were careful to consider the roles of other factors that could explain the change in performance. Because they had a large sample (228 individuals with complete data), they were able to use regression analysis and control for the impact of age, sex, education, years of service, years in current position, bargaining unit, grade level, previous training courses attended, span of control, various psychological measures, and the flexibility and openness of the individual's organization. None of these factors had a significant relationship with the level or change in performance.[5] The follow-up inter-

---

4. The authors of the case noted that a control group design with random assignment was not feasible because training is defined as a union benefit.

5. The evaluators also determined that there were no significant differences in the observed characteristics of the trainees who stayed in the program compared to those who left.

views were a useful approach for documenting the specific ways in which training improved performance.[6] Although the performance ratings used here were subjective, the authors felt that this was not a problem because the individuals were evaluated on the basis of a large number (82) of very detailed and specific items. By conducting posttraining evaluations at two different times (that is, at three and six months), the evaluators could determine if initial gains persisted; of course, it would be preferable to reevaluate the participants at a later time. The one drawback of this case study is that, like many others, it cannot rule out the impact of other factors, such as increased experience, that may have contributed to the observed increase in performance.

INTERNATIONAL OIL COMPANY (CASE 17). This case, described in Phillips (1994), refers to a training program for dispatchers at International Oil's central dispatch in Los Angeles. The company introduced the training program in response to an increase in delivery costs from order errors as well as customer complaints about these errors. The training program was evaluated by tracking data on pullouts (when a dealer cannot take the full load ordered and the truck has to pull out and return to the terminal to adjust the product mix for the next station on the schedule), dealer complaints, and dispatcher absenteeism, before and after training. The data were tracked for 11 months prior to the training program and 11 months after. The company had already calculated the cost of a pullout. Using this information, it was able to calculate the difference between pullout costs before and after training. By using information on managers' salaries and the average amount of time it took a manager to resolve a customer complaint, the company estimated the cost of a dealer complaint. This was used to measure the cost savings from the reduction in dealer complaints that occurred in the 11 months after the training. Finally, the value of the reduction in dispatcher absenteeism was quantified by using data on dispatchers' salaries. Combining these savings produced the total benefit for the program. The cost of the program was underestimated because data on the trainer's salary and the cost of the training facility were unavailable; hence, the resulting ROI, 501 percent, is likely to be an overestimate.

This is an interesting case because it demonstrates how data from company records can be used to successfully quantify the outcomes of a training program. Because the company had a history of tracking pullouts and dealer complaints, it could tap into this database and monitor changes over fairly long periods before and after the training. Other companies that utilized internal databases to facilitate the training evaluation were case 1, Garrett Engine; case 18, Magnavox; case 19, Arthur Andersen; and case 20, CIGNA. The weakness in this case is that there was no attempt to consider other factors that may have changed over time and that could be responsible for the improvement in performance. For example, the dispatcher's efficiency de-

---

6. The researchers felt that these discussions with the trainees enabled them to reject the Hawthorne effect as the explanation for their finding.

pends on both the truck drivers' behavior and the dealers' ability to accurately measure the amount of gasoline in their tanks. It is possible that the reduction in pullouts occurred because there were more experienced truck drivers or dealers in the later time period than before the training.

5. EVIDENCE FROM ECONOMETRIC STUDIES

A number of studies in the labor economics literature have attempted to estimate the ROI on training. These studies fall into two categories: those that use data on individuals from one or two companies, and those that use organizational-level data from a large number of companies. The findings from this literature are reviewed in this section and summarized in table 3.

Individual-Level Data from Company Databases

Bartel (1995) obtained data on 19,000 employees from the 1986–1990 personnel records of a large manufacturing company in order to estimate the company's rate of return on its investments in training its professional employees. As discussed in part 4, estimation of the ROI may be flawed if the company does not randomly select employees for training; for example, in the Midwest Banking case, the company targeted its best prospects for the training program. Because the receipt of training may have been related to the prospects' individual characteristics, Bartel used the extensive information in the personnel database to determine those factors that can predict which employees receive training. Bartel found strong evidence that assignment to training was indeed based on individuals' relative status in their jobs. Her estimates of the impact of training on wage growth were adjusted to take account of this fact, resulting in a 1.8 percent increase in wages for each day of training. Bartel also found that individuals who received training experienced an increase in their job performance scores, thereby confirming the robustness of the relationship between training and productivity.

Because Bartel had access to company records, she was able to calculate the cost of a day of training, combining information on both direct costs and the cost of time taken away from work. By assuming that the company had a value added/wage ratio equal to one, Bartel estimated that the company's productivity gains from training equaled the estimated wage gains.[7] Rates of return were calculated based on various assumptions regarding the rate at which skills depreciate per year. Assuming an annual depreciation rate of 10 percent, which implies a half-life of 5.4 years for the investment, resulted in an internal rate of return of 41.8 percent. Doubling the depreciation rate to 20 percent, which implies a half-life of 2.9 years, produced an internal rate of return of 26.1 percent.

These rates of return are considerably smaller than the returns estimated in the previous case studies. The reason is that a large panel database

---

7. This is actually a very conservative assumption. Most companies have value added/labor costs ratios that exceed one.

Table 3. Econometric analyses of personnel databases and large samples of firms.

Author	Dataset	Sample Size	Performance Measure	Findings
1. Bartel	One company	19,000 employees	Wages and performance ratings	ROI ranged from 26.1% to 41.8%
2. Krueger and Rouse	Two companies	1,000 employees	Wages	100% payback after 13 years
3. Bartel	Columbia Human Resource Survey (1986)	155 manufacturing businesses	Value-added per worker	Implementation of formal training raised productivity by 6% per year.
4. Holzer, Block, Cheatham, and Knott	Survey sent to Michigan firms applying for state training grants (1988–1989)	157 firms	Scrap rate	Doubling of worker training reduced scrap rate by 7%; this is worth $15,000.
5. Black and Lynch	EQW National Employers Survey (1994)	617 manufacturing establishments	Net sales	Percentage of formal training that occurs off the job has significant effect in cross-section; may be due to positive effect of productivity on training.

enables the researcher to eliminate at least some of the bias that may result from nonrandom assignment to training programs, as well as to measure the impact of training on performance net of any unobserved individual characteristics.[8] Bartel's work could have been improved if she had been able to incorporate more detailed information about changes in the employees' job tasks and work environment. In addition, she only estimated the impact of training during the first year after training and was unable to directly observe the rate at which the training impact depreciated.

In a similar study, Krueger and Rouse (1994) collected data from two New Jersey companies, one in manufacturing and one in the service sector, that sought help from a community college in designing on-site training for lower skilled workers. They collected pretraining and posttraining wage data on the workers, as well as detailed personal characteristics and information on turnover, absenteeism, and performance awards. Like Bartel, Krueger and Rouse estimated the impact of training on wages by using a model that eliminated the impact of any unobserved individual characteristics. In the manufacturing company, they found that the return to training was about 0.5 percent, although there was no effect of training in the service sector. To check whether the positive effect in the manufacturing firm was because training participants were on faster earnings trajectories or better workers, they estimated the effect of training on the workers' pretraining wage level and growth. The results showed that participants did not have significantly different levels of pretraining wages, or pretraining wage growth, from nonparticipants.

Like Bartel (1995), Krueger and Rouse (1994) had access to company records that enabled them to calculate the cost of training. The total cost of training (direct expenses and release time) was approximately 4 percent of the average trainee's annual compensation. They assumed that completed job tenure was 16 years and the value of training depreciated by 3 percent per year. Using a 6 percent real discount rate, Krueger and Rouse concluded that the program paid for itself, but this result may be due to the relatively low depreciation rate that they used.

Organizational-Level Data from Large Samples of Firms

Bartel (1994) utilized data from a 1986 Columbia Business School survey that covered 495 Compustat II business lines.[9] Because the businesses reported the year in which they implemented their formal training program, Bartel was able to identify those businesses that introduced training programs after 1983. She found that businesses that had output levels in 1983 that were below what would be expected given their input usage and their industry were more likely to introduce a formal training program after 1983. Bartel then found that the businesses that implemented formal training programs after 1983 experienced an 18 percent increase in productivity

---

8. Admittedly, the selection bias correction technique may not produce the same results as utilizing a true experimental design.

9. For those firms that operate only one business line, a "business line" corresponds directly to the company. When a parent company operates several business lines, a business line generally corresponds to a division of a company.

between 1983 and 1986 (that is, a 6 percent annual increase) compared with those businesses that did not. Implementation of other human resource policies (for example, job design, performance appraisal, employee involvement) during the same time period did not have a productivity-enhancing effect, thereby enabling Bartel to reject a Hawthorne effect explanation for her findings. Unfortunately, data on the cost of the training programs were largely missing, so Bartel was not able to conduct a cost-benefit analysis.

Holzer, Block, Cheatham, and Knott (1993) utilized data on firms that applied for training grants under the Michigan Job Opportunities Bank-Upgrade in 1988 and 1989. They found that a doubling of worker training in any year produced a contemporaneous reduction in the scrap rate (a measure of output quality) of 7 percent. They calculated that this was worth about $15,000 per year. Unfortunately, about half of this effect disappears in the next year, and presumably even more would be gone by subsequent years. Because Holzer et al. did not collect information from the firms about their training expenditures, they were unable to conduct a cost-benefit analysis.

Black and Lynch (1996a, 1996b) used data collected from the National Center on the Educational Quality of the Workforce (EQW) National Employers Survey, which the U.S. Bureau of the Census administered as a telephone survey in August and September 1994 to a nationally representative sample of more than 3,000 private establishments with more than 20 employees. They found that the number of workers trained had no impact on productivity, but the percentage of formal training off the job was positive and significant for the manufacturing sector, whereas computer training was positive and significant in the nonmanufacturing sector. Once they accounted for the fact that a firm's decision to train may be a function of its productivity level, the positive relationships between training and productivity disappeared.

6. CONCLUSIONS AND RECOMMENDATIONS

More than half of American businesses do not evaluate the results of their training programs but focus instead on reactions, learning, and behavior changes. Even among those companies that do consider business results, only a fraction actually monetize productivity gains and calculate a return-on-investment. Many of the ROI studies that I reviewed used faulty methodologies that resulted in estimated ROIs that were too high to be believed. Practitioners who are considering conducting an ROI analysis for their firm's training investments can learn from these mistakes. Following is a list of guidelines that should be followed in order to conduct a sound ROI analysis.

1. Identify the relevant performance measure. In some of the case studies, we saw examples of direct measures of performance (for example, equipment downtime for the maintenance teams in Garrett Engine, loan volume for the consumer loan officers in Midwest Banking, and

pullout costs for the dispatchers in International Oil Company). In many case studies, especially those involving supervisory training, the performance measures were somewhat indirect (for example, the turnover of subordinates in Penske Truck Leasing and Vulcan Materials, the safety record of subordinates in Wood Panel Plant). Sometimes the performance measure was a supervisor's subjective evaluation (Information Services, Southeastern Bank, U.S. Government, Hughes Aircraft, New York State Employees).

Before evaluating a training program, a company should ensure that it can define an employee's performance and that this performance can be measured. In other words, can the company distinguish in a specific way between top performers and weak performers? A company should select those items from figure 1 that are most relevant to the particular employee group and use them to measure performance gains. It may be easier to make these measurements for production workers than service or supervisory employees; but if the company has already established and uses a performance metric for evaluating the latter employees, it should be the appropriate metric for training evaluation as well.

2. Avoid subjectivity. A number of the cases used highly subjective data, either a supervisor's estimate of the value of skills or the trainees' self-reports of skill or behavior changes. Human resource practitioners have been encouraged to use this approach if hard data are unavailable, but as we have seen, these data are highly questionable and could introduce either a positive or negative bias. Companies should be encouraged to avoid the use of subjective calculations and strive, where possible, to use objective measures.

3. Calculate the dollar value of performance. Some companies did not monetize the performance changes that occurred after training and hence were unable to calculate a return-on-investment. Others used the 40 percent conversion factor (that is, each standard deviation in performance is worth 40 percent of salary) that is popular in the personnel psychology literature. Where possible, companies should seek objective ways of calculating the dollar value of performance. Some good examples from the cases are Garrett Engine, which calculated the cost of machine downtime, and Midwest Banking, which utilized the profit per loan.

4. Use existing company databases. In the case studies, we saw a number of examples of companies that were able to use information from existing company databases to facilitate the training evaluation. Garrett Engine already collected data on the cost of machine downtime; International Oil Company regularly tracked pullout costs; Magnavox maintained monthly data on productivity, scrap, and rework; and Arthur Andersen tracked fees and chargeable hours. These data provided a ready source of information about worker performance before and after training. They are preferable to data that are collected for the express purpose of evaluating a training program; the latter could be biased because of a predisposition to finding a training effect. Use existing databases, where available.

5. Isolate the effect of training. Admittedly, it is difficult to eliminate the effect of other factors on performance. There are two issues here. The first problem is that trainees may differ from nontrainees. One way to resolve this problem is to use a control group design where employees are randomly assigned to training. An alternative approach is the one used by the econometric case studies in which detailed panel data can be used to eliminate selection bias. The second problem is that the posttraining experiences of the trainees and the nonparticipants could differ in ways that could influence observed performance. To avoid this problem, evaluators need to carefully collect data on factors that are known to affect an employee's performance. This requires first identifying those factors and then systematically gathering the data.

6. Monitor performance changes at multiple points in time. Training can have an initial positive effect on performance that could dissipate over time because of depreciation or the waning of a Hawthorne effect. Ideally, performance should be measured at several time intervals after the training is completed.

7. Use extrapolations cautiously. Often, companies use data on small samples of trainees and extrapolate the findings to large numbers of employees to obtain very large ROIs. A good example of this was the Hughes Aircraft case in which data for 20 trainees were extrapolated to 300 employees. In the absence of a randomly selected sample of trainees, this approach is dangerous. Hence, where possible, companies should be urged to use random assignment in order to be able to rely on extrapolated results.

    Another type of extrapolation, unrelated to the issue of random assignment, is where a company observes posttraining performance for a short period of time and assumes that the performance gain will last for a much longer time period. Magnavox took a four-month average and extrapolated it to one year, even though the productivity gain occurred only in the first month after training. This type of problem can best be handled by extending the time period over which performance is monitored, thereby eliminating the need to rely on extrapolated results.

8. Use the net present value method or the internal rate of return method. An accurate ROI calculation requires accounting for the time value of money. Net present value and internal rate of return are the only methods that accurately do this. Where possible, the net present value technique should be used instead of the internal rate of return technique because it gives more accurate results when comparing projects of two different sizes or projects that have payout streams of different magnitudes and lengths.

APPENDIX

Description of Cases Not Discussed in Text

INFORMATION SERVICES (CASE 2). This case, described in Phillips (1994), comes from Information Services, a marketer of information, software, and services in the area of strategic planning, financial planning, and information systems management. An interpersonal skills training program was designed for professional (for example, business analysts) and support (for example, secretaries, data entry operators) personnel in three of the company's locations. A sample of similar individuals from another location was randomly selected for the control group. Behaviors of the trained and control groups were measured immediately before and approximately one month after the training. The behaviors measured were dealing with problems, communicating with co-workers, and working with superiors. Ratings were obtained from the employees themselves as well as their supervisors.

The major challenge was to convert the behaviors into monetary benefits. The company used the average annual salary for each of the employee groups and multiplied it by the percentage of time each employee (as reported by the employee) undertook each of the activities listed above. This yielded the dollar value of the time the employee spent in each activity. Then each pretraining skill rating for the employee was multiplied by the cost figure to give the return to the company for that skill prior to training. The same was done for the posttraining skill rating to give the return to the company after the training. The difference between the posttraining and pretraining figures indicated the benefit to the company resulting from the training. They found significant differences between the trained and control groups in the improvements in skill ratings. Although there were 85 trainees, these calculations were only done for 42 individuals. Based on the total benefits for the 42 people and the total cost (direct and indirect) of training all 85 trainees, the company calculated an ROI of 336 percent. This assumes that there were no benefits for the other 43 individuals, but it does not allow for the fact that the skill ratings for this group may have worsened.

Although this case has the attribute of using randomly assigned experimental and control groups, it suffers from a number of problems. First, the posttraining behaviors are measured only one month after the training problem, and it is not clear that the benefits will continue after the first month. Second, the behavior ratings are highly subjective. Third, the time allocation data are subjective and may be biased if the message from the training program was to spend more time on "productive" activities. Fourth, there is no consideration of factors in the posttraining environment that could explain the posttraining performance differentials.

INSURANCE COMPANY OF AMERICA (CASE 3). This case, described in Phillips (1994), is about a newly revised training program for underwriters at Insurance Company of America. The goal of the new program was to reduce the time to proficiency (that is, the time it took a new underwriter to reach the proficiency level of an experienced underwriter). Trainees were randomly assigned to take the new or the original training programs. Six months after training, both sets of trainees completed a comprehensive test, as did experienced underwriters (those with three or more years of experience). Test scores were compared to determine if the graduates of the revised training program approached the performance of experienced underwriters faster than graduates of the original training program. The evaluators found that trainees who completed the revised training program learned more and became productive sooner than trainees who completed the original training program. This result remained even after controlling for such factors as characteristics of the trainee (for example, education, work location, relevant job experience), quality of the instructor and training conditions.

Unfortunately, the company would not report specific data about the return-on-investment from the new training program, although the case talks in general terms about the cost savings from developing productive workers more quickly and the fact that the new program required less trainer preparation time and less administration time, implying a relatively high return-on-investment. One limitation of this evaluation effort, that the authors themselves identify, is that it did not consider factors outside the classroom that affect job performance. Factors in this category would be items like supervisor's guidance, supervisor's feedback, and nature of the underwriter's workload.

PENSKE TRUCK LEASING COMPANY (CASE 4). This case, discussed in Phillips (1994), is about a training program for supervisors that was implemented to reduce Penske Truck Leasing's high turnover. All program participants were maintenance supervisors who supervised seven to eight mechanics and fuel island attendants. Thirteen locations were selected for training, and 11 locations were selected as the control group. Two or three supervisors were taken from each location, but the unit of analysis was the location, not the individual. Pretest, or baseline measures of turnover, were tracked for nine months prior to the training. Posttest measures were tracked for seven months after the training. An average monthly value was computed for the pretest and posttest periods. The experimental and control groups had virtually identical turnover rates at pretest. The training group showed a 46 percent drop in turnover at the posttest, although the control group remained unchanged.

Unfortunately, the monetary value of the reduced turnover was not calculated and data on costs were not presented. As a result, it is impossible to determine the ROI on this training program. Also, there is no consideration of other factors that could explain the changes in turnover, such as employee characteristics and length of tenure, so it is hard to safely conclude that training alone was responsible for the turnover reductions.

FINANCIAL SERVICES COMPANY (CASE 5). This case, described in Phillips (1994) is about an anonymous financial services company that faced turnover rates of 48 to 63 percent among its branch manager trainees. The company decided to institute a training program for its district sales managers to teach them how to better identify and select candidates that would stay with the firm. One-third of the company participated in the training program, and the remaining two-thirds constituted the control group. Six months after the training program, the company began tracking the monthly turnover rate for the experimental and control groups. The tracking continued for six months. It found a significant reduction in turnover for the experimental group compared with the experience of the control group. The dollar value of the reduction in turnover was quantified, and in conjunction with data on the cost of the training, resulted in an estimated ROI of 2,140 percent. The large ROI resulted from a 28 percent drop in turnover coupled with the company's estimate that, prior to the training program, turnover cost $10 million per year! Even the authors of the case admitted that this ROI is likely to be exaggerated because of the assumptions made in calculating cost savings. The sensitivity of ROI to these assumptions is demonstrated by the fact that, if we assume that turnover cost the company $1 million per year, the ROI from the training program would be 124 percent.

Another problem is that when evaluating the posttraining performance of the two groups, the supervisors were likely to remember or know which of their subordinates had attended the training program. This could have introduced some bias into the estimate of training's impact on performance.

A SOUTHEASTERN BANK (CASE 6). This case, described in Mathieu and Leonard (1987), is about the evaluation of a training program in supervisory skills that was offered to head tellers, branch managers, and operations managers. Employees either volunteered for the training or their supervisors nominated them. The authors of the case constructed a post hoc quasi-experimental design to estimate the effects of training on individuals' performance. For each of the 65 trainees, an individual was selected from the company's personnel list who matched the trainee in terms of salary, tenure, gender, and age, and could serve as a control. As a proxy for a pretest measure, the authors used the most recent performance appraisals completed prior to training for trained individuals and appraisals from the corresponding time period for members of the control group. They found that the training group and the control group did not differ significantly on the performance appraisal measure.

Six months after the training program was completed, supervisors of employees in the trained and control groups were asked to assign dollar values to the bank on three levels of performance, that is, the 15th, the 50th and the 85th percentiles. Following the approach of Schmidt, Hunter, and Pearlman (1982), this information was used to compute values of the standard deviation of job performance in dollars. The supervisors were also asked to evaluate the performance of their subordinates, some of whom had been trained and some of whom were in the control group. This assessment was used to calculate the difference in job performance between the trained and untrained workers. Combining these data with information on the cost of the training program enabled the authors of the case to calculate the utility value of the training. They reported a utility value of $34,627 after the first year. Using data on expected tenure of the employees and assuming that the effect of training on job performance declined by 25 percent per year resulted in a five-year utility value of $99,298. I used the cost data reported by the authors to calculate an ROI on the training investment. The resulting numbers are 129 percent after one year and 370 percent after five years.

The authors recognized that a truly random experiment would have been preferable to their quasi-experimental approach. Their control group was created on the basis of four observed characteristics, and unmeasured characteristics (such as personality, ambition, intelligence) could play a role in explaining the performance differences of the two groups; their estimates of training's impact on performance are likely to be biased.

U.S. GOVERNMENT (CASE 7). This case, described in Phillips (1994), refers to a training program delivered by the U.S. Office of Personnel Management for supervisors with less than one year of tenure. One week before the training course and six weeks after the program, the managers of the trainees rated them on various skill dimensions. There was a statistically significant improvement in skill.

In order to quantify the value of these skills, managers were asked to estimate the percentage of job success accounted for by the new supervisors' effectiveness in the skill areas covered in the training program. This percentage was multiplied by the average annual salary of the participants, which yielded the dollar value of performing successfully in the skill areas. Then the trainees' average level of skill before the training program was divided by the required level of skill, which showed that participants were performing at 77 percent of job requirements prior to the course. The ratio of trainees' average level of skill after the training program to the required level showed that they had improved to 87 percent of required performance. These percentages were then converted to dollar values by using the dollar value of performing successfully in all skill areas. The difference between the post- and pretraining dollar values represents the average benefit per person attributable to the training. This, combined with data on the average cost per participant, produced an ROI of 150 percent.

This case suffers from a number of problems. First, is the element of subjectivity in managers' estimates of the value of the skills, as well as their rating of the trainees' skills. Second, the change in behavior is only measured six weeks after the training program, and there is no attempt to determine if the skill improvements persisted. Third, since no control group was used, it is impossible to rule out the contributing effects of other factors such as experience on the job.

WOOD PANEL PLANT (CASE 9). This case, described in Robinson and Robinson (1989), is about an unnamed wood panel plant that implemented a training program for its 48 supervisors because of three problems: 2 percent of the panels produced each day were rejected because the stain was either streaked or of unacceptable color, poor housekeeping (10 defects per week), and preventable accidents (24 per year). The training program was designed to teach the supervisors how to discuss quality problems with employees, how to discuss poor work habits with employees, and how to recognize employees for above-average performance. Twelve months after the training, all three measures showed improvement. The number of product defects fell to 1.5 percent; the number of housekeeping defects fell to 2, and the number of preventable accidents fell to 16. The dollar value of product defects and preventable accidents could be quantified, thus enabling a calculation of the dollar benefits of the training program based on these two dimensions. Using this in conjunction with the direct and indirect costs of the training led to a calculated ROI of 680 percent.

The main problem with this case is that there is no attempt to consider other factors that could be responsible for the changes that were observed one year after the training program. The composition of the employee group may have changed as well as the pace of work, the types of panels being produced, and the quality of the stain itself.

MULTI-MARQUES (CASE 12) This case, discussed in Phillips (1994), is about a training program in work process analysis for supervisors in the administrative services department of a large commercial bakery in Quebec. The training focused on teaching the supervisors how to make better use of their time by instituting various systems that would help to monitor the work flow. Three months after the training, the supervisors were asked to indicate how the time they spent in various tasks changed. The time saved was valued at the average hourly salary of the supervisors, and this was extrapolated to an annual savings estimate, based on the number of times the task is performed during the year. Combining this annual savings with the cost of the training program led to an ROI of 215 percent. This case demonstrates three pitfalls discussed previously. First, it relies on the participants' self-reports to identify productivity gains. Because the participants were told that the purpose of the training program was to make them more efficient in the use of their time, it is not surprising that they reported time savings. Second, it does not properly define performance. The time savings create a return for the company only if a head count reduction is achieved or if the supervisors spend their time in more productive tasks. No evidence of either is presented. Third, the results are extrapolated from a three-month period to a full year.

THE COCA-COLA BOTTLING COMPANY OF SAN ANTONIO (CASE 13). This case, described in Phillips (1994), is about a training program for 64 supervisors at Coca-Cola Bottling Company of San Antonio. The program focused on motivation, performance appraisal, and effective time management. Three months after the program ended, the participants were brought together and asked to identify the results achieved from applying the concepts and skills learned in the course. Some examples of these are increased sales, reduced waste, better route planning, and less absenteeism. The participants then converted these benefits into dollar values and also estimated the cost of implementing the changes. Benefits were totaled and, when viewed in conjunction with the cost of the training program, led to an ROI of 1,447 percent.

This case demonstrates the element of subjectivity that we have seen in other cases. The participants themselves were asked to identify gains that were attributable to training and to estimate the dollar value of these gains. In addition, because the participants knew they would be brought back together three months after the training, there was tremendous peer pressure to identify a positive result. Finally, there was no attempt to see if the productivity gains continued beyond the three-month evaluation point.

VULCAN MATERIALS (CASE 14). This case is described in Carnevale and Schulz (1990). Vulcan Materials implemented a training program to improve first-line supervisors' supervisory skills in order to reduce production worker turnover. Six months after the training program, Vulcan determined that turnover had been reduced, resulting in savings of $100,000. Managers of the production workers' supervisors were asked to rate their confidence that the training program was responsible for the turnover reduction. Using their 50 percent confidence level, the $100,000 savings was reduced to $50,000. Because the cost of training was $10,000, this resulted in an ROI of 400 percent.

As with other cases, this case suffers from managers' subjectivity bias in determining that 50 percent of the improvement was due to the training. In addition, the turnover reduction is only measured at one time, and there is no attempt to analyze whether it persisted after the six-month mark.

ROCHESTER METHODIST HOSPITAL (CASE 15). This case, discussed in Blomberg, Levy, and Anderson (1988), is about the evaluation of a management development training program for managers in Rochester Methodist Hospital. One year after completing the program, a 30 percent random sample of the managers who had attended the program were asked the following question: "If you were to assign a dollar value or worth to the application of the management development training, what would that dollar value be? How did you arrive at that figure?" The authors of the case reported total savings of $213,000. Unfortunately, there is no information about the cost of the training program, so it is impossible to determine the ROI. This case also demonstrates the problem that the trainees' estimates of the impact of the training and the value of the training are likely to be highly subjective.

ARTHUR ANDERSEN & COMPANY (CASE 19). This case, described in Phillips (1994), is about a training program that Arthur Andersen designed to improve its tax professionals' abilities in the area of state and local taxation. Information on fees and chargeable hours was obtained from the company's organizational database and was tracked for 12 months before and 12 months after the training event. This was done for offices that sent individuals to the training program and those that did not. The results showed that individuals who participated in the program were generating more fees. Although this group had already been on an upward trend prior to the training, the level increased following the training. Arthur Andersen did not calculate the ROI on this investment; it used the payback method instead. By calculating the difference between projected fees and actual fees, and comparing this to the cost of the program, it determined that payback was almost 100 percent at the end of the 12-month period after the training.

One good feature of this case is that the company also compared the pretraining and posttraining performance of the offices that sent individuals to the training program with the performance of offices that did not participate in the program. It found that, prior to the training, the participating offices were already performing at a higher level than the nonparticipating offices. The revenue for the nonparticipating offices remained flat over the entire two-year period, whereas the revenue for the participating offices increased significantly after the training. This lends support to the argument that the training was responsible for the observed increase in performance of the participating offices. It is important to note, however, that the offices were not chosen randomly for participation; the case suggests that the participating offices were already doing a substantial amount of work in the state and local tax specialty. Hence, it is likely that the significant benefits from the training may not have been replicable to other offices.

CIGNA (Case 20). Paquet, Kasl, Weinstein, and Waite (1987) describe the evaluation approach that CIGNA uses for its management training program. CIGNA uses repeated measures of work-unit performance before and after training from actual business records. Prior to the training program, the manager develops a productivity measure that is appropriate for his or her work unit. This is then tracked for at least three months before training, and then for four months after training. The managers have to submit actual work-unit records to substantiate any pre- and posttraining differences. The case reports separate ROIs for individual managers. For example, a premium collections manager was able to significantly improve the percentage of premiums collected on time. Because the company used a time-series design, it was able to compare the actual improvement to the predicted improvement based on the pretraining trend. This could then be translated into a dollar value for the company because late premiums represent a lost investment opportunity. In particular, the company gained extra investment income of $150,000 and reported an ROI of 5,900 percent because the cost of training this manager was only $2,500.

This case demonstrates the advantage of the time-series design in that results for several time periods prior to the training can serve as the benchmark for evaluating posttraining results. It also shows the value of using actual business records to track results rather than relying on subjective estimates. The problem with this case, however, is that the trainees were put on notice that productivity would be tracked, and they were certainly motivated to show strong results in the four months after the training. The real question is whether these results continued after the four-month mark.

REFERENCES

Ban, Carolyn, & Sue Faerman. (Spring 1990). "Issues in the Evaluation of Management Training." *Public Productivity and Management Review,* volume 13, number 5, 271–286.

Bartel, Ann P. (October 1994). "Productivity Gains from the Implementation of Employee Training Programs." *Industrial Relations,* volume 33, 411–425.

Bartel, Ann P. (July 1995). "Training, Wage Growth and Job Performance: Evidence from a Company Database." *Journal of Labor Economics* volume 13, 401–425.

Bassi, Laurie J., & Scott Cheney. (1996). *Restructuring: Results from the 1996 Benchmarking Forum.* Alexandria, VA: American Society for Training & Development.

Bassi, Laurie J., Anne L. Gallagher, & Ed Schroer. (1966). *The ASTD Training Data Book.* Alexandria, VA: American Society for Training & Development.

Bishop, John. (July 1994). "The Incidence of and Payoff to Employer Training." Cornell University Center for Advanced Human Resource Studies, Working Paper #94-17.

Black, Sandra, & Lisa Lynch. (May 1996a). "Human Capital Investments and Productivity." *American Economic Review,* volume 86, 263–267.

Black, Sandra, & Lisa Lynch. (September 1996b). *How to Compete: The Impact of Workplace Practices and Information Technology on Productivity.* Washington, DC: U.S. Department of Labor.

Blomberg, Robert, Elizabeth Levy, & Ailene Anderson. (1988). "Assessing the Value of Employee Training." *Health Care Management Review,* volume 13, number 1, 63–70.

Carnevale, Anthony, & Eric Schulz. (July 1990 Supplement). "Return on Investment: Accounting for Training." *Training & Development Journal,* S1–S32.

Godkewitsch, Michael. (May 1987). "The Dollars and Sense of Corporate Training." *Training,* 79–81.

Gordon, Jack. (August 1991). "Measuring the 'Goodness' of Training." *Training,* pp. 19–25.

Haislip, Otis, Jr. (February 1987). "How to Treat Training as an Investment." *Training,* 63–66.

Hawthorne, Elizabeth M. (1987). *Evaluating Employee Training Programs.* New York: Quorum.

Hequet, Marc. (March 1966). "Beyond Dollars." *Training,* 40–47.

Holton, Elwood F. III. (Spring 1966). "The Flawed Four-Level Evaluation Model." *Human Resource Development Quarterly,* volume 7, number 1, 5–21.

Holzer, Harry, Richard Block, Marcus Cheatham, & Jack Knott. (July 1993). "Are Training Subsidies for Firms Effective? The Michigan Experience." *Industrial and Labor Relations Review,* volume 46, 625–636.

Huselid, Mark. (1995). "The Impact of Human Resource Management Practices on Turnover, Productivity, and Corporate Financial Performance." *Academy of Management Journal,* volume 38, 636–672.

Kirkpatrick, Donald. (1994). *Evaluating Training Programs: The Four Levels.* San Francisco: Berrett-Koehler.

Kirkpatrick, Donald. (January 1996). "Revisiting Kirkpatrick's Four-Level Model." *Training & Development,* 54–59.

Krueger, Alan, & Cecilia Rouse. (August 1994). "New Evidence on Workplace Education." *NBER Working Paper No. 4831.*

Lombardo, Cynthia A. (December 1989). "Do the Benefits of Training Justify the Costs?" *Training & Development,* 60–64.

Mathieu, John, & Russell Leonard. (1987). "Applying Utility Concepts to a Training Program in Supervisory Skills." *Academy of Management Journal,* volume 30, 316–335.

Merlo, Nicholas S. (November 1988). "Subjective ROI." *Training & Development,* 63–66.

Mosier, Nancy. (Spring 1990). "Financial Analysis: The Methods and Their Application to Employee Training." *Human Resources Development Quarterly,* volume 1, number 1, 45–61.

Paquet, Basil, Elizabeth Kasl, Lawrence Weinstein, & William Waite. (May 1987). "The Bottom Line." *Training & Development,* 27–33.

Phillips, Jack J. (1991a). *Handbook of Training Evaluation and Measurement Methods.* Houston: Gulf Publishing.

Phillips, Jack J. (Autumn 1991b). "Measuring the Return on HRD." *Employment Relations Today,* volume 18, number 3, 329–342.

Phillips, Jack J., editor. (1994). *Measuring Return on Investment, Volume 1.* Alexandria, VA: American Society for Training & Development,

Phillips, Jack J. (February 1996a). "ROI: The Search for Best Practices." *Training & Development,* 42–47.

Phillips, Jack J. (March 1996b). "Was It the Training?" *Training & Development,* 28–32.

Phillips, Jack J. (April 1996c). "How Much Is the Training Worth?" *Training & Development,* 20–24.

Pine, Judith, & Judith C. Tingley. (February 1993). "ROI of Soft-Skills Training." *Training,* 55–60.

Robinson, Dana Gaines, & Jim Robinson. (August 1989). "Training for Impact." *Training & Development Journal,* 34–42.

Robinson, Dana Gaines, & Jim Robinson. (1989). *Training for Impact.* San Francisco: Jossey-Bass.

Schmidt, Frank, John Hunter, & Kenneth Pearlman. (1982). "Assessing the Economic Impact of Personnel Programs on Work Force Productivity." *Personnel Psychology,* volume 35, 333–347.

Scovel, Kathryn. (April 1990). "What's Topping the Charts in Management Training." *Human Resource Executive,* 37–40.

Shelton, Sandra, & George Alliger. (June 1993). "Who's Afraid of Level 4 Evaluation? A Practical Approach." *Training & Development,* 43–46.

Sheppick, Michael, & Stephen Cohen. (November 1985). "Put a Dollar Value on Your Training Programs." *Training & Development,* volume 39, number 11, 59–62.

About the Editors

Laurie J. Bassi is vice president for research at the American Society for Training & Development. Under her leadership, the Research Department identifies and tracks key business and labor market trends, conducts survey research, engages in a major ongoing study benchmarking training within a select group of firms, performs empirical and case study analysis of high-performance work systems, and reviews important developments in academic research.

Prior to joining ASTD in January 1996, Bassi was a professor in both the Department of Economics and the Graduate Public Policy Program at Georgetown University. She has also served as executive director of the Advisory Council on Unemployment Compensation and as deputy director of the Commission on Workforce Quality and Labor Market Efficiency, and has been a research associate at the Urban Institute. In addition, she has been a consultant to many major foundations, associations, government agencies, and research organizations.

Bassi is the author, co-author, and editor of many reports, scholarly journal articles, and books. She received a Ph.D. and master's degree in economics from Princeton University, a master's degree in industrial relations from Cornell University, and a B.A. in both economics and mathematics from Illinois State University.

Darlene Russ-Eft is division director of research services at Zenger Miller, an international consulting, training, and education company headquartered in San Jose, California. She is responsible for overall management of the research function at Zenger Miller, which includes services in research, evaluation and needs assessment. She has ongoing responsibility for consulting with clients about methods for measuring the effectiveness of consulting, training or other interventions, management audits, and climate surveys. She has responsibility for all corporate and product research activities.

Prior to joining Zenger Miller, she was a senior scientist at the American Institute for Research in Palo Alto, California. In that role, she was the principal investigator or project director on a variety of research projects. Before that, she was a research fellow at the Human Performance Center of the Department of Psychology, University of Michigan. Russ-Eft is currently an adjunct faculty instructor at the University of Santa Clara, University of California, Berkeley, and University of California, Santa Cruz. She holds Ph.D. and M.A. degrees from the Department of Psychology at the University of Michigan and a B.A. from the Department of Psychology at the College of Wooster.

An active member of numerous professional organizations, Russ-Eft is the author and co-author of many articles and essays about research issues, which have appeared in major journals. She is a speaker at both regional and national psychology and training association meetings. She is a member of the Board of the American Evaluation Association, an associate editor of *Human Resource Development Quarterly,* a member of the Research Committee of the Instructional Systems Association, and the immediate past chair of the Research Advisory Committee of the American Society for Training & Development. Russ-Eft was recently named a 1996 Editor of the Year by Times Mirror for her research work.